ELECTRONIC COMMERCE

ONLINE ORDERING AND DIGITAL MONEY

Second Edition

ELECTRONIC COMMERCE

ONLINE ORDERING AND DIGITAL MONEY

Second Edition

PETE LOSHIN
PAUL MURPHY

CHARLES RIVER MEDIA, INC.
Rockland, Massachusetts

Publisher: Dave Pallai
Interior Design/Comp.: Reuben Kantor
Cover Design: Marshall Henrichs
Printer: InterCity Press, Rockland, MA.

CHARLES RIVER MEDIA, INC.
P.O. Box 417
403 VFW Drive
Rockland, Massachusetts 02370
781-871-4184
781-871-4376 (FAX)
chrivmedia@aol.com
http://www.charlesriver.com

This book is printed on acid-free paper.

Pete Loshin & Paul Murphy, *Electronic Commerce: Online
Ordering and Digital Money 2/e*
ISBN: 1-886801-67-3

Printed in the United States of America
     99 00 01 7 6 5 4 3 2

CHARLES RIVER MEDIA titles are available for site
license or bulk purchase by institutions, user groups,
corporations, etc. For additional information, please
contact the Special Sales Department at 781-871-4184.

CONTENTS

PREFACE

On January 24, 1848, gold was discovered near the confluence of the American and Sacramento rivers in Northern California. As news of wild fortunes leaked out, people from all over the world descended on the previously unknown corner of the America, creating the gold rush of the 1840s.

Today, a gold rush is also under way. However, instead of picks, shovels and sifting pans, the tools are computers, electronic switches, routers, telephone lines, and programmers. Things are happening, not at the confluence of the American and Sacramento rivers, but on your desktop.

Despite the obvious tangible differences between the California gold rush of the 1840s and today's electronic commerce opportunities, both events have one thing in common—an undeniable level of excitement. A spirit of opportunity.

Today, merchants, software companies, and financial institutions are racing to provide the products and services that will make online purchasing as common and convenient as ordering by telephone or fax.

Finding the best electronic commerce solution for your business or personal online shopping needs will be guided by several factors. Despite the daily flow of new products and alliances, services, and several years of hard work already behind us, it is still too early to announce the winners in the race to provide an electronic online marketplace. In addition to the search for more efficient and secure applications, there are still questions about what type of networks will be used. Many companies — and technologies — are still in their first year of operations.

No matter whose products and services will be used, though, the foundation of the digital marketplace has already been laid. Logistics dictates that, in these early years, electronic commerce will be heavily oriented toward products that can be delivered as well as ordered through Internet connections (anything that can be digitized, from music to news to software to pictures), while the realities of the market require ease of use for both merchant and consumer. The continued perception of a lack of security and reliability inherent in the Internet's network architecture calls for the creation of commercial transaction methods and software that add both, for peace of mind all around.

This book introduces the issues involved in bringing business to the Internet — the obstacles to online commerce, as well as the advantages. Once the issues have been laid out, we will explain how advances in cryptography make it possible to transmit business information across unreliable and unsecure networks, reliably and securely. Once the general concepts have been presented, different current commercial schemes and systems are discussed in their proper perspective.

After the various schemes have been examined, other relevant and related issues can be discussed, including digital currencies, techniques for marketing on the Internet, and related services available to the online merchant.

Appendices include an Internet and networking glossary, a guide to locating the most current and complete electronic commerce resources on the Internet, and a guide to the included CD-ROM.

Chapter 1: Introduction and Concepts

The idea of doing business electronically over networks is nothing new: We think nothing of ordering products from catalogs or TV by phone, or requesting information by fax, or using ATMs for banking. The promise of the Internet is to allow business to be transacted directly between consumer and merchant, with no intermediaries, instant response, and virtually no overhead costs. The issues raised by electronic commerce include transaction security, authentication and certification of orders, and fulfillment.

This chapter introduces the Internet and presents the benefits that can accrue from using the Internet for commerce, as well as the problems that must be resolved before such commerce is possible.

Chapter 2: Security Technologies

Online commerce is impossible without working on the security and reliability problems. While some are attacking the problem by taking the sensitive material offline, many others are using public key cryptography to encrypt sensitive information, to digitally —sign" orders and responses, and to make sure that messages have been transmitted unmodified.

This chapter explains why the Internet is inherently unsecure and unreliable, as well as why that does not necessarily keep transmissions from being secure and reliable. It also introduces the concepts behind public key cryptography, and explains how public key applications are implemented within the Internet to produce frameworks for secure commerce.

Chapter 3: Electronic Payment Methods

Many different approaches can be taken to the problem of transferring money from one individual to another, ranging from existing methods such as bank draft authorization and credit cards, to indirect use of existing methods (such as registering your payment information with a third party who processes all transactions, or registering it with the vendor outside of the public network and using an account number online), all the way to the use of digital currencies that permit the digital movement of cash endorsed by digital signatures.

This chapter examines the different general methods for processing electronic transactions. A brief discussion of the (apparently) more mundane methods of exchange, such as cash, check, and credit card, will highlight some of the obvious and not-so-obvious advantages and disadvantages. Electronic transaction options will then be examined, including the following.

- Encryption of payment information transmitted from buyer to seller
- Use of an intermediary to handle transaction settlement and keep consumer payment private, even from merchants
- Electronic checking, using digital signatures to authenticate the exchange of value between two individuals as if a check were used
- Electronic currencies, using digital signature technology to authenticate the exchange of value between individuals with no intermediaries at all (allowing truly private exchange of money)

This chapter examines these alternatives in the context of actual systems and schemes that use them, though Chapter 5 introduces a more comprehensive listing of industry players, and Chapters 6 through 8 highlight some of these companies and products in greater detail.

Chapter 4: Protocols for the Public Transport of Private Information

A universal medium of exchange is necessary to make electronic commerce work. Like a standard currency, a standard for transactions makes it possible for everyone to participate. Transactions are most often made through the World Wide Web, and add-on protocols, which define the exchange of sensitive information across the Web, have been defined and implemented. The Secure Sockets Layer (SSL) is a solution offered by Netscape Communications Corporation for use in its own secure Web products. The Secure Hypertext Transport Protocol (S-HTTP) is an extension of the Web's basic protocols that also allows the transmission of sensitive information.

There are other solutions and other protocols; many of the organizations offering electronic commerce solutions also offer their own protocols for moving transaction information among the buyer, the seller, and interested third parties such as banks and credit card authorizers. Some of these will be discussed, primarily to highlight how they differ from each other.

We also outline the basics of the still-developing Secure Electronic Transaction or SET protocol currently being developed by MasterCard and Visa.

Chapter 5: Electronic Commerce Providers

Billions of dollars are at stake in this industry, and there are many organizations looking for at least part of the bounty. Ranging from financial heavyweights such as Visa, MasterCard, and Wells Fargo Bank, to software giant Microsoft, to newcomers such as First Virtual, DigiCash, and Netscape, the players today may not be the winners tomorrow — but that's the way to bet.

This chapter introduces a selection of the companies now offering electronic commerce products and services. Company contact information, product profiles, corporate background, and other pertinent information are included.

Chapter 6: Electronic Payment Systems

Anything that makes it possible for a consumer to spend money online can be construed as an electronic payment system. As discussed earlier, these can be electronic checking systems, third-party systems (a third party handles the payment information, collecting money from the consumer through a credit card or checking account and then paying money to the merchant), or digital currency systems that allow direct interchange of values. These systems all share the requirement of some kind of prior action on the part of all participants, both merchant and consumer.

Profiled in this chapter are representative payment systems, all in current use.

Chapter 7: Online Commerce Environments

Online commerce environments, unlike payment systems, tend not to make assumptions about customers, nor do they necessarily require the consumer to take any specific prior action to be able to use them. The simplest example would be a secure Web server that encrypted the customer's credit card information prior to transmitting it to the merchant across the Internet. Though a credit card is required, no special preparation is necessary prior to making an order, and the merchant handles the rest — possibly processing the process by hand through a — traditional" credit card authorization process.

More commonly, though, secure server vendors will be seeking to maximize the benefits of electronic commerce by automating payment authorization, order fulfillment, account management, and other functions. Commerce environments can also coexist with payment systems by facilitating their use; just as traditional merchants now accept payment by various credit and charge cards, checks, and cash, electronic merchants will be able to accept payment through a variety of different payment systems.

Like the preceding and following chapters, this one examines in more detail a sampling of currently available electronic commerce software.

Chapter 8: Digital Currencies

Digital currencies can be considered a special case of the electronic payment system, though they are not necessarily limited to the World Wide Web, the Internet, or even networks in general. Government agencies around the world are keeping especially close watch on these systems, since they could enable the virtually instantaneous and anonymous transfer of unlimited funds, making a mockery of tax and currency-transfer statutes.

This chapter examines a widely available prototype for digital cash, and discusses in greater detail how digital cash works.

Chapter 9: Strategies, Techniques, and Tools

Though there has been a flood of books discussing strategic marketing on the Internet, given that Internet marketing is in its infancy, there are no time-proven strategies yet available for anyone. This chapter discusses some of the options open to both consumers and merchants, as well as ways to safely and happily transact business across Internet connections.

Appendix A: Internet Glossary and Abbreviations

The Internet's history as a research project done largely for the U.S. military may have something to do with its propensity for often opaque acronyms, and as a new technology it comes with its own unique terminology. This appendix should help the technical and nontechnical reader alike to decipher some of these terms and acronyms.

Appendix B: Electronic Commerce Online Resources

Information about the Internet has always been some of the most easily obtained material on the Internet. There is a wealth of information about transacting business through Internet connections, as well as pointers to participating organizations, and and this appendix should be useful to anyone who wants to locate the latest news.

Appendix C: Guide to the CD-ROM

This appendix offers a brief guide to the contents of the included CD-ROM, as well as instructions for using it.

ONE

INTRODUCTION AND CONCEPTS

"We are an all-IBM shop, but thanks for calling."

— A TYPICAL END TO A PHONE CONVERSATION FROM A SALES REPRESENTATIVE
OFFERING NON-IBM HARDWARE AND SOFTWARE TO A LARGE CORPORATION.

There are thousands of definitions used to describe the Internet. One of the most popular is the concept of a standard. For years, the major forces in the computer (personal, midrange, and mainframe) industry were building proprietary systems, and customers were committing to one-vendor solutions. The ability to share information freely was slowed by this practice.

At the most fundamental level, the Internet is a series of standards for three basic tasks:

- Sharing a file with one or more parties
- Sharing email with one or more parties
- Allowing the user of one computer system to log onto another computer system.

From these three functions, Internet applications like the World Wide Web, file transfer, telnet, and others are created.

The growth of the Internet is accredited to the widespread acceptance and implementation of the Internet standards. After all, if everyone is using the same basic method to send and receive email, files, etc., it does not matter what systems are used.

In the business world, although we have different currencies, we already have existing standards for exchanging money. Chances are you used a credit card or check to pay for this book.

The focus of this book is to shed light on the collision of these two industries/standards. The ultimate goal for the electronic commerce industry is to make conducting business with your computer as pain- and worry-free as using your credit cards or checkbook.

NETWORKS AND COMMERCIAL TRANSACTIONS

The idea of doing business electronically over networks is nothing new: We think nothing of ordering the products we've seen advertised on television or in printed catalogs with a phone call or a fax, and ATMs are always within reach for quick, easy, and automatic banking. Corporations advertise through broadcasting networks, and consumers flock to local outlets of national and international franchise networks. As the world becomes increasingly interconnected, particularly through the Internet with its open protocols, forward-looking businesses will be able to make their products available to a global market, the largest possible market, without having to create and maintain their own private networks for sales, delivery, and customer support.

Although the techniques for attracting consumer attention, describing products, and delivering them electronically will all be of interest to those who wish to participate in this new market, this book simply explains how business transactions can be executed across an unreliable and unsecure medium like the Internet, and discusses some of the methods currently being planned and implemented—in other words, how you will be buying and selling in the future, and how it will work.

The number of businesses devoted to promoting commerce on the Internet has been growing exponentially since the end of 1994, but they all share the goal of making commercial transactions over the Internet safe, simple, and secure—and earning a profit in the process. The methods employed to achieve these ends are somewhat more various, but can be categorized as either creating secure and reliable channels to carry transactions across Internet connections (which are inherently unsecure and unreliable), or using more traditional channels to carry sensitive information.

Electronic merchants need to feel confident they can safely market and deliver their products, get paid for all products purchased, and not lose any product to theft. Electronic consumers need to feel confident they can safely select and take delivery of products, pay for them, and not be concerned about compromise of payment information (such as credit card or bank account numbers). Everyone wants to feel confident that the individuals they deal with across the Internet are who they say they are, to avoid losses to fraud.

The Internet and Other Novelties

The apparent overnight success of the Internet blindsided a lot of people. In fact, the Internet has its roots in internetworking research that began in 1969 (the same year people first walked on the Moon), and it has been steadily doubling in size roughly every year. Consider some of the other technologies introduced since 1969 that have become ubiquitous: the videocassette recorder (VCR), cable access television (CATV), automatic teller machine (ATM), compact disc (CD), personal computer (PC), and cellular telephone, to name just a few.

The Internet functions as a medium for data transmission in much the same way that the international telephone network functions as a medium for voice (and other signal) transmissions. The telephone system

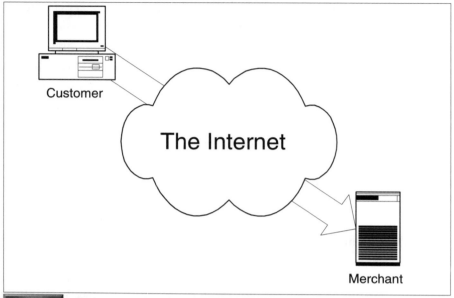

FIGURE 1-1 *Consumers can gain access to an Internet merchant's system across the Internet without having to know anything about the intervening networks.*

consists of connections (and the required supporting hardware and cabling) to people, organizations, and devices (answering and fax machines, computers, and others), but does not include those things—nor does it include the signals being sent over it. Similarly, the Internet can be said to consist of the connections (and the required supporting hardware and cabling) between networks, but not the data stored on and made accessible from those networks.

As shown in Figure 1-1, the standard representation of the Internet is as a cloud, to stress the fact that there is something going on between systems communicating across the Internet. That something encompasses any number of intermediate computers and networks (and will be discussed in slightly more detail in Chapter 2), but it is not necessary to know exactly what it is to be able to use it.

There are no worldwide organizations "running" the Internet, any more than there are such organizations "running" the global telecommunications network. Instead, there are standards bodies for both networks, who define the rules (or protocols) to be used by anyone connecting to those networks. If the rules are properly implemented, then the telephone, fax, or computer will be able to pass signals to and from the network. In other words, if your telephone company conforms to the CCITT (Consultative Committee on International Telephony and Telegraphy, a standards organization for telecommunications) protocols, you can talk to anyone else connected to the global telephone network, as long as their telephone company also conforms to those protocols. If you subscribe to a telephone service that has implemented its own proprietary protocols, however, you may find yourself limited in whom you can connect to (or at least in how you can make a connection).

The same goes for the Internet: The Internet Advisory Board (IAB *See* Internet Architecture Board) provides oversight to the Internet Engineering Task Force (IETF *See* Internet Engineering Task Force), which is responsible for evaluating and defining Internet protocols. If you are using a computer connected to a network that conforms to the Internet protocols and is connected to the global Internet, you can exchange data with any other computer connected to the global Internet, as long as that computer also conforms to the Internet protocols. If you connect to some other type of internetwork, you may have problems connecting to the Internet.

> **NOTE:** *The Internet protocols are also known as TCP/IP, for the two most central protocols defining internetwork transmissions: the Transmission Control Protocol (TCP) and the Internet Protocol (IP). These protocols, and the many others included in the TCP/IP suite, define how Internet traffic is passed between computers and between networks; how information is passed between communicating systems; and how the Internet functions as a network of networks.*

Using the right protocols won't guarantee connectivity, though, unless you actually have some point of connection to the desired large network. Your organization could have a telephone and a computer

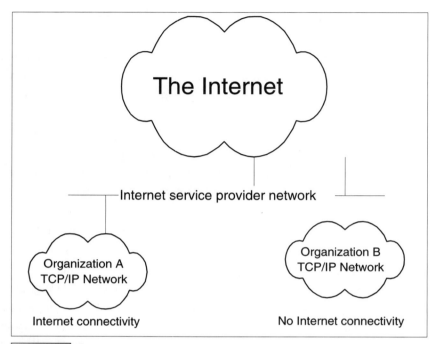

FIGURE 1-2 *You can connect to the Internet as long as you are using the right protocols AND are connected to the Internet.*

on every desk, with both connected to the organizational switchboard and network—but without a connection between the organization and the outside world, you could use those facilities only for internal communication. As shown in Figure 1-2, an organizational internetwork has to be connected to the Internet for it to be accessible outside the organization using the Internet protocols.

Networks and Electronic Transactions Today

When considering online commerce, it is important to maintain a perspective and define a context. Broadcasting networks, particularly television networks, have a long history of being used to market products, although viewers cannot use that same medium to place orders. With widespread use of credit cards, consumers and merchants have been happily transacting business over the telephone network for many years. Highly sensitive banking transactions have been routinely processed through ATM networks since the late 1970s.

Once participants in the electronic marketplace understand the mechanisms set up for transacting business across the Internet, buying and selling online will be at least as simple and trusted a method as buying by phone or in person.

A Model for Commercial Transactions

Understanding the ways in which commercial transactions take place online, across the Internet, requires understanding the way in which any commercial transaction takes place. There will be differences between different types of transactions. Although the way a large corporation buys raw materials in bulk from its supplier is different from the way the schoolchild buys candy at the corner drugstore, both transactions share certain characteristics.

Let us examine some of the issues involved in electronic commerce by taking a look at what happens in the course of any commercial transaction. We'll focus on the issues involved in simple retail transactions, since virtually everyone is familiar and comfortable with this type of transaction.

Establishing Trust

Before any purchase can be made from a retail store, a customer must enter it. Most shops are open to the public, so all it takes is for a customer to walk in. However, this is not always the case: The merchant may control access to the goods it offers in several different ways. It can sell to any and all comers through an open storefront, or it can restrict its sales to a certain clientele (wholesalers may sell only to resellers; exclusive merchants may do business only with referred customers). The merchant can decide which customers to give access to its merchandise, and how that access is provided.

The consumer also makes choices prior to entering a store. The consumer must determine, often by just looking in a display window, whether the establishment carries the product being sought and whether the establishment is a reliable place to do business. To entice customers, the merchant may display brand names of the products carried, stickers on the door indicating payment methods accepted, and sample products. Additional customer acceptance can also be gained through use of a well-known company name, by being a branch or a franchise holder of a nationally known company.

The degree to which the merchant will restrict access to its products will vary, depending on the type of business. An automobile dealer will require a driver's license before permitting a test drive; although most bookstores don't mind strangers browsing through their books, some encourage it with tables and comfortable chairs for browsers. Likewise, buyers may be more careful about selecting vendors of products that can affect their health or well-being (such as prescription drugs or safety items) or are expensive (such as automobiles or computers) than they are about buying products that are relatively benign (household items or musical recordings) or inexpensive (newspapers or chewing gum).

The merchant and the consumer each establishes a level of trust in the other. The merchant trusts that the consumer is a potential purchaser, capable of selecting and paying for some product offered; the consumer trusts that the merchant may be offering the desired product and will be capable of delivering (and servicing, if necessary) that product if needed. As we will see later, if the two parties actually come to an agreement, a higher level of trust may be required.

There are other identity issues that both buyer and seller are concerned with when first initiating contact. Many products have distribution limits. For example:

- Prescription drugs may not be dispensed to anyone without a legitimate prescription.
- Alcoholic beverages may not be sold to minors, and may be subject to other sales restrictions (may not be sold on Sundays, for example) depending on the locality.
- Firearms and ammunition are subject to a wide range of restrictions, varying by locality.
- Tobacco products may not be sold to minors.
- "Adult" entertainment products may be subject to local restrictions on sales to minors.

Establishing trust between parties in a commercial transaction that takes place across a public network is difficult. While the merchant can use judgment during in-person transactions (the white-haired customer does not have to show ID to buy a six-pack of beer), online transactions offer no opportunity to exercise judgment because it is difficult to correlate identities on the Internet with actual individuals. Electronic merchants cannot afford to trust everyone—or even to trust anyone.

The same goes for the consumer. There is no way to tell how long a Web page has been in existence, or whether it will be there tomorrow. Constructing a counterfeit Web page, representing itself as part of a large corporation, is much easier than constructing a counterfeit retail outlet, restaurant, or supermarket, and potentially more lucrative.

Online transactions require mechanisms for establishing trust between prospective buyers and sellers.

Negotiating a Deal

Determining the item to be purchased, and the price to be charged, are trivial matters in most retail stores. The buyer selects the desired item, and the price is usually clearly marked either on the item itself or near its display area. In most cases, this is all that is necessary.

However, when the desired item is not immediately available (the desired color, size, flavor, version is not in stock), the retailer may have to order the product or offer an alternative deal, perhaps selling a similar item for a similar price or extending a special price to be applied at a later time (like rain checks offered by supermarkets on products that are on special but out of stock).

The validity of the merchant's offering price, as well as the exact identity of the item desired by the consumer, is easy to determine in a retail store. Electronic transactions sometimes require special mechanisms to ensure that the buyer did, in fact, place an order, and that the seller did, in fact, offer the product for the specified price.

Such mechanisms are a requirement if electronic transactions are to be kept free of fraud. When you select an item from a store's shelf, pay for it, and walk away with it, there is no question about what was bought and at what price. When you order products by phone from a catalog, you can refer to the price in the catalog (but you still make a leap of faith that the order-taker accurately records your purchase order and will not abscond with your credit card number). Ordering products over the Internet does not offer an explicit method to reference the offering price, nor does it offer an explicit method to reference the original order.

Neither the buyer nor the seller should be able to repudiate the offered price or the products ordered; mechanisms to accomplish this are available for electronic commerce.

Payment and Settlement

At the heart of any transaction is the exchange of values, generally some standardized currency traded for some product or service. Probably because we are so accustomed to purchasing items in person, the process seems to be straightforward: the buyer gives cash, a check, or a credit card and receives in return the product being purchased and a receipt.

Translating these actions into electronic form takes some doing. Many participants will want the entire process to be private; after all, most consumers would not announce their credit card numbers out loud in a crowded store—and some would prefer to purchase certain items or services anonymously. There are mechanisms which allow payment information to be kept private, by encrypting it, by keeping it entirely offline, or by using third parties to settle transactions.

In the store, the transaction is completed as soon as the buyer pays for an item: The buyer can then walk away with the purchase. Over the Internet, unless the product being purchased is available digitally (information, pictures, software, or other information-based products), the buyer must trust the seller to deliver the goods. One way the consumer can avoid problems is by patronizing trusted Internet vendors; another way is to use a major credit card company that will back up the consumer in the event of a problem with a vendor.

The vendor takes a smaller risk when selling online, since credit cards can be authenticated through automated connections to settlement companies. This is similar to the authentication done in person when a clerk uses a credit card authorization terminal ("swipe box") to verify a credit card. Both parties to an online transaction can benefit from the use of digital signatures, which will be discussed in Chapter 2.

Payment Vehicles and Currencies

A great deal of attention is focused on consummation of the online transaction—as it should be, since this is the point at which values are exchanged. The offline buyer has many options for transacting exchanges, of which the most common are cash, universally accepted and totally anonymous; personal check, providing an audit trail and a paper record of the transaction; and credit, charge, or ATM card, offering audit trails, guarantees for recourse through the sponsoring credit card company, and no-questions-asked credit extension.

When presented in person, all these payment methods are subject to some degree of scrutiny. Merchants may examine large-denomination bills for counterfeits (or refuse to accept large bills); may accept personal checks only if the customer offers sufficient personal identification (or cash checks only for frequent customers); and may verify identity and signature when accepting credit cards (as well as getting payment authorizations through settlement companies).

Similar mechanisms for using electronic currencies, personal checks, and credit cards are available for electronic transactions. Digital currencies are being developed to allow anonymous transactions across public networks such as the Internet. Digital signature technologies permit the authentication and certification of digitally transmitted documents like personal checks. These transactions, including credit card transactions, can all use special encryption methods to ensure reliability and privacy.

Finally, digital currencies need not be limited to digital representation of actual currencies. Other units of exchange may be used, whether they are barter units, airline frequent flier miles, or some other unit of exchange. Likewise, since there is no reason to limit currencies to a single "real" currency, international currency exchanges and transfers could become virtually instantaneous and untraceable: a prospect that many governments would prefer not to have to contend with.

Products and Delivery

You can't stuff a food processor or football or even a computer down a wire, so merchants selling products with a physical presence electronically still have to physically deliver them to the customer. Merchants who wish to sell physical items need to inspire a greater level of trust in their customers; after all, those customers must wait for a delivery, and they may not be convinced the product will arrive until it arrives. Merchants may allay some of these fears by giving the buyer detailed delivery information (when the product will be packed and shipped, how the product is to be shipped, approximate delivery date or time).

Digital products, however, that can be delivered electronically increasingly are being sold electronically. Figure 1-3 shows the relation between online accessibility and scale of various digital products. Information products such as news articles, information from

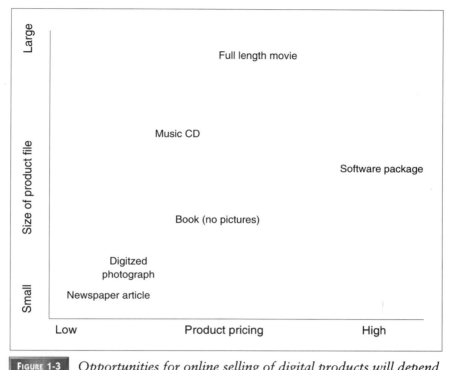

FIGURE 1-3 *Opportunities for online selling of digital products will depend on price as well as the completeness of the product purchased when compared to traditional retail outlets.*

databases, and other traditional text or data items can all be delivered immediately after purchase over a network connection.

It isn't always practical to sell information products this way, though. The text of a 300-page book may only consist of about half a megabyte of data, and transferring that amount of data across a typical 28.8-Kbps (thousand bits per second) dial-up connection would take at least three minutes or so. However, graphical elements such as photographs, drawings, and tables can add significantly to the amount of data to be transmitted. In either case, book readers still find it preferable to read the printed page rather than on screen. Whether or not selling books electronically is a good thing, it is not yet entirely practical.

Photographs and other images can be digitized and sold electronically. Small black-and-white snapshots may take only a few seconds to transfer across the typical modem connection; larger photos scanned at higher resolutions and in color may take up to a minute or more. There is already a brisk trade in images across the Internet, particularly those with an erotic content.

There are many more information products than books and images, however. Recorded music and movies, now sold mainly on compact disc and video tapes, could be sold digitally. Downloading the contents of a CD, which contains up to 600 megabytes, is impractical even with a very fast network connection. On-demand sales of single-play video or audio is a more promising application, though not yet practical.

Finally, software itself is an excellent example of a digitizable product. Despite the fact that software vendors go to great lengths to give a physical presence to their products — by putting them in boxes, adding manuals, folders, quick reference cards, and other collateral materials — the software could just as easily be sold on a single CD-ROM, complete with online manuals, licenses, and special offers. There are a number of options, including distributing the software directly across the network (as is now done with many shareware programs), or freely distributing the actual software on CD-ROM and selling "keys" online to unlock the software for installation.

Delivery of digital products online raises issues that parallel those raised by online transactions. Some vendors may want to ensure that a third party cannot eavesdrop on the product transmission and gain use of the material being sold without paying for it. Buyers want to ensure that they are getting the material they requested, from the source from which they requested it. Everyone wants to ensure that the material received by the consumer has not been altered in any way by any third parties. These issues can be resolved by the same tools that make secure and reliable transactions possible online.

THE INTERNET ENVIRONMENT

As mentioned earlier, electronic commerce is not an entirely new idea. Nor is the online transaction. Dial-up computer services, like those provided by CompuServe since 1980, usually include services and products that can be ordered online. Electronic funds transfer (EFT) is another relatively mature field that is only now reaching a mass market as ATMs, gas stations, and supermarkets increasingly accept credit, debit, and charge cards.

In 1993, when the World Wide Web protocols were first being proposed as Internet standards, few people outside the research and academic world had even heard of the Internet, let alone used it. Today, the Internet and the World Wide Web are such a part of daily life that major mainstream publications no longer define Internet-related terms like Web site, home page, or news posting.

The Internet Advantage

Despite the Internet's long existence as a noncommercial research network, its commercialization owes its apparent success to several factors:

- The Internet is an open system.
- The Internet itself does not belong to anyone.
- The World Wide Web is the Internet's "killer app."

The Internet Is Open

All the Internet protocols are open and public, and anyone can use them to write software implementations that can interoperate with other computers and networks running the Internet protocols. Most of the competition between vendors of Internet and TCP/IP software is based on performance, ease of use, and compatibility. None of these vendors is foolhardy enough to announce a new version of their software that provides even the most attractive of new features at the cost of compatibility with other TCP/IP implementations.

LAN (local area network) operating system vendors such as Novell and Microsoft have traditionally kept their product specifications private and incompatible, but have lost the benefits of having an entire community of researchers and developers working on interoperable implementations, as has happened with the Internet protocols.

Because of this openness, a wide range of implementations are available, from freeware and shareware versions of Internet application and networking software through high-performance, high-function versions of Internet software sold by companies like FTP Software and SunSoft. The result of this competition is lower costs barriers to small companies and individuals who previously could not afford to connect to the Internet.

The Internet Does Not Belong to Anyone

Part of the openness of the Internet is derived from the fact that you do not have to belong to any special group, pay any special fees, or become anyone's customer to access any Internet content. True, there are fees to be paid to the Internet Service Provider (ISP) for initiating service, charges for connect time, and perhaps other value-added services such as e-mail accounts, but the ISP functions in the same way as a telephone company, providing access and connectivity only.

In contrast, the more traditional online services (like America Online, CompuServe, and Prodigy) charge users fees for connect time, as well as to access certain value-added content and activities. More important is the limitation on the participation in any AOL, CompuServe, or Prodigy forums. For example, only CompuServe members can read or submit to CompuServe forums. The same is true for AOL and Prodigy members.

Connectivity through the Internet allows any connected individual to browse any freely available content, without regard to memberships. At least as important is that anyone with a dedicated Internet connection and a computer can be not just an information consumer, but also an information provider. And instead of communicating with an online service population, people with Internet connectivity can potentially communicate with anyone else connected to the Internet: 30, or 40, or 50 million people, or more, depending on when you read this.

The online services have recognized that, when given the choice, users would prefer full Internet access to more limited online service access. To meet this need the online services are also offering true Internet service.

For new computer users going online for the first time, the traditional online services offered by AOL, CompuServe, and Prodigy are very attractive, as they offer hand-holding and support for the online "freshman." Eventually the majority of users will migrate to full Internet access. However, the flow of new online users is not likely to slow down in the near future, and many people do stay with the traditional online services for one reason or another. Building a successful electronic commerce application will require implementing the needs of these users and the proprietary functions of the online services they use at least until the turn of the century.

World Wide Web, Killer App of the Internet

Most Internet applications were developed by computer scientists more often concerned with performance and extensibility than with usability. Applications such as *telnet* (for running terminal sessions on remote computers) and *ftp* (the File Transfer Protocol application, for transferring files between two computers) required from the user a high level of awareness about the operating systems of the local and remote computers. While not entirely unusable by the less technically sophisticated, these applications nevertheless had a sufficiently high cost of entry (long learning times) to turn off many potential users.

Even before 1993, there were enough different information providers on the Internet to make it a complicated matter to find a desired resource. Various applications were developed to make searching the Internet simpler, but none was sufficiently compelling to users. One application, Gopher, held promise. Gopher servers simply made various Internet resources available through a common interface, using menus instead of requiring entry of explicit commands. The resources could be file repositories or remote computers allowing guest logins, or they could use any other allowable Internet application; Gopher simply provided a simple character-based system, with a menu-based front end to those resources.

No serious contender for a killer application appeared until the World Wide Web began and graphical browsers became available. It had always been a hassle to track down sources of information on the Internet, connect to the server, and attempt to locate the desired data. The World Wide Web offers improvements both to the end user, who can point and click to navigate the Web and locate interesting or necessary information, and to the information providers, who can offer access to their own data as well as other related providers to a much wider audience. Even more attractive is the ease with which regular users can create and publish their documents for Internet consumption.

The result was an application that appealed to a huge potential user base: those wanting access to free or cheap information and entertainment, but without the hassles of figuring out how to work all the different computers and programs.

The World Wide Web

In 1989, the World Wide Web began to take shape as the ultimate networked hypertext document. The idea was to use a markup language to create documents, relying on *tags* (function-oriented labels that define how a part of a document behaves) rather than using traditional word-processing formatting options to control the way the document is displayed. The result is that parts of each marked-up document behave the way they are supposed to, no matter how they are being displayed. For example, if a line is tagged as a title, it can be printed out in a specified font and size appropriate for hard copy, but when it is displayed on a monitor it may appear in a different specified font, size, and color appropriate for that particular video display monitor.

This is a very dry and technical way of saying that Web documents can be created in such a way that a person using virtually any kind of computer (with a character-based or graphical user interface) can access virtually any information, resource, or device connected to a World Wide Web server. The user starts up client software and connects to a home page, and then can surf on to other Web documents by traversing links on the home page and other connected pages. The result is a world-wide web of connections between information services on the Internet.

Connected services are often provided directly through Web documents, but the protocols allow any type of Internet application to be accessed, including more traditional file transfer servers and terminal sessions on larger host systems.

Although backward compatibility with existing services and systems is important, the Web owes its success to an extraordinarily simple user interface. Rather than requiring an explicit search for Internet resources using arcane tools, all the services are available in a graphic format and the user simply points and clicks to access them. As it becomes trivially easy for increasing numbers to access a Web site, it also becomes an especially attractive avenue for companies looking for new ways to market their products.

World Wide Web document development, server maintenance, specifications, and standards are all important topics, but are also mostly beyond the scope of this book. Some pointers for more information about the World Wide Web standards and protocols are provided in Appendix B.

World Wide Web Standards

The World Wide Web is defined by a handful of protocol specifications. Software developers use those specifications to implement the Web browser and Web server programs. The interaction between browser and server is defined by the Hypertext Transfer Protocol (HTTP). Web browsers send messages conforming to this protocol to Web servers; these, in turn, return the requested information.

Traditional Internet addressing conventions are for locating computers attached to specific network interfaces. Special Internet host names and addresses are used, but these are sufficient only to locate a computer — locating a specific resource on a computer can be equally complicated, requiring the user to search through (sometimes unfamiliar) operating system directories, folders, and files. The Uniform Resource Locator (URL) protocol specifies how individual resources (files, documents, or even a specific section of a document) are to be identified within the World Wide Web. Web browsers use these URLs in HTTP requests to remote servers. They identify to the server exactly what resource is being requested.

Information transmitted from servers to browsers comes from Web documents stored on the server that have been specially tagged using Hypertext Markup Language (HTML) tags, which define the different functional pieces of each document. As mentioned earlier, tags allow different parts of a document to behave differently; most important are the abilities of text and graphics to behave as pointers to other parts of a document, other documents and resources, and especially resources on other Web servers. HTML documents consist of plain text (ASCII) files and may point to graphics files, other types of multimedia files (for example, sound or full-motion video files) stored in standard formats, or other network resources (URLs).

It isn't possible to put all the information that a person browsing the Web would like from your site into HTML-formatted files. Large databases, in particular, work better when they stay in their original formats. The Common Gateway Interface (CGI) specifies mechanisms for passing information from the person browsing your Web server to other resources available through that server, in particular by collecting information from the remote user in Web forms and then passing that information along to the other resource.

This type of interchange is vital to allow the remote user to access resources such as databases, but it is equally critical to collecting information (and then using it correctly and automatically) for the purposes of transacting business through the World Wide Web. Designing forms to collect orders through a Web site is not enough; there must be some mechanism outside the server to handle that information. The user's order needs to be processed: If a physical product has been ordered, inventory and shipping information must be handled; billing information must always be processed. CGI provides the link between the Web server and the rest of the commercial process. Tools such as CGI will be discussed in Chapter 3.

Finally, the security protocols relevant to the World Wide Web include Secure Sockets Layer (SSL) and Secure Hypertext Transfer Protocol (S-HTTP). These will be discussed in greater detail in Chapter 4, but very simply they add security to existing protocols between the browsers and servers that support them.

Browsers and Servers

Web browsers (or clients) must be able to send HTTP requests and receive HTTP replies from servers. The most popular browsers are fully graphical, although nongraphical browsers are a necessity for character-based operating systems. Browsers range from spartan text-only implementations like Lynx for UNIX and other operating systems to full-featured commercial products like Netscape Navigator and Microsoft Internet Explorer. Browser functions can also be integrated into more complete network or communications packages (like Netcom's Netcruiser or Wollongong's Emissary), or even into operating systems (like IBM's OS/2 Warp).

There is no shortage of Web browsers for any taste or budget. All should provide access to any Web-connected resource, although some will offer extra functions or features such as integration with other Internet tools (e-mail, network news), options for saving or copying retrieved data to files, and display-customization options. Performance enhancements, like the ability to "cache" or save documents already retrieved, can also differentiate browsers.

Just as Web browsers are available for virtually every computer and operating system, Web server software is also widely available. To offer Web services, a computer must be connected to the Internet, be running a Web server program, and have Web documents available. Web servers can contain highly graphical content without being able to display that content locally: The server system need only be able to run the server software and store the hypertext documents and files.

Although a basic PC with a full-time dial-up telephone link to the Internet is sufficient to act as a Web server, it would not be sufficient to serve very many simultaneous users. More often, Web servers are set up on higher-performance systems with higher-performance connections to the Internet (i.e., T-1). Individuals and organizations wishing to provide Web services have the option of setting up (and managing and maintaining) their own system, or paying an Internet presence provider to run their Web sites for them. Secured or commercial-grade servers for the World Wide Web are discussed in Chapter 7.

Selling on the World Wide Web

With its easy-to-use and graphical interface, the World Wide Web seems an ideal medium for commerce. The biggest obstacle to commercialization of the Internet, its funding by government agencies for research purposes only, disappeared rapidly in the early 1990s as those subsidies expired and were not renewed. Obstacles such as a lack of market penetration and lack of mechanisms for secure transactions are rapidly disappearing, as consumers and businesses are flocking to the Internet and developers are turning their attentions to the problem of securing the Internet for commerce.

Keeping in mind the previous discussion of commercial transactions, selling on the World Wide Web parallels selling in the real world. Very simply, the customer enters the merchant's Web site and views product and company information. If the merchant successfully sells a product and fosters sufficient trust in the customer to generate an order, the customer will place an order.

The merchant's overall presentation, on- and offline, determine the consumer's level of trust. The Web page presentation content — products, descriptions, pricing, and delivery — will help the consumer to make a decision. The rest of the transaction is carried on across the

World Wide Web, but may require additional mechanisms connected to it. For example, the purchase of a digital product such as the text of an article can be carried on entirely through the Web page: The buyer selects the desired article and enters a credit card account number, and the Web server transmits the article. Assuming that some security mechanism is in place to keep the credit card account number private, no other network mechanisms are required (remember, of course, that the vendor in this instance would have to collect the sale information and process the credit card transaction manually).

Commerce over the World Wide Web requires more than transaction security: It requires mechanisms for processing sales as well. Those mechanisms cover the process from the point at which the sale information has been captured through the Web, moving information to the appropriate systems within the merchant's organization as well as outside, to companies that provide services like credit card authorization, to banks providing electronic banking services, and to other organizations involved in electronic transfers of value.

Chapter 2 discusses the actual mechanisms behind secure transactions, while Chapter 4 examines how these mechanisms are applied to protocols defining secure applications for use over the Internet.

Other Internet Sales Venues

For many years before anyone even imagined the World Wide Web, electronic mail and network news existed. And for many years before Internet access providers started selling dial-up access, people were doing business with each other by e-mail and network news.

Acceptable Use Policies (AUPs) prohibited commercial use of those parts of the Internet supported with government funds until the government moved out of the Internet business, but in practice this was interpreted to mean activities engaged in purely for profit. Personal possessions were routinely advertised in the appropriate news forums, although trying to sell magazine subscriptions or aluminum siding in lists devoted to computer operating systems was highly inadvisable. Used cars, computers, memory, and telephone answering machines were routinely sold online, generally through postings on lists devoted to personal items for sale.

Setting aside some of the "religious" discussions that "for sale" posts often incited (Is it appropriate to advertise a used network hub for sale on a network discussion group? Is puppy-farming a hobby or a business?), the problems of transacting business across an unsecure, unreliable, and public medium became glaringly obvious.

First was the problem of fraud. Negotiating prices and delivery options by e-mail is quite easy; making sure that payment and delivery both occur is hard. Unless the parties were able to meet physically, there was no satisfactory solution to this problem. With no control over online identities, it is difficult or impossible to determine exactly who has sent an e-mail message, and unscrupulous individuals have taken advantage of this fact. Buyers often found that they had sent a check or money order off to a post office box, but never received the disk drive or monitor they thought they bought. Sellers often shipped their used equipment off to a remote address and then never got the check that was forever in the mail.

Obviously, there were enough honest individuals buying and selling to make it worthwhile, and there were ways to check up on uncertain quantities: One was to get phone numbers, addresses, and references for faraway buyers and sellers — but this added significant costs in time and money. Another option was to limit all sales to cash, in-person transactions, which also limited to the number of potential buyers, but eliminated the problems of nonpayment and nondelivery.

Credit card sales, though far from common, did happen. Some individuals had set up as corporations for the sale of specialized books, software, music CDs, and other products; when buying from these people, it was possible to send a credit card account number by e-mail. Despite it being transmitted in clear text between any number of different hosts through the Internet, we are not aware of any instance of a credit card number being intercepted on the Internet and misused. Either no one is willing to admit having sent credit card numbers by e-mail (it is widely considered to be pure folly to do so), or thieves looking for credit card numbers have easier ways to steal them than by attempting to put a packet sniffer on an Internet backbone and digging them out of the gigabytes of e-mail, news posts, and World Wide Web graphics image downloads.

Commerce by e-mail is becoming more viable an option for those without World Wide Web access as more security and authentication products become available. These will be discussed at greater length throughout this book; they are generally equally applicable to the World Wide Web and any other Internet application, including e-mail.

ONLINE COMMERCE SOLUTIONS

As the previous sections make clear, commercial transactions over the Internet are not only possible; they are easy, as long as the proper tools are used. The rest of this book addresses these solutions, describing their general terms as well as providing overviews of some of the specific implementations announced and currently being delivered.

Beyond the basic issues of security (as manifested in authentication of offers, authorization of buyers and sellers, and verification of content), merchants and consumers also need to understand how these methods (as well as the use of digital currencies) can all be fitted into a commercial environment for the processing of orders.

Public Key Cryptography

Development of public key cryptography has paralleled the development of the Internet over the past 25 years or so. This should not be surprising, because improvements in the average computer's processing power have been rapid, constant, and remarkable — and both internet-working and cryptography require lots of computer power.

Cryptography is, literally, "secret writing" and refers to the arts and sciences of codes and secrets. Traditional cryptography relied on the use of keys and coding algorithms (procedures used to process text). The algorithm, which was generally kept secret, manipulated the message to be coded in a repeatable way; the key, also kept secret, provided a starting point for encoding and decoding texts. For example, a simple algorithm uses replacement. To encode, replace each plain-text letter with the letter a certain number further down the alphabet (wrapping around to the start of the alphabet after the letter "z"). There are 25 distinct and usable keys for this algorithm. If the key selected is "1," then the word

```
rabbit
```

would be rendered as

```
sbccju
```

This code has been implemented as a cereal-box giveaway, and it becomes trivially easy to break when the message is more than a very few words: The letter distribution and patterns are sufficient for rapid solution of this type of puzzle.

Private key codes like this may depend on the algorithm as well as the key remaining unknown. Much more sophisticated codes have been developed as computing equipment has been increasingly relied upon for cryptographic purposes. Developments have included methods that make distribution and pattern solutions (without the code-breaker having any knowledge of the algorithms or keys used), but all codes are breakable with sufficient time and resources.

Public key methods, which will be discussed in greater detail in Chapter 2, rely on schemes that employ two separate keys — one private and the other public — employed in a well-known algorithm. All the information needed to break the code is available to any code-breaker, as long as the code-breaker has the time and computer resources required. Depending on the way the code has been implemented, this could keep today's most advanced supercomputer occupied for many, many years. Since most encrypted information loses its value to code-breakers rather quickly, this approach to security works quite well.

Public key methods are useful beyond encryption: They make it possible for an individual to digitally sign a digital document, and they make it possible to verify that a digital transmission has been completed unmodified from the original. All these functions are vitally important to electronic commerce, and all will be discussed in greater detail in Chapter 2.

Security Standards

As mentioned earlier, the Secure Sockets Layer (SSL), originally proposed by Netscape Communications Corp., and the Secure HTTP (S-HTTP) specification add significant security functions to the World Wide Web. These and other proposed standards (like that announced by Visa/MasterCard in late 1995) generally incorporate the public key cryptographic tools described earlier and in Chapter 2 to provide security. SSL and S-HTTP are described in greater detail in Chapter 4.

Commerce Models and Environments

The movement of money between buyer and seller is rarely simple even in the traditional storefront. Credit cards, debit cards, and charge cards all represent different payment methods; add to the mix cash, personal and third-party checks, traveler's checks, and money orders, and it is no longer simple to figure out where the money is and where it is going.

Electronic commerce systems include many of the same options as nonelectronic commerce, but add different methods of transmission. Electronic payments can be as simple as the unencrypted transmission of a credit card account number, or as complex as the encrypted transmission of a digitally signed electronic check. Third-party payment processors and electronic currencies add to the complexity. Chapter 3 introduces the various options for implementing electronic transfer of values, and it builds a conceptual foundation for the reader to better understand the vendors and products described in Chapters 5–8 and how they interact with each other. Chapter 9 discusses some tools, services, and products related to the implementation and support of electronic commerce.

TWO

SECURITY TECHNOLOGIES

Three may keep a secret, if two of them are dead.

—BENJAMIN FRANKLIN, POOR RICHARD'S ALMANAC (1733)

S ecrets have always been hard to keep, and we have more secrets today than ever, what with Social Security numbers, credit card accounts, and Personal Identification Numbers (PINs) for accessing practically everything. With computers to keep records and collect data, the informed person is examining what information is solicited, what is shared, and what is kept private. The Internet is open — meaning transmissions can be overheard, intercepted, and forged. However, some simple tools can eliminate (for all intents and purposes) the risks inherent in communicating over an open link. This chapter explains why the Internet is unsecure and examines the tools used to secure it. Internetworking protocols and cryptography don't make for easy reading, but they do build a base for understanding the issues of online commerce.

WHY THE INTERNET IS UNSECURE

The Internet is simply an implementation of protocols, rules of operation, or standards that define the way connected computers communicate with each other. When every connected system follows these rules, they can all communicate with each other — even if they use different hardware, software, or operating systems. Connected systems can even be connected to different types of networks, but as long as they all run the Internet protocols, they will be able to interoperate.

The people upon whose work the Internet is based intended to prove the feasibility of internetworking, not to produce a commercial product for internetworking. As a result, the things consumers of commercial computer products look for, such as easy-to-use interfaces and secure operations, have long been missing from Internet Protocol suite implementations.

In the early days of the Internet, the overwhelming majority of people connected to the Internet were academics or researchers, and Internet traffic was restricted to not-for-profit uses. Users then, as now, were advised not to trust any sensitive information to the Internet. Most computers connected to the Internet were UNIX boxes, with the remainder being large, multiuser systems — all of which had their own security implementations. One of the most important functions fulfilled by Internet news groups was dissemination of security information and warnings about risks uncovered in different operating systems and TCP/IP implementations. The prudent network manager used heavily monitored Internet firewalls to strictly filter data being sent in and out of the organizational network; this is still recommended today.

Securing personal computers on a network is considerably more difficult than securing UNIX workstations and mainframes: There are as many points of entry to the network as there are personal computers, PC security tools range from nonexistent to barely adequate, and the PC users themselves are notoriously lax in their security practices.

```
Tracing route to openmarket.com [199.170.183.2] over a maximum of 30 hops:
 1 486 ms 212 ms 166 ms dial2.primary.net [205.242.92.16] 2 151 ms 168 ms 133 ms
bigrtr.primary.net [205.242.92.254] 3 149 ms 140 ms 140 ms ATM1-0-STL.dmnd.net
[206.114.210.7] 4 210 ms 308 ms 179 ms 902.Hssi3-0.GW1.STL1.ALTER.NET [137.39.168.5]
5 270 ms 360 ms 469 ms 127.Hssi5-0.CR1.CHI1.Alter.Net [137.39.69.45] 6 594 ms 401
ms 394 ms 106.Hssi4-0.CR1.BOS1.Alter.Net [137.39.30.57] 7 195 ms 215 ms 320 ms
Fddi0-0.GW2.BOS1.Alter.Net [137.39.35.7] 8 284 ms 189 ms 249 ms
OpenMarket1-gw.customer.ALTER.NET [137.39.207.226] 9 298 ms 397 ms 212 ms
screen1.openmarket.com [204.254.94.3] 10 373 ms 535 ms 703 ms bb-router-2.openmarket.com
[204.254.94.126] 11 406 ms 381 ms 252 ms openmarket.com [199.170.183.2]
Trace complete
```

FIGURE 2-1 *Once data is transmitted past the organizational network, it can pass across many different computers and networks, where eavesdroppers may be able to intercept it. To demonstrate this, the following is the result of a trace route (tracert.exe) from the computer used to write this book to Open Market, Inc.*

In any case, the Internet is definitely an open network. Once data is transmitted beyond the organizational network, it may be handled by any number of different intermediate computers (called routers) which make sure the data is delivered to its intended destination. Data is also likely to travel across Internet backbone networks, which move vast quantities of data over large distances. Information is vulnerable at many points, including the originating computer (which may have been tampered with at some point to subvert it), the local or organizational network (local traffic is almost trivially easy to listen to and requires little more than a connection to the same network), and some intermediate system or network out on the Internet—and the same risks exist for the networks and systems on the receiving end. Figure 2-1 shows the type of route data may take between two hosts on the Internet.

Smart network managers and administrators take great care before connecting any corporate system on the Internet, implementing elaborate and extensive filtering systems and firewalls. Another growing issue for many companies is the creation and enforcement of a security policy and acceptable use policy. Before one dismisses this attitude as overly paranoid, it must be put in the context of other information risks:

- Long-distance telephone calling card accounts (along with personal identification numbers, PINs) are routinely looted by watchers (some using binoculars) at airports and train stations.
- Intruders routinely take advantage of unprotected systems not just to search for valuable or interesting information, but as stepping-stones to further attacks on other systems.
- More than 20,000 credit card numbers stored on a computer at an Internet service provider were compromised by an intruder in early 1995.

The service provider had not implemented sufficient security to prevent the attack, which apparently had not taken advantage of any inherent Internet weakness, but exploited security weaknesses in the actual computer. The point is that property must be protected, whether it is information or has a physical existence, because immoral people will try to steal it if they possibly can. Those apparently paranoid network managers realize that any corporate resource exposed on the Internet is at risk, and the solution is eternal vigilance.

It's the Protocols

The Internet protocol, TCP/IP, is a layered protocol with seven layers. In many circles these are referred to as the seven layers of OSI. The seven layers are formed in a hierarchy with the lowest level, level one, focusing on the raw physical connection between two devices. The highest level of the protocol works with the actual application such as the Web, Internet mail, or file transfer protocol.

For the purposes of this discussion, we will discuss four of the levels, as shown in Figure 2-2. Understanding a little about the way information moves around the Internet will help explain why the Internet itself is unreliable and unsecure — but can still allow reliable and secure messages to be sent and received.

The different layers represent different kinds of interactions. They are useful in the design of internetworks because they separate and

Application Layer	Handles interaction between the applications running on communicating systems.
Transport Layer	Handles the connection between the processes running on communicating systems.
Internet Layer	Handles the connection between systems communicating across an internetwork.
Link Layer	Handles the connection between systems communicating across a local area network or other link.

FIGURE 2-2 *The Internet reference model helps engineers implement applications to allow any two computers to communicate across the Internet.*

distribute important functions in an efficient way. The specific type of network cable my computer is connected to is a vital part of Internet traffic — but only as it concerns moving that traffic from my Internet service provider to my actual computer. Likewise, my computer operating system and version of e-mail software is important, but only as it relates to the display of e-mail that I receive from the Internet.

The lowest level at which the Internet functions involves connections across the local area network (between the network connections of computers physically linked together) — in other words, actual signals that pass along a wire (or wireless) link. Because the Internet is actually a network of networks, this layer operates only at the local level between computers connected to the same wire.

Called the Link or Network Layer, this level may be an Ethernet cable LAN installed in a corporate office, or a telephone link between a home PC user and an Internet service provider. In theory, the link layer can control just about any communication medium (one April Fool's Internet specification describes IP as implemented with carrier pigeons), but is largely irrelevant to Internet security. Any security mechanisms that might be in place on a local network or telephone connection work only as long as the data remains on that local area network or phone link. As soon as the data is forwarded to another network, it has to be made accessible to systems on that network.

The next layer is the Internet Layer. This is where connections between computers are handled, using the Internet Protocol. Internet addresses uniquely identify each and every connected computer on the Internet and are used to deliver data. The source computer addresses its information to the destination computer. If the destination system isn't on the same physical wire as the source system, intermediate router computers (which have connections to more than one network) pass the information on until it arrives at the destination system's home network.

The Internet Protocol is known as a "best effort" protocol: There are no mechanisms defined through IP to guarantee delivery of any particular piece of information. That type of mechanism would require any recipient system to notify the origination system in the event that it received the data, but also in the event that expected data was not received. That type of transaction is relatively easy when the communicating systems are sitting on the same local network — but when data has to be passed across any number of different networks by routers, it becomes burdensome to offer any kind of delivery guarantees. As a result, the Internet Protocol leaves delivery guarantees (as well as security) to a higher layer.

The Transport Layer is next, handling the connection between the actual programs running on the source and destination systems. This turns out to be important because each computer can have more than one active link to another computer, so there must be a way for each individual session to be differentiated. Because there are different types of network application programs that need to be run in the Internet, there are two different protocols defining the way the programs can interact: the User Datagram Protocol (UDP) and the Transport Control Protocol (TCP).

These two protocols carry two different types of Internet traffic. The Transport Control Protocol is the workhorse of the Internet: Applications that require a "virtual circuit" (the functional equivalent of a direct connection between two computers) use TCP to ensure that information being sent has been received by the remote system. TCP supplies reliability for Internet applications that require it: any application that offers users some degree of interaction with remote network resources. For example, interactive terminal sessions (telnet) and file transfers using the File Transfer Protocol (ftp) both use TCP—as do World Wide Web protocols (usually).

The User Datagram Protocol, like the Internet Protocol, is an unreliable, best-effort protocol. Most often used by applications that don't support direct interaction or that don't require every single message to get through, UDP is a much more efficient protocol: It takes less programming to implement it, and it uses far fewer network resources to communicate between programs using it. Neither of the Internet's transport protocols currently implements security features—those are left for a higher layer.

The highest layer is defined by the interaction between end user and network resource. Called the Application Layer, its relevant protocols define the different applications available to users in the Internet. For instance, the World Wide Web application is defined by the Hypertext Transport Protocol (HTTP), and the most common method for file transfer is defined by the File Transfer Protocol. Each Internet application is defined by its application protocol, which prescribes how commands are passed from the user to the remote system, and how requested information is passed back to the user.

Security and reliability may both be built into the application layer, if desired. Doing so means that no intermediate routers need to worry about the reliability or security of the data they transfer from network to network (which would mean additional computations for verifications)—they just make sure it arrives at its destination. Once the data reaches its destination, the target computer can then make sure the data it receives is reliable and secure.

By using several different layers, data can move efficiently across the Internet. The program at the Application Layer collects information (from the end user or the network resource), wraps it up (encapsulates it), addresses it to the destination resource, and passes it down to the Transport Layer. The Transport Layer wraps the data up and addresses it to the target program on the destination system, then passes it on down to the Internet Layer. The Internet Layer program wraps the data up and addresses it to a particular computer on a particular network, then passes it down to the Network Layer. If the destination computer is on the same network as the source computer, the software at the Network Layer simply sends the data directly to the destination; if not (as is usually the case), the data gets sent to an appropriate router, to be forwarded to the destination network and host.

The software operating at any given layer is concerned only with moving data chunks to its destination at the same layer: Network Layer software moves chunks of data between connections on the same physical wire; Internet Layer software moves chunks of data between two specific computers connected to the Internet; Transport Layer software moves chunks of data between two programs; and Application Layer software moves data between a user and a resource. When Network Layer software receives a chunk of data, it unwraps it and passes it up to the next layer; this process continues until the actual application data is unwrapped and passed to the user or network resource.

This is a very abbreviated summary of how the Internet protocols work, but it is enough to show how data moves around the Internet, as well as where some of the security risks lie.

Where the Risks Are

It should be stressed from the very start that the greatest threat to security in any organization almost invariably comes from within. Insiders have the access, they know what is valuable, and they know what is most damaging. The same goes for the Internet, at least for now: The hacker who stole 20,000 credit card numbers did not exploit any weakness in the Internet protocols; he exploited the weakness in the security of the computer where those numbers were stored.

What the Risks Are

In any case, there are still some serious risks that you take on when you transmit data across the Internet:

- Interception by third party (someone other than the intended recipient reads mail you send)
- Forgery (someone sends mail and signs your name)
- Modification (someone intercepts your mail, changes it, and sends it on to its final destination)

Interception of your network traffic is only a problem if you are sending sensitive information, like credit card numbers or electronic cash. However, most traffic is largely pretty boring or irrelevant except to the parties involved. One sure way to keep eavesdroppers in the dark is to not speak publicly about private matters: This works as well on the Internet as it does in a restaurant.

Forgery can be a much more serious risk. The nature of the e-mail protocols makes it a relatively simple matter for someone to send a message that appears to be coming from someone else. The possibilities for mischief (at least) are infinite, from sending poison pen letters to someone's boss to ordering a dozen pizzas electronically in someone else's name. With no physical evidence, e-mail forgery is relatively easy to get away with, which eliminates one restraining factor that might keep someone with insufficient moral compass from doing it.

Another insidious threat is that someone will intercept transmissions, modify them, and send them on to their destinations. For instance, a criminal could intercept a message from a vendor and change the payment instructions, directing payment to the criminal's account. Again, the devious mind can come up with any number of other options for mischief.

Internet Security Holes

Once you've secured your own computer system — using access codes or passwords, physically restricting access to it, and making sure that it is not left unattended while connected to any remote services — you can start to worry about the risks from your Internet connection.

The first place your data goes when it leaves your computer is a router connected to the Internet. If you are linked through an organizational Internet connection, your own system may actually be visible to anyone else connected to the Internet; more likely, though, your organizational Internet connection will sit on the other side of a firewall system. Firewall gateways function by hiding organizational systems from the rest of the Internet, while still providing access for approved applications to send and receive data. Organizations that use firewalls also usually put their public access systems, such as World Wide Web servers, just outside their firewalls and keep sensitive material off those servers.

What if you don't have a corporate connection, but rather use a dial-up connection (SLIP or PPP) to an Internet service provider across a telephone line? In theory, your computer is vulnerable to attacks any time you are connected. Your system at those times can act as a server — but only if you are running a server program.

The larger issue is what happens to your Internet transmissions when they leave (or before they arrive at) your computer. Anyone with access to the router through which you receive your Internet traffic (or the network to which it is connected) has the ability to eavesdrop on your sessions. Security depends on the integrity of participating network and system managers, as well as on their ability to keep out intruders.

As someone who has been entrusted with access to sensitive systems like these, I would like to believe that anyone who has been given that kind of access is an upstanding, moral person. But, although the vast majority of people are upright, there will always be a few bad apples who will betray their trust for money, for power, for ego, or just for fun.

This security risk exists at every interconnection, so if you purchase your Internet service from a local reseller, chances are that your transmissions get passed from the local company to a regional company, who passes them on to Internet backbones. There may be quite a few intermediate networks and systems between your computer and the computers you communicate with, each with its own support staff that must be trusted to be capable of running both a secure network (to keep outside intruders out) and a moral one (to keep insiders from selling out).

A Bigger Risk

Security methods that use digital signatures and encryption can, in general, be considered secure, for all practical purposes. The cost of a brute-force attack against this type of mechanism would be astronomical, far in excess of any conceivable potential benefit to the attacker.

However, whenever the user must provide his or her own password, attacks on individual accounts are possible, just as they are in any system that uses passwords for access. This means that customers must take as much care in protecting the passwords to their secure commerce services as they would in protecting their own wallets:

- The password should not be easy to guess (like a name or birth date).
- The password should not be written down near the computer from which it will be used.
- The user should not give out the password to anyone, ever.
- The user should not leave an active session running on an unattended, unprotected system.
- Passwords should be changed periodically.

As long as precautions are taken, and passwords protected properly, they will keep the system secure. If the passwords are not protected, however, the only thing they provide is a false sense of security. It should also be noted that requiring users to maintain (and remember) a separate user ID and password for every commercial site they connect to makes it increasingly difficult for users to actually follow basic security principles and more likely that they will fail to do so.

Fighting Back

Despite the ominous description of the Internet and firewalls, there are steps you can take to recover some peace of mind in connecting a corporate network to the Internet. The firewall software market is evolving on a daily basis. There is tremendous competition in this field, yielding great results for end users.

One great product of the development is virtual private networking or VPN, often referred to as tunneling. Fundamentally, VPN gives the network/firewall administrators of two firewalls the ability to create a virtual encrypted path between the two firewalls. Assuming each firewall is equipped with the VPN feature, the two administrators enter the IP address of the other firewall into their home firewalls. The two firewalls exchange messages and create a special encryption algorithm or code. When data is sent from one firewall to the other, the originating firewall will detect that the data (packets) are headed to a participating firewall and use the previously arranged encryption algorithm to encrypt the data. Upon arrival at the destination firewall, the data will be recognized and the shared algorithm will be used to decode the data once inside the firewall. And, of course, while the data passed over the Internet, the data was encrypted, and the only device on earth that could quickly decode the information was the destination firewall.

The first installations of VPN were limited to firewalls from the same manufacturer. However, to promote interoperability, the IPSEC standard has been created and is being implemented by leading fire-wall vendors.

VPN is only practical for business-to-business transactions such as one between a railroad and an auto manufacturer. However, the functionality will be applicable as more servers managing electronic commerce transactions automatically communicate with banks and similar high-security sites. VPN also holds opportunities for midsized and large companies looking to create secure wide-area networks over the Internet.

What It All Means

The bottom line is that the Internet is a public network, and anyone concerned with transmission security needs to approach the Internet in the same way one would approach communicating by any other public means. Internet communications are functionally equivalent (at least as far as security goes) to communicating in a public hall. Conversations between you and your neighbor can be overheard by anyone who wants to eavesdrop; if you want to talk to someone at the opposite end of the hall, you've got to rely on intermediaries to carry the message between you.

A BRIEF INTRODUCTION TO CRYPTOGRAPHY

Modern cryptography offers solutions to the problems of an open network. This section introduces some of the basic concepts of modern cryptography, on which most online commerce schemes depend. This section simply raises some of the pertinent cryptographic issues as they relate to passing commercial transactions across an open channel; discussion of the actual algorithms, implementations, and the mathematical basis for private and public key cryptography are all far beyond the scope of this book, but the interested reader will find some excellent references in Appendix B.

Cryptography

As an individual, if you've got something "sensitive" to say to someone, chances are you can find a way to do this without resorting to secret codes: A whisper in the right person's ear, a confidential chat in a bar, or a discreet letter are all reliable ways to share a secret (keeping the secret later is another story). You've got control over who is listening, and you need not worry about anyone trying to read your mail (unless you are a criminal kingpin, revolutionary leader, or subject of some other investigation).

If you did want to protect your sensitive communications, chances are you'd try to use some kind of code or cipher, replacing the "real" words with "code" words, or shifting characters to hide the real meaning of your messages.

Chances are that some form of cryptography first came about shortly after the invention of writing, although the earliest surviving ciphers date from the time of Julius Caesar.

Governments and military organizations have always needed to protect their communications (lives depend on it). And since the stakes are so much higher, there is more risk that the messages will fall into the wrong hands—so there is greater incentive to hide the meaning of the message. If there were a method of passing messages that could not be detected by anyone but the intended recipient, then cryptography would be unnecessary. As it is, with radio transmissions being highly public, cryptography has become indispensable.

By offering reliable and secure communications methods like a (relatively) sacrosanct postal service and (usually) bug-free telephone service, governments have been able to argue that their law-abiding citizens had no need for cryptographic services. Only the government had the power to read your mail and listen to your telephone conversations, so that was OK. In an increasingly digital world, though, there are more opportunities for practically anyone to listen in—and those opportunities are more lucrative.

A criminal would much rather discover your credit card number than find out how your vacation went or what subjects your children are flunking. Making a purchase across the Internet may put your credit at risk, but using cryptography can help protect it. It should be noted that the individual consumer in the United States is liable for no more than $50 when a credit card is compromised, so the greatest risk is taken on by the credit card companies and the merchants. While individual credit card accounts may be susceptible to hijacking when transmitted over the Internet, there is far greater risk of theft from concentration points, like the computers where the account numbers are stored. And while criminal hackers may be responsible for some thefts, insiders familiar with those systems are more likely to exploit them.

The Objective of Cryptography

The whole point of cryptography is to keep information out of the hands of anyone but its intended recipient. Even if the message gets intercepted, the meaning won't be apparent to the interceptor—unless the interceptor is able to decipher it.

Cryptography as we know it uses encryption to transform plain texts into encrypted texts. Ideally, encoding or decoding them should not require too much effort, but decoding without the keys should be hard enough to discourage anyone from trying to do so. The fact is that encryption schemes can always be broken, if you have enough time and resources. The idea behind modern encryption methods is to make it so costly in time and resources for an interceptor to interpret a message that it is not practical to even attempt it—while keeping it easy for an authorized recipient to read.

The strength of the encryption scheme needed is determined by how long you want to keep your secret. For example, if you're planning a surprise birthday party in two weeks, you might trust a scheme that required a month of continuous effort to break; a corporation would want a stronger method to protect long-term plans or trade secrets.

Codes and Ciphers

The terms "code," "cipher," "encryption," and "decipher" all have quite specific meanings. Strictly speaking, a code actually uses some method of interchanging vocabularies so that each code word represents some other noncode word. Codes require special code books which act like dictionaries; if the code book is lost, encoded text cannot be interpreted—and anyone with the code book can read encoded text.

Ciphers are the basis of encryption schemes. Ciphers act on each character of a message, transforming it according to some repeatable rule, or algorithm. Keys are special numbers which help initialize the algorithm; different keys used with the same algorithm will produce different versions of encrypted texts.

At this point, keep in mind the objective of cryptography: keeping secrets secret. As was mentioned earlier, encryption is used when you cannot guarantee that a message will not fall into the wrong hands. Ideally, you want to keep the plain text of the message secret, but you know that is not always possible. If you encrypt it, you prefer that the algorithm you are using not become known to the bad guys, because that would mean they could try every possible key to break your cipher—but really good algorithms don't grow on trees, and there are plenty of ways to figure out which one is being used (this will be discussed in the next section). So, you'll settle for a key that can be kept secure, and an algorithm that's tough to break even if you know which one it is.

Traditional ciphers use a single key, which the sender and the recipient share (and try to keep secret from anyone else). The sender runs the algorithm using the key to turn the plain-text message into an encrypted message, and the recipient runs the same algorithm in reverse (using the same key) to decrypt the message. This is known as symmetric cryptography.

Breaking Encryption Schemes

Encryption schemes are vulnerable on several fronts: You can analyze encrypted text for things like word and character frequencies, or trick someone into sending some particular message and then figure out what was done to that message, or find out what the encryption algorithm is and do a "brute-force" attack on it by trying every single possible key. The last method is a completely reliable way to break any encryption scheme — as long as you have enough time.

Cryptographers accept that all ciphers are vulnerable to brute-force attacks, and they design ciphers with this in mind. The key to security is usually the cipher key size. A cipher key can be compared to a combination lock: If you have the correct key, you can unlock the message. The three-digit combination locks often found on luggage offer minimal protection, since there are only 1000 different options. Sometimes you'll hit on the right combination in only a few tries (for example, if the combination was "007"), and sometimes the combination will be more elusive (for example, "999"); on average, though, you'll break the lock after trying half the total possibilities. At about a second per combination, this means I can open your briefcase, on average, in about eight minutes (and it shouldn't take more than about 17 minutes).

This level of security may be acceptable for keeping your co-workers away from the doughnuts in your briefcase, but not for much else. Adding another digit to the lock increases the number of possible combinations by a factor of ten; doubling the number of digits to six increases the number of possible combinations to one million. A brute-force attack on a six-digit combination lock, at a second per combination, takes an average of almost 6 days (and could take as long as 11.5 days). Add another two digits, and you'd need over a year and a half, on average, to break in.

Of course, with computers in the picture, you can use much larger numbers — and much more complicated algorithms. Adding to the length of the key you use doesn't necessarily make encrypting or decrypting messages more difficult if you know the key, but does make it much less practical to apply brute-force techniques. I may want to steal your credit card number, but if it would take me a century using ten of the biggest supercomputers in the world running at full tilt to do it, I won't bother (since the account will undoubtedly have expired by then).

Another risk is that computing technology will continue improving sufficiently to make practical brute-force attacks on currently adequate encryption schemes. Increasing the size of the key makes it more secure over a longer period of time, but it also makes it harder to implement right now. The bottom line is that a good encryption scheme must represent a compromise between security and practicality.

Encryption schemes are also vulnerable to non-brute-force attacks. Although it is possible to prove that a cipher can be broken through some application of analysis or a smart search for keys, there is no way to unalterably and conclusively prove an algorithm is secure from attack. However, making details of the algorithm public, as discussed in the next section, can help improve the odds that it's secure.

Securing Algorithms

Keeping your algorithm a secret may be a tempting way to keep the algorithm secure, but it turns out that is not the case. If your algorithm is to be used in a commercial product, it doesn't take long for it to be reverse-engineered. Someone buys the product, runs sample texts through it, and figures out what your algorithm does. Security through obscurity seldom works, particularly in commercial products: Software vendors had their copy-protection schemes defeated almost immediately after they introduced them; cable operators lost revenues when their inadequate encryption was broken and illegal cable boxes were widely distributed; early cordless-telephone security features were trivially easy to defeat.

More recently, cryptographers have made their algorithms public either by publishing them in academic journals or by patenting them; in either case, one objective is to subject them to trials by fire. Mathematicians earn bragging rights, among other things, for breaking algorithms that were thought to be secure; getting credit for creating a strong encryption scheme is a major incentive for publishing. Algorithms that can withstand direct attacks are much stronger (and more elegant) than those that fall apart as soon as you know how they work. As indicated earlier, the less you have to keep secret, the easier it is to maintain security.

Distributing Keys and Keeping Them Secret

Up to now we have been considering secret key algorithms: If you have the key, you can read any encrypted messages. One major weakness with this approach is that you need to have a dependable way to pass keys around to the people who need them. You have to treat the key with at least as much care as you do the messages; losing a single message may be harmful, but losing the key means losing all messages. Another weakness is that if you want to send a secure message to a group, you've either got to rely on everyone involved keeping a single key secure among them, or you've got to assign a separate key to each individual and use it for all communications.

While the simplest answer is to hand-deliver all keys, and have a single key for each pair of people who want to exchange secure messages, it soon becomes clear that this solution doesn't scale up well at all. You and I can communicate securely with a single key; add my brother to the mix, and I need one key to talk to him, one to talk to you. You need another key to talk to him; each of us now has two keys, and there are three keys in all. Adding new participants in our little secret circle adds more keys; if we were running a company and wanted to assign secret keys to our customers, we'd soon be in the business of assigning and distributing keys.

Online commerce requires that you be able to securely exchange messages with anyone, whether you know that person or not. Private key solutions are available, but by and large they require some degree of trust either in the parties exchanging messages, or else in some intermediary agency with access to both parties' secret keys. As it happens, public key cryptographic techniques make this unnecessary.

Data Encryption Standard

One widely distributed secret key solution is the Data Encryption Standard, or DES. The United States National Bureau of Standards published DES in the late 1970s for commercial uses. For instance, Automatic Teller Machine networks use DES to encrypt consumers' PINs (Personal Identification Numbers) when they are transmitted through shared networks and data communications lines.

DES is considered safe against all but brute-force attacks, which are considered to be impractical against DES for all but the very largest and most determined organizations (like major governments, for example). More to the point, DES can be implemented reasonably efficiently for bulk encryption like that required by electronic commerce applications.

While there are software implementations, the DES standard specifies that only hardware-only implementations comply with the standard.

The Public Key Solution

Public key cryptography relies on the fact that it is relatively easy to perform modular arithmetic, even on large numbers, and that it is relatively difficult to find the factors of very large numbers. This means that you can use a very, very large number that has only two factors as the basis of an encryption scheme, where you encrypt using one of those factors, and you can decrypt the resulting ciphertext only using the other factor. Decrypting the text using the same key it was encrypted with does not reverse the process.

Modular Arithmetic

Modular arithmetic is similar to regular arithmetic, but it adds division by some number and is concerned only with the remainder resulting from that division. For instance, the expression

8+17

is equal to 25; calculating this value **modulo** (or **mod**) another number (called the **modulus**) simply produces a remainder:

```
25 mod 10 = 5
```

because 10 goes into 25 two times, with a remainder of 5;

```
25 mod 15 = 10
```

because 15 goes into 25 once, with 10 left over.

Any regular arithmetic expression can also be calculated modulo some other number, including raising to powers. For example:

```
5² mod 10 = 5
```

This turns out to be extremely useful because you can represent a piece of data as a number and then encrypt it by raising it to a certain power, and then finding the remainder when dividing the result by another number. For the moment it's enough to know that doing modular arithmetic on very large numbers can be a lot easier than evaluating the underlying expressions themselves. For instance, the numbers in the expression:

```
some large number^some other large number
```

don't have to be very large before they begin to tax the capacities of most computers to evaluate. The expression

```
1000¹⁰⁰⁰
```

is easy to evaluate, but would take up a couple of pages in this book. Change the expression to

```
1013⁹⁶⁷
```

and all of a sudden this is a very difficult number to figure out, even with a computer.

However, if the number used as the exponent is chosen carefully, calculating the remainder after dividing by a carefully chosen modulus will actually prove fairly simple.

Factoring and Large Numbers

Although doing modular arithmetic on powers of large numbers can be relatively easy (certainly well within the capacities of the average desktop personal computer), factoring large numbers is not easy. Factoring, or determining what numbers can be evenly divided into another number, is hard to do and becomes harder to do reliably as the number to be factored becomes larger. Some factors are easy: If the number in question ends in a zero, one of its factors is 10 (and two more are 2 and 5); all even numbers are divisible by 2, and all numbers ending in 5 are divisible by 5.

There is no way to look at a large number and quickly determine whether it is prime, or whether it has factors. The brute-force solution to factoring is to try dividing the number in question by every smaller number. If a number is the product of two prime numbers, especially if those two prime numbers are already big numbers, the number of divisions needed to find the correct factors becomes astronomical, even though the numbers in question remain relatively easy to work with.

Public Key Encryption

By choosing two large prime numbers and properly manipulating them, you can extract two keys; multiply them to get the number to evaluate the modular expressions. You can now encrypt a message by chopping it up into small chunks, converting those chunks to numbers, raising those numbers to the power of one of the keys, and calculating the result modulo the sum of the two original primes.

As a result of the nature of modular exponentiation, the two keys work together to create an encryption algorithm. You can encrypt a message with one of the keys, but you must use the *other* key to decrypt it, doing the same process on the encrypted text. That means that this is an asymmetric encryption scheme: Encrypting with one key cannot be reversed without the other key, as shown in Figure 2-3. In practice, one of the keys is called a public key and can be safely distributed publicly; the other key is called a private or secret key and is not for distribution.

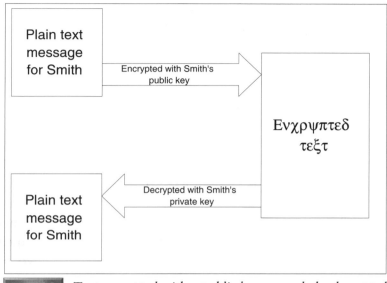

FIGURE 2-3 *Text encrypted with a public key can only be decrypted by the private key, and vice versa.*

This is, very simply, the idea behind the dominant public key encryption scheme. Named for its inventors, Ron Rivest, Adi Shamir, and Len Adleman, RSA was patented, and it is now owned by RSA Data Security, Inc. (RSADSI). Because it has held up against attacks by cryptographers, mathematicians, computer scientists, and amateurs over the nearly 20 years since it was first published, it is widely held to be a secure encryption method.

How It Works

Very simply, once you've got your public and private keys, you can communicate securely and reliably. Individuals with public keys often add those keys to the bottom of any document or e-mail they distribute; companies using public keys can include those keys in network application software like security-equipped Web browsers.

Although public key encryption is practical on personal computers, it is still requires a lot of computing power. As a result, it is often implemented as a method of exchanging a single-session, traditional secret key between participants, rather than encrypting the entire transmission with a public key. Encryption of that key is done with the recipient's public key; only the recipient is able to decrypt that transmission. Once both parties have the secret key, each is able to encrypt and decrypt the communication (much more efficiently, too, since symmetric cryptography is easier to do on the fly than public key or asymmetric cryptography).

Encryption solves the security problem, but authentication of content and sender are also solved with RSA. Let's say you and your sweetheart are separated geographically and can only converse by e-mail. If you were to send a proposal of marriage by e-mail, your partner might want you to digitally sign it, just to be sure it's you (you might have a malevolent hacker as a rival). Doing so is a simple matter of using a digest function to summarize the contents of your message mathematically, and then encrypting the result using your own private key. The result can be decrypted by anyone using your public key; your paramour simply runs the same digest function on the signed message and decrypts the signature. If the result matches, it proves that no one but you could have sent the message; if they don't match, your friend will know that the message sent was not the same as the message received.

Of course, a consumer can verify the validity of a product offering made across the World Wide Web just as easily, and vendors can also confirm and authenticate electronic orders made by their known customers.

It should be noted that the RSA method is not perfect; public keys may be made public, but only work reliably if there is a reliable way to guarantee that the public key someone advertises actually is their own. There are also some reasonably well-known weaknesses that can be eliminated by taking certain precautions. However, RSA public key techniques are stronger and more secure than many easier methods.

Why It Works

If the numbers you select as keys are too small, someone could intercept your encrypted messages and apply a brute-force attack with some chance of success. However, by choosing numbers sufficiently large (100 digits and up), solving the cipher (essentially, finding the factors of the modulus) requires factoring a huge number — which, while theoretically possible, approaches impracticality as the size of the numbers used goes up.

As new techniques are devised for factoring large numbers, RSA loses its effectiveness. In addition, computing power has already increased sufficiently since RSA was first formulated to make brute-force attempts against smaller key sizes possible. One group in 1994 factored an RSA modulus that was 129 digits long (using hundreds of workstations over a period of about 8 months); the same group would have needed about 200 years to break a 150-digit public key. The implication, of course, is that it won't take very many years for the computer industry to produce much cheaper workstations capable of much faster computing — at which point the public keys will have to be much bigger numbers to continue to be secure against a concerted effort.

Legal Issues

The United States government classifies cryptographic devices as munitions and restricts their export. RSA represents a very strong method of keeping secrets, and the government would prefer that it not fall into the wrong hands. Unfortunately, the RSA algorithm has been globally disseminated in professional journals, and the cat is out of the bag — pretty much anyone who wants it can have it.

Reality, however, does not get in the government's way, so any software or hardware that implements strong encryption methods has to be approved for export from the United States. Vendors of such products have few options: move their operations off-shore and *import* the products into the United States; go through the process of getting proper certification of the products for export; or weaken the product to make it acceptable for more general export and get proper certification.

Noncompliance with the export law is not usually seen as an option, since the penalties range up to 10 years in federal prison and fines of up to $1,000,000. The government's position is that our enemies, terrorists, drug lords, and other organized criminals can use strong encryption techniques to hatch plots against the United States, and we will have put the tools in their hands and be powerless against them. Given the reality of the situation, that it's too late to keep the technology out of the wrong hands, and the fact that limiting distribution of this type of tool hampers domestic and foreign online trade, easing of these restrictions may be on the horizon.

KEY DISTRIBUTION AND CERTIFICATION

The preceding discussion about private and public key cryptography has avoided the issue of how to manage key distribution. As with all the other aspects of cryptography, there are well-known problems pertaining to secure and reliable key distribution. To illustrate, a simple scenario:

- Bob and Alice are two acquaintances who communicate by e-mail on occasion.
- Evil Robert, impersonating Bob, sends a forged piece of e-mail to Alice, requesting a secure communication channel using public key encryption.
- Included in this forged message is Evil Robert's public key (which he represents as Bob's public key).
- Alice receives the message and encrypts a reply using what she believes to be Bob's public key (but which is actually Evil Robert's public key).
- Evil Robert receives the message, decrypts it with her own secret key, and is able to communicate with Alice while pretending to be Bob.

Of course, this scenario can be easily defeated if Jones could somehow verify that the public key matches the person who sends it.

Trusted Key Distribution and Verification

With the wider application of public key cryptography for the purpose of commerce, mechanisms for the trusted publication and distribution of public keys are necessary. Simply having a merchant (or customer) send a copy of a public key will not do, since a forger could sent her own public key while pretending to be someone else.

One solution is for some (respected) organization to offer key-publishing services. Those who wish to can report their keys and their identities, and anyone else can find a key by looking for a person's name. To add further trust, people can have other people certify their public keys. In other words, one person (or organization) can vouch for another one by adding their own name and public key to the listing. The greater the resulting "pedigree" to your public key, the greater amount of trust others can put in your digital signature.

THREE CRYPTOGRAPHIC APPLICATIONS

As may already be obvious, cryptography, and public key cryptography in particular, plays a vital role in making online commerce a secure option. Three applications of cryptography will be almost constantly mentioned throughout this book (and elsewhere), so these are explicitly defined and summarized here.

Encryption

Requiring the use of a key to "unlock" data is called encryption. The key can be a secret key, used symmetrically, or it can be one of a public key pair, used asymmetrically. The longer the key, the less likely it is that a brute-force attack on the encrypted data will be successful (assuming that the encryption algorithm is not susceptible to other types of attack).

Public key pairs include a private key and a public key. When sending a public-key-encrypted message, the sender encrypts the message with the recipient's public key. The resulting message can now only be decrypted using the recipient's private key.

In practice, public key cryptography is very secure, but very costly in terms of computer resources. As a result, it is often combined with secret key cryptography. For example, a sender can use public key encryption to encrypt a secret key to be used for bulk encryption purposes. Both participants could use a single secret key, or they could use a single key to generate some other set of keys to use for their communication. The exchange of the secret key uses the very secure public key encryption, while the bulk encryption of the remainder of the communication would use some other encryption method.

An eavesdropper could capture the encrypted communication, and thereby attempt to break the encryption. However, by using very long secret keys, using them only for one communication session, and not reusing them, this method can be made quite secure.

Digital Signature

If the sender encrypted data using the sender's own private key, the resulting message could be decrypted by anyone who had the sender's public key. This process can't be considered a way to protect the message from anyone, since anyone with access to the sender's public key can decrypt it. However, it does offer a method of signing a document digitally.

Encrypting a message in this way will ensure that it can only have come from the person whose public key will decrypt it—however, it also ensures that every such message must be decrypted. As has been mentioned, since public key encryption uses lots of resources, this becomes impractical. Also, there is the problem of keeping track of and certifying public keys.

A better option for digital signatures is to use a digest function to summarize the contents of a particular message in a smaller, more manageable chunk of data. This chunk can then be encrypted using the sender's private key, and appended to the message. The recipient can then use the same digest function on the received message and use the sender's public key to decrypt the digest included by the sender. If the two digest results match, then the message has been certified as signed. If the results don't match, then the message cannot be certified as signed.

Nonrepudiation and Message Integrity

There are two by-products of the use of digital signatures. Nonrepudiation is a cryptographic term describing the situation when the originator of a message cannot deny having sent it. Normal electronic mail is deniable, since it is (relatively) easily forged and easily modified. Electronic mail that has been digitally signed, however, is nonrepudiable. If the digital signature checks out properly, the owner of the signature is the only entity capable of having signed the message.

The other important by-product of digital signatures is a guarantee of message integrity. If a message has been digitally signed and transmitted, verifying the signature also verifies that the message has been received unchanged from the source. A signed message that has been intercepted, modified, and forwarded on to its original destination will not produce a verified signature.

The ability to verify a digital signature also confirms that the signed message was delivered intact and unchanged. Furthermore, the person signing the message cannot later deny having sent it.

THREE

ELECTRONIC PAYMENT METHODS

"A New Way to Pay Old Debts"

—PHILLIP MASSINGER (PLAY TITLE, 1632)

UPDATING TRADITIONAL TRANSACTIONS

The typical modern consumer uses a handful of different methods to pay for goods and services on a regular basis:

- Cash
- Credit
- Personal check

This list is far from complete, leaving out choices like debit cards, money orders and bank checks, traveler's checks, barter systems, tokens, and other instruments used by consumers — organizations have their own instruments available, including purchase orders, lines of credit, and others. However, most consumer transactions can be handled by cash, credit cards, or personal checks.

Internet-based electronic commerce methods also focus on secure transmission of credit card information, electronic checking and digital currencies.

> **NOTE**: *Credit cards like MasterCard, Visa, and Discover allow consumers to extend themselves credit on purchases; charge cards like the American Express card do not extend credit. Debit cards are tied to checking accounts, and the amounts charged are debited immediately from the account. However, for the purposes of electronic transactions they are used similarly, and for the purposes of this book the term "credit card" should be taken to cover all credit-card-like plastic payment tokens (unless otherwise specified).*

Adapting Existing Methods

Credit cards are the easiest method of the three to adapt to online transactions, in part because people are already accustomed to using them remotely, whether for telephone transactions or for mail orders. Credit card transactions simply require that the consumer provide a valid credit card number and expiration date (and often a billing address) when placing an order — that information can be, and often has been, provided through standard Internet applications like e-mail. This exposes the credit card to eavesdroppers monitoring for sequences of digits specific to credit cards along the message's route. Although I have not heard of any actual instance of an eavesdropper stealing credit information in this way, it is definitely possible. Securing Internet credit card transactions can be as simple as applying secure encryption (as described in Chapter 2).

Adapting cash for use over an open network is considerably harder, in part because most people associate cash with the physical exchange of currency, but doing so makes it possible to spend anonymously. There are other problems to solve in the process of digitizing cash, where actual currency is replaced by digital "coins" represented as chunks of data. These will be discussed in greater detail in Chapter 8, but one of the most prominent schemes uses public key encryption as well as digital signatures, deployed within a framework managed by a central bank.

Checking across a network is conceptually simpler to grasp, in part because the check itself is simply a document with very specific information (bank, account number, payee, and dollar amount) which has been signed by the account holder. Turning a hard-copy check into an electronic check requires that the electronic check be transmitted securely and signed digitally. In some ways the process is similar to digitizing cash, but is simpler because there is no need to even consider the anonymity of the person "writing" the check.

Building a Commercial Environment

It's one thing to engineer and implement a technique for making purchases electronically, and another to make it useable and accessible. So much commercial activity is centered on the World Wide Web because it seems to provide an easily accessible forum for merchants to display and distribute their products, and an easily accessible environment for consumers to shop and make purchases. Since the World Wide Web was not designed for commerce but for information publishing, making it safe for commerce requires adding on security features and protocols, to be described in Chapter 4. These techniques only make it possible to transmit information securely — they do not address transmission of payments, nor do they do anything to further the transaction once payment information has been received.

An online commerce environment must go beyond the simple transmission of payment information, but it must start there, usually with an Internet server capable of transmitting data securely. Although the payment information is usually the only portion of the transaction that must actually be transmitted securely, some systems offer methods of guaranteeing information such as shipping instructions, offering prices, and other order information through digital signatures. Security goes beyond encryption of ordering information, however, and it is necessary to guard against criminals who masquerade online as merchants authorized to accept consumer credit card information. Even more important is to secure the merchant's server system where credit information is collected.

As an entire solution, the commerce environment should be as flexible as possible, accepting different payment methods consistent with the market and the business. Next, it should help the merchant collect information about customer (wherever relevant and possible). It should be integrated into the general business environment, generating actions to be taken as a result of the order:

- Product delivery instructions
- Transaction settlement
- Account activity reports
- Confirmations
- Order status reports
- Gathering of marketing information

Some merchants will be able to do business on the Internet simply by purchasing and installing a secure World Wide Web server, and manually processing orders received over the Internet in the same way they process mail or telephone orders. Merchants who do not expect a large volume of orders from the Internet will prefer to operate in this way, since it costs less than the more holistic approaches—however, merchants wishing to maximize the benefit of selling online will invest in a more complete commercial environment. Secure servers and related commerce environment products are discussed in more detail in Chapter 7.

Offline and Online Transactions

In general, direct commerce solutions that use the Internet directly to transmit transaction information protect that information with some kind of encryption method. This neutralizes what is perceived to be, but actually isn't, the greatest threat to Internet transactions — the eavesdropper. Data encrypted with a sufficiently strong method is immune to likely threats (the cost of computer resources required to decrypt your credit card number ranges from millions of dollars to many billions of dollars, depending upon whether the decryption must be complete in a matter of decades or faster). There are easier ways to steal credit card numbers.

However, it is not strictly necessary to transmit any sensitive information over open networks when there are much more secure channels that can be used to carry sensitive information. For example, many people feel more comfortable discussing business with associates in person than discussing business over a telephone. Barring the relatively extreme instances of those whose business is under government scrutiny, personal conversations inspire a high level of confidence that no one is listening in: Eavesdroppers in most cases would most likely be noticed.

Although telephone conversations have a greater potential for eavesdropping (legal and illegal taps, someone listening in on an extension, cellular and cordless phone scanners), with a minimum of care a telephone conversation can be relatively secure. The same type of consideration can be applied to fax transmissions, as well as to postal mail and other delivery services. The result is that there are other channels across which sensitive information can be sent. Some Internet commerce solutions take advantage of the relative security of these alternative media to eliminate the need for software security solutions.

These solutions require that the consumer make a telephone call, send a fax, or send a hard copy with sensitive information like credit card numbers, consumer names, and billing and shipping addresses.

SECURE ONLINE TRANSACTION MODELS

It may be simplest to contract with some other company, like an electronic mall operator, Internet service provider, or some other organization, to manage servers, orders, and content. However, that company itself must use some method or methods of accepting and processing orders. As has been mentioned, the simplest method of doing direct business online on the Internet is to set up a secure World Wide Web server, then create content pages and program forms to take orders.

Secure Web Servers

The current battle for domination of the secure World Wide Web server and Internet browser markets is between Netscape and Microsoft. However, Web browsers and servers from any vendor are expected to interoperate with the servers and browsers of any other vendor — this is the whole point behind using Internet standards. (The Netscape and Microsoft secure servers and browsers will be discussed in greater detail in Chapter 7.)

A secure World Wide Web server must, by definition, support some type of security protocol. At the moment, the two most important of these are the Secure Hypertext Transport Protocol (S-HTTP) and the Secure Sockets Layer (SSL), which was initially developed by Netscape and offered to the Internet community as a proposed standard in 1995. These protocols, as well as some others, will be discussed in greater detail later in this chapter and in Chapter 4. However, one of their primary advantages is their relative unobtrusiveness to the consumer using an SSL- or S-HTTP-enabled browser.

Secure Server Purchasing

The resulting browser/server interaction is, to the consumer, very closely mapped to the interaction that occurs when a consumer makes a purchase from a catalog. The consumer browses through graphical and textual descriptions of the merchant's products, selects a purchase, and usually clicks on a button that says something like "BUY NOW" to make a purchase. If the consumer is using a secure browser supported by the secure server, that button will produce a form on the consumer's screen, which the consumer must complete. Delivery and payment information will usually be required, and at some point after this information has been provided the product will be delivered. If the customer is using a browser that is not secure or that uses a protocol not supported by the server, then some other method must be employed to consummate the transaction (alternative methods will be discussed later in this chapter).

Delivery information represents name, address, delivery address, e-mail address, and any other information necessary or desirable to deliver the product. If the product happens to be a physical item, then a physical destination, preferred shipper, and telephone number may be necessary. If the product is a digital item, then it may be transmitted directly to the consumer via the browser, by e-mail, or through some other application such as file transfer.

Secure Server Selling

Merchants want to make it economical, pleasant, and easy for consumers to buy their products, and doing so with a secure Web server is no different. There is a broad spectrum of options to choose from to balance price against a pleasing shopping experience; these issues are beyond the scope of this book — but ease of use is definitely a factor for the consumer using a secure browser.

First, the merchant needs to publish product offerings on the Internet with a secure server. Servers are available that support SSL, S-HTTP, and both. Because the Internet is an open network, based strictly on the proper and widespread implementation of standards, it doesn't make sense for merchants to limit their potential customers by using only one standard. By supporting both SSL and S-HTTP, they support transactions with consumers whose browser uses either of those standards.

However, the merchant must go beyond merely setting up the server. As with mail orders, there must be a mechanism for processing the information contained on an order form. The Internet programming community has created and offers several utilities to manipulate data. One of the first was the Common Gateway Interface (CGI), which uses scripts or lines of code to perform different tasks. More recently, Java and ActiveX have arrived on the market, offering growing levels of sophistication and power in managing data between users and the Web sites they are visiting. World Wide Web forms prompt the consumer for some kind of information, and on receipt of the form, either the data is reported back to a data base, or the Web site massages the data, with CGI, ActiveX, or Java to take the user through another task.

In the simplest case, the information provided by the consumer might be dumped into a data file to be manually processed later. The merchant would go through this file, processing credit card information and shipping the product off to the indicated delivery address. This may be an acceptable solution for low-volume applications — merchants who do not anticipate a large flow of online transactions, for instance. It is not acceptable where the product sold is digital in nature: If the product is delivered immediately, there is no guarantee for the merchant that the payment information is correct, but waiting to ship the digital product may not be acceptable to the consumer who assumes immediate delivery.

More often, the merchant will use interfaces of some type to automate transactions. For example, banks, credit card clearing organizations, and credit card companies are all increasingly willing to authorize transactions executed over the Internet. Companies selling physical products over the Internet use e-mail confirmations and shipping notices to keep customers up to date on the status of orders, and all merchants can use network applications to notify their internal organization of orders.

Required Facilities

The merchant must understand (and the educated consumer should understand) that purchasing products over the Internet requires a significant investment in software, hardware, and services. Surprisingly, the software and hardware components are probably the smallest part of the investment, while the "services" can be acquired from any number of different providers.

The majority of Internet merchants will be unlikely to set up their own secure servers, because doing so can be complicated for the Internet novice, and also because there are so many companies now offering such services. However, merchants who are aware of what their options are can be smarter consumers of these services, and customers who are aware of how their online orders are processed can be smarter online consumers.

Hardware

Technically, any computer that can run an implementation of TCP/IP (including a World Wide Web server program) and that can be connected to the Internet can be a World Wide Web server. More realistically, the system should have a great deal of processing power to handle many simultaneous or near-simultaneous requests for information. It should have a hard disk sufficiently large to store all the information to be published in the Web server as well as system software. It should have a sufficiently fast Internet connection to support the maximum expected load on the system. And, it should have security features sufficient to protect it from unauthorized access. Perhaps surprisingly, a graphical user interface, or any graphics capability, is not technically necessary on the server—it does not have to display any information locally, but rather sends and receives data across the Internet.

In practice and at a minimum, this translates to a fast, current personal computer capable of running an operating system such as Windows NT (or possibly Windows 95), using an Ethernet connection to an Internet router. A UNIX workstation or PC-architecture server system is preferred, though. The Internet connection itself should probably be at least a dedicated telephone line running at 56 Kbps (thousands of bits per second). Internet routers are often included in

Internet service packages, but they are often simply fast personal workstations with special networking software and hardware.

Some organizations using the Internet may prefer to simply get a server and an Internet connection, and leave their internal networks out of the loop. However, those who do opt to connect their organizational networks to the Internet along with their Web server will almost certainly want to invest in some kind of firewall architecture to protect their network from intruders. This is likely to add to the cost of the hardware required for an Internet connection, but is necessary whether they are running a Web server or not.

There is also a blossoming software industry enabling the presentation of data already existing on an internal computer system in a Web server without reentering the data. This will be very useful for companies looking to offer online order processing of inventories experiencing a high level of turnover.

Total initial cost, depending on the systems selected, can be anywhere from $1000 on up. A typical implementation, using a low-end PC server/high-end personal workstation, should cost somewhere between $4000 and $10,000, including router, network cards, and cable.

Software

As mentioned earlier, a TCP/IP implementation is necessary for the Web server. This may be built in to the operating system, or it may be a part of the Web server package, but in any case it is necessary. Likewise, a Web server package is required. This is the software that responds to requests from browsers on the Internet and sends out the desired information. Security, as mentioned before, should be part of the operating system.

Savvy system administrators make sure that there is no other software on Internet servers. This guarantees that if an intruder should compromise that system, no software is available to the intruder for further mischief. For example, network software installed and configured on a server allowing access to organizational data could be used by an intruder to access, modify, or delete that information.

Services

The raw materials are relatively cheap, but the knowledge of how to put it all together is (at least right now) expensive. And there is quite a handful of different things that need to get done to set up a server:

- Obtain Internet service
- Administer Internet link and servers
- Create Web server content
- Process transactions

Obtaining Internet service is simply the process of getting connected to the Internet, and keeping that access up and running. In some ways it is comparable to getting a telephone connection — the ISP simply offers connectivity, not content.

Some Internet service providers will also manage your link and your server hardware. This should mean they will keep the systems up and running and manage access to and from those systems. This often includes security and firewall services.

Creating and maintaining Web server content is critical and is a task often farmed out to consultants. While this approach may be effective for getting a Web site online quickly, maintaining and updating content must be an ongoing task. Fortunately, there are many tools available to make Web authoring easy, and these will tend to drive down the cost of managing Web content.

Finally, transactions using credit cards must be settled. Most people will be familiar with the "swipe" machines used in stores where credit cards are accepted. These transmit information about the transaction to a clearing company, which then provides an authorization code indicating whether the transaction will be processed. This same process can be linked to a secure Web server, for a price. This is just one of the services included in online commercial environments, to be discussed later in this chapter and in Chapter 7.

Electronic Malls

Setting up a Web site for buying and selling can be complicated and expensive; it is not for everyone. However, some companies have been setting up electronic, or virtual, or online malls. The shopping mall is a familiar and comfortable model for consumers and merchants, and it is relatively straightforward to simulate using the World Wide Web. Mall operators allow individual merchants to "rent space" on the mall. The financial arrangements may vary, but generally include some kind of monthly charge, charges for storage space required, and also usually some charge for each transaction.

As with other Internet commerce service providers, digital malls provide a way for individual merchants to sell online without having to assemble all the parts themselves. The parts are still all there, and merchants investigating online commerce options should consider the systems and networking expertise of the service provider as well as the commercial facilities.

ONLINE COMMERCIAL ENVIRONMENTS

As should be apparent from the preceding discussion, simply having a secure World Wide Web server is far from a complete online commerce solution for merchants (although having a secure World Wide Web browser can be a complete solution for the online consumer). There is an entire "back end" infrastructure needed to support electronic sales and fulfillment. This includes links to credit card authorization networks, as well as integrating alternative payment methods into the solution. Merchants maximize their potential sales by making it easy for all customers to buy, and this includes accepting different payment methods.

Companies offering online commerce environments strive to produce an integrated and complete solution for Internet merchants. This may include software tools for creating World Wide Web documents and commercial offerings, secure Web server software, Web site management tools, and links to commercial transaction settlement services for credit cards as well as other digital payment methods.

Merchant Requirements

As part of the ability to sell products electronically, the online commercial environment should provide at least some of the following abilities:

- Automatically process transactions received through the Internet and send payment information to credit card authentication services, also via the Internet
- Automatically process responses from the credit card authentication service
- Get digital signatures or other proof of approval of the order from the customer
- Generate necessary transaction tracking information, including electronic receipts, customer statements, and internal documentation of orders
- For nonelectronic material, have a link to the delivery company (e.g., FedEx) for delivery status between the vendor and the customer
- Be able to handle occasional telephone or fax transactions as well as online transactions

Online commerce environment vendors must offer at least some of these functions because they are necessary to transact business online. Many of the functions described in the preceding section (Required Facilities) may also be provided in an online commerce environment, but these are offered as a convenience to merchants—the merchant can just as easily supply its own facilities, or contract them out to some other vendor.

Customer Requirements

The successful online commerce environment makes no demands at all on the customer, other than requiring the ability to access the online sales facility and the intention to buy something offered. However, the environment should permit the customer to use whatever payment method is desired, consistent with good business practice. In practice this means major credit cards, as well as an appropriate selection of electronic payment methods.

Customers, like merchants, will want some kind of audit trail or account statements, particularly when purchasing information products. The ability to provide receipts, monthly billing statements, and account status reports will be important to customers evaluating online business partners.

Chapter 7 will discuss an online commercial environment that includes some of these services.

DIGITAL CURRENCIES AND PAYMENT SYSTEMS

While secure commerce servers are intended to protect transaction data being sent over the Internet, digital currencies and other types of digital payment mechanisms are intended to carry value in a protected digital form over the Internet. Digital currencies and payment systems do not necessarily compete against secure Internet servers or commercial environments, but can complement such products by adding another way to exchange values.

Two approaches are taken by companies offering this type of service. One is to link a customer payment method (credit card, checking account, or some other source of funds) to an online identity, managed by the service provider. Merchants selling to a participating customer can then authenticate the payment information through the service provider, who may also provide authorization and clearing services. This type of service may seem to overlap somewhat with commerce environment services. The difference is that the payment system usually requires participants to register in some way with the payment system sponsor, while commerce environments usually permit the customer to use a credit card or a payment system. The payment method may also become merged into the applications themselves as new protocols are introduced which define procedures for transacting business using existing, nondigital payment methods.

The CyberCash and First Virtual payment systems are discussed in greater detail in Chapter 6.

Digital checking can also take advantage of the same techniques, in much the same way that debit cards are used the same way as credit cards — consumers present the card to the merchant, who must get an authorization for the purchase. The charges are paid immediately out of the consumer's checking account, rather than at the end of the monthly billing cycle.

A different approach is used for actual digital currencies, as opposed to payment systems. Usually, anyone can participate by opening an account with a financial institution offering digital currency service. Client software is used to withdraw money from the account, check on balances, and maintain a "digital wallet" that holds the value on the participant's computer. Cash exchanges between a user and the bank use the same types of cryptographic technologies described in Chapter 2. Digital signatures guarantee cash transfers, and transactions may be encrypted.

New technologies for transfering cash without hard currency or a traditional check are also appearing on the market and will be covered in Chapter 8.

OFFLINE SECURE PROCESSING

All of the options discussed so far in this chapter require some type of online security, whether it is a secure channel between the customer and the merchant or encryption of some or all data sent from one application to another. As entrepreneurs and developers investigated the methods for doing business online, it became apparent that there were two general approaches:

- Use cryptographic techniques to secure the channel and enable online, real-time transaction initiation and completion
- Use alternative, secure channels to transmit sensitive data

To some developers, the advantages of using cryptography — all related to the securing of a previously unsecure channel — are outweighed by the costs of implementing it. These costs include the following:

- Licensing fee for patented cryptographic tools
- Creation and distribution of new Internet browsers and servers
- Maintenance of public key certification facilities
- Increased computing overhead needed to transact business exchanges
- Difficulty in distributing cryptographic technologies outside of the United States due to export restrictions on strong cryptography

It has been argued that by taking the sensitive data out of the online Internet loop, companies can provide relatively secure commercial services on the Internet without the costs associated with implementing a secure channel or secure payment protocol. Most important is that implementing this type of system independently of the underlying application means that the end user — the customer — does not have to upgrade or buy any special software to support new security protocols. All existing channels are capable of supporting commerce, whether through a World Wide Web server, file transfer or terminal emulation, or even e-mail. What's more, any future application or network can also be supported just as easily, with no need for modification.

This approach was first used by First Virtual Holdings Incorporated in 1994 and is described in more detail in Chapter 6. In this approach, customers must telephone, fax, or mail (all relatively secure, or at least familiar, methods) their credit card payment and shipping address information to the sponsoring organization. They are then provided with an account ID, which they can use to order goods from participating merchants. The information about an order, including order status, can be transmitted in the clear, while the sensitive information, such as payment information, is kept entirely offline.

Although this approach has some interesting and attractive features, it is not likely to dominate the electronic commerce world. It is likely to continue to be used in certain specialty and niche markets, but some assumptions that motivated this approach are proving wrong. For example, as larger numbers of new Internet users come online, it becomes easier to implement new Internet browsers supporting commercial security features. Also, the United States government is granting export licenses for some electronic commerce applications of varying strength.

Private Data Networks

The use of the Internet for the exchange of business data is a growing, unstoppable trend. Internet-based transactions are in the future for most, if not all, companies. However, many companies are still reluctant to use the "open" Internet to conduct mission-critical business transactions. A genuine problem faces many companies, as they want to groom existing systems and bring on new applications, but do not want to close out future possibilities. An alternative is available.

A solution for many companies may lie in the use of private data networks to pass Internet data. For example, a large distribution company clearly sees the Internet as a transaction medium in the next few years. They are proceeding with plans to build an online catalog and order processing application but, at first, will not hook it to the Internet. Instead, they will connect it to a private third-party network.

This is not a new technology. For years, companies such as CompuServe, Advantis, AT&T, and, more recently, BBN Planet have offered private data networks for companies that are looking for a large network, but would like to avoid the cost of building such a network from scratch.

In this scenario, users access the application and information with a standard Internet browser, and the distribution company will employ all of the required security methods, including firewalls, secure browser support, and electronic commerce servers. The only difference is that when the customers connect to the distribution company, they will dial a toll-free number and be connected to a third-party company, which will in turn be connected to the distribution company. The third party will have a network in place that functions exactly like the Internet, but that will not be accessible to the general public.

In the future, management opinions may change, the nature of the application may change or new Internet technologies could be deployed, and the company will have the option of connecting the application to the open Internet.

FOUR

Protocols for the Public Transport of Private Information

Abraham Maslow's hierarchy of needs theory suggests that a person's basic needs, such as food and water, must be satisfied if they are to be satisfied with something more complex such as a job or family. Never has Maslow's assertion been more appropriate than in the world of electronic commerce. No matter how attractive the shopping venue, it will fail if customers do not have the fundamental confidence in the process to complete the transaction.

The Internet is rapidly becoming the universal medium for exchange of transaction information, but before we can fulfill our Buck Rogers futuristic dreams, the electronic commerce community must take steps to secure transactions *and* educate consumers about security. The electronic commerce community has taken great steps to adopt security protocols and standards, which are necessary to make the traditionally unsecured channels, such as the Internet, attractive to the average consumer.

SECURITY PROTOCOLS

Until very recently, people wishing secure communications over the Internet had to find products implementing security at the application level. In practice, this meant that communications had to be protected explicitly by the user before being sent across the Internet, usually in the form of encrypted e-mail. Although this approach is quite effective when properly used, the consensus of consumers and merchants is that such an approach to security is unacceptable. Only when security is built into Internet applications and requires an absolute minimum of interaction by the user will it become acceptable to a mass market.

The Secure Hypertext Transport Protocol (S-HTTP), an extension of the World Wide Web protocol, adds security features just below the application layer. The Secure Sockets Layer (SSL) protocol was originally proposed and implemented by Netscape Communications and has also been implemented by other Web browser vendors. SSL operates at the transport layer, which means it can be used for private Internet transmissions between systems and programs supporting it.

MasterCard International and Visa International are cooperating in support of secure credit card transactions on the Internet, and companies involved with electronic commerce have generally pledged to comply with the standards they produce.

Figure 4-1 illustrates how these different security solutions fit into the Internet data architecture. The Secure HTTP option adds security directly to the application, while the Secure Sockets Layer adds security to the entire stream of data between server and client because it operates just above the transport layer. Secure Courier and other transaction-level protocols operate on the transaction data itself, so it can be transmitted between merchants and financial institutions without compromising that data's security or authenticity even while it awaits transmission from intermediate systems (like the merchant's server).

There are other mechanisms and protocols devised for transmitting transaction information across the Internet, and there will undoubtedly be more in the months and years to come. However,

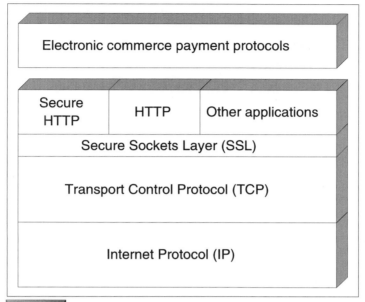

Electronic commerce payment protocols		
Secure HTTP	HTTP	Other applications
Secure Sockets Layer (SSL)		
Transport Control Protocol (TCP)		
Internet Protocol (IP)		

FIGURE 4-1 *Internet commerce security protocols can operate at different levels, and thus can all be used together if desired.*

these protocols should represent the type of standards that will eventually define the way business is done over the Internet.

These protocols will be discussed briefly, mostly to examine how they use the Internet, the World Wide Web, and security technologies to make secure commerce possible over the Internet.

SECURE HYPERTEXT TRANSFER PROTOCOL

The Secure Hypertext Transfer Protocol (S-HTTP) is the logical extension of the Hypertext Transfer Protocol (HTTP), which is the basis of the World Wide Web. HTTP defines the interactions between Web browsers and Web servers, determining how requests from browsers (also known as clients) are handled by Web servers. Very simply, a Web browser sends requests for information stored on a Web server, and if that server is connected and the information is available, the server will respond by sending the information back to the browser.

HTTP did not originally include any security features at all, other than those provided by resources accessed through the World Wide Web. For example, HTTP can be used to provide a more user-friendly interface to File Transfer Protocol (ftp) and terminal emulation (telnet) services, both of which challenge users for user ID and password before providing service. However, the content of telnet or ftp sessions is transmitted in plain text, and eavesdroppers could intercept the content being sent.

S-HTTP Security Features

The S-HTTP protocol was designed to add security at the application level. The objective was to add support for a wide range of security mechanisms on top of the interactions between Web browser and Web server. Protection mechanisms include the following:

- Digital signature
- Message authentication
- Message encryption

These mechanisms are used as negotiated between browser and server. Any one or more of these mechanisms may be used. The protocol also allows unprotected transmissions.

The S-HTTP specification includes support for many cryptographic formats, including private key and public key cryptography, as well as key distribution schemes like Kerberos. S-HTTP supports use of prearranged and predistributed private keys between individuals, public key encryption in one direction (using the server's public key only and not requiring the browser to have a public key), and two-way public key encryption. Each interaction between an S-HTTP browser/server pair is negotiated to determine what protection is available, needed, and capable of being used. Option negotiation can be driven by the requirements of the browser or the server, so either end of the transmission can request protection of some sort for that transmission.

The S-HTTP specification was written to offer the widest latitude in implementing security, with a variety of different cryptographic methods to ensure compatibility across national boundaries (using technologies approved for export from the United States) or between browsers and servers supporting other technologies.

Secure HTTP Data Transport

S-HTTP *encapsulates* the HTTP interactions between browser and server. This means that data being sent from browser to server (or vice versa) is contained within a special S-HTTP chunk of data. Figure 4-2 shows the concept of encapsulation. This chunk uses the same basic

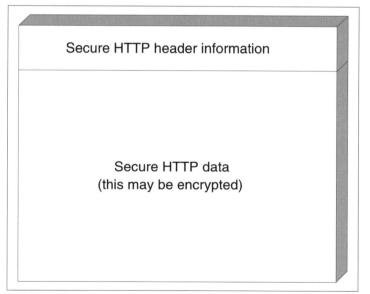

Secure HTTP header information

Secure HTTP data
(this may be encrypted)

FIGURE 4-2 *An S-HTTP message sent from a server to a browser includes data that is "wrapped" by a header with handling and contents information about the data.*

format as HTTP (which is also the basis for data sent via e-mail and Usenet news communications), indicating the source and destination systems and other information required by TCP/IP.

Encapsulated data sent across the Internet is comparable to a package that has been wrapped in plain brown paper and addressed for delivery by an express service. The contents of the package are irrelevant, and intermediate handlers do not know (nor do they need to know) exactly what is inside. However, the package will have delivery instructions printed on the outside — *headers* are the parallel structure for Internet data. When a package of data arrives at its destination, the recipient program takes the headers off and interprets the data inside as appropriate.

The typical HTTP session starts out with a user starting up a Web browser. This browser may be pointed to a home page at a remote Web server. On startup, the browser application program sends out an HTTP request to that server for the information on that home page. Assuming the server (and specified home page) is able to respond, it sends back the requested hypertext document (a document created with the Hypertext Markup Language — HTML).

S-HTTP Explained

For the details of the S-HTTP implementation, the reader is referred to the appropriate Internet RFC and Internet-Draft documents (see Appendix B for more details). This section summarizes the extra headers that S-HTTP defines for data connections between servers and browsers on the World Wide Web.

Secure HTTP Header Lines

There are two required header lines for S-HTTP, one identifying the type of content contained within the S-HTTP message ("Content-Type") and the other identifying the general cryptographic implementation being used ("Content-Privacy-Domain").

Other headers are optional and have the following uses:

- Indicating data representation of enclosed data (what format the enclosed data takes)
- Transmission of session keys and other information relating to the enclosed data
- Message Authenticity Check (MAC) to authenticate and provide an integrity check to the message

The Content–Privacy–Domain header allows the use of digital signatures alone, encryption alone, both signatures and encryption, or neither. Encryption options include use of public key pairs, or encryption with a prearranged key (previously exchanged offline or by some other mechanism).

S-HTTP Message Contents

The message sent by an S-HTTP browser or server can itself be simple data (a protocol request or response to a request). It could also be HTTP data (a response to an HTTP request for a Web document) or another S-HTTP message (a message that has been digitally signed could actually be an encrypted message).

The contents of an S-HTTP message are interpreted by the receiving entity (browser or server) based on how the data package is labeled and what kind of security treatment has been negotiated.

S-HTTP Security Negotiation Headers

S-HTTP adds a set of security negotiation headers used to negotiate security options. Four different issues are negotiated between server and browser:

- Property, or what kind of security option is being selected (what kind of cryptographic scheme, such as bulk encryption) to apply to a transfer

- Value, or what specific implementation (which specific algorithm, such as RSA public key encryption) to apply to the transfer
- Direction, or whether the system negotiating (sending the header) wants the other system to send the specified security-enhanced transmissions, or is willing to receive specified security-enhanced transmissions (in other words, each entity is allowed to indicate the maximum level of security it is capable of sending or receiving)
- Strength, or how strongly the system negotiating wants the negotiated option: it can require a security enhancement, make it an option, or refuse to use it

The negotiating process allows two S-HTTP-compliant participants (a browser and a server) to negotiate secure transmissions using the cryptographic facilities that both support, and that both require to transmit sensitive information securely.

Related Protocol Extensions

Data is requested and delivered across the World Wide Web using HTTP and S-HTTP; after all, those are Hypertext Transfer Protocols. However, there are two other important protocols without which the World Wide Web would not exist: the Uniform Resource Locator (URL) protocol, defining the syntax of Web documents and locations; and the Hypertext Markup Language (HTML) protocol, defining the syntax of the documents themselves.

URLs follow a very specific format, usually consisting of three parts: the scheme designation (indicating the protocol used by the underlying document), the Internet host and domain name of the resource hosting system, and the location on that system of the resource document file. Most current World Wide Web resources look something like this:

```
http://www.mcompany.com/home.html
```

This example indicates a file called `home.html` residing on a server called `www.mcompany.com` using the HTTP protocol. (URLs can now use a protocol designator of SHTTP to designate a resource using Secure HTTP.)

The Hypertext Markup Language uses tags, as discussed in Chapter 2, to indicate the different functional portions of a hypertext document. For example, a paragraph of text is set off by a paragraph tag; a bullet list of items is set off by tags indicating that it is a bullet list.

Security enhancements are not necessary for every piece of data sent from a secure server to a secure browser, so new HTML tags have been defined to mark certain hypertext elements as requiring some kind of security treatment, and to store supporting security information. This information includes the type of security enhancements to use when sending data, cryptographic options to be negotiated, and other options.

Secure Sockets Layer

In a way, S-HTTP can be considered to be typical of a traditional Internet application solution: It adds security and reliability functions to an application, at the application level. In other words, the browser on one side and the server on the other negotiate their own security independent of the underlying network protocols. The result is that the underlying network protocols need not be reliable or secure to support reliable and secure interaction at the application level, and it is not necessary to make any changes to the basic underlying network implementation.

However, another approach to security is to add a layer on top of the existing network transport protocol and beneath the application. The Secure Sockets Layer (SSL) protocol takes this approach by adding

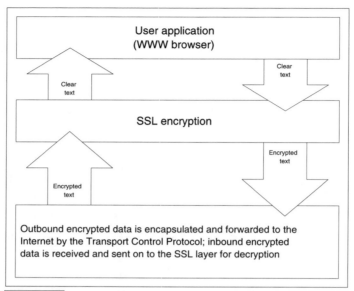

FIGURE 4-3 *The Secure Sockets Layer operates between the Internet application and the network transport layer, encrypting data passing between the client and the server.*

an intermediate step, requiring negotiation of secure transmission options, to the establishment of a network connection. Data flowing between the client and the server on that connection is encrypted before transmission and decrypted before it can be used by the receiving system, as shown in Figure 4-3.

One advantage of this approach is that SSL can be applied to any Internet application, not just the World Wide Web (although it was initially implemented only under HTTP). A second advantage is that once the SSL connection has been negotiated between a server and a client, the resulting data communication channel is private, authenticated, and reliable.

SSL links are initiated with a handshaking exchange between the server and the client, during which the two systems exchange necessary cryptographic information to support the secure channel. After this information has been exchanged, the application programs must subject their transmissions to the required cryptographic treatment and then send them on to a destination application program—which must then subject that data to the cryptographic treatment necessary to decrypt and authenticate it.

SSL was originally developed by Netscape as the basis of its secure World Wide Web server. It is implemented in leading browsers that have been distributed widely. Netscape has made the SSL specification publicly available as an Internet draft document to ensure compatibility between its browsers and servers and other vendors' products. Because by definition Internet applications must be able to interoperate with other implementations of the same applications in order to succeed, there is no benefit to Netscape in making SSL proprietary—if it were not widely implemented, there would be no benefit to purchasing servers or browsers from Netscape.

SSL Record Specification

As with other underlying network protocols (and similar to the way in which S-HTTP encapsulates HTTP data), SSL encapsulates the data transmitted between the client and the server in an SSL record. However, the SSL header is only two or three bytes long; it is primarily used to indicate how much data has been encapsulated and whether that includes data padding to fill out the SSL record. Data padding is often necessary to make sure that the "real" data can be properly encrypted with certain types of cipher.

SSL requires a reliable network transport protocol (one which provides some level of confidence that data is being received by the destination host), which means that data is transmitted using the Transmission Control Protocol (TCP) across the Internet. The TCP headers identify the source and destination of the data, while the application headers that have been encapsulated with the rest of the application data (in other words, the HTTP headers and data) remain secure until it reaches its destination.

Initiating an SSL Session

An SSL session begins after the TCP session is initiated. SSL uses a handshaking protocol, with the client and the software exchanging specific pieces of information in order to build a secure channel for transmitting data. The very first exchange between client and server is in plain text and contains enough information for the two systems to initiate an encrypted and authenticated data stream.

Figure 4-4 shows a typical exchange of SSL information between a client and a server. Because SSL requires the use of TCP, which itself uses a reliable three-way handshake protocol to initiate a connection, the server begins the session by awaiting the opening transmission from the client. This is called a "client-hello" message and includes some challenge data (data which is to be used later to authenticate the server) and specifications of supported ciphers.

Upon receipt of this message, the server responds with a random connection ID, its own cipher specifications, and its own digitally signed public key certificate. In response, the client sends off two messages in succession: First, it sends a "client-master-key" message, in which a master key is delivered to the server as the basis for further communication. This master key is encrypted with the server's public key, meaning that it can only be decrypted with the server's private key. The client follows this message with a "client-finish" message, indicating that it is ready to start receiving SSL data. This message includes the connection ID supplied by the server, but encrypted using the client's private key, meaning that it can be decrypted using the client's public key — this authenticates the message as coming from that client.

Completing the handshake, the server responds with a "server-verify" message, followed by a "server-finish" message. The server-verify message functions as the server's digital signature and includes the challenge data mentioned above in the client-hello message — but it is encrypted with the server's private key. This message can be decrypted using the server's public key, and this authenticates the server to the

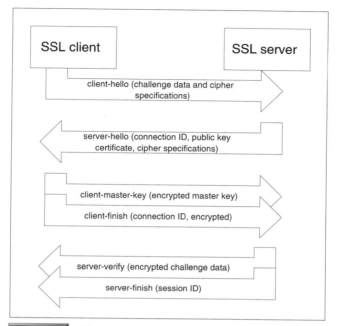

FIGURE 4-4 *The SSL client and server exchange information in a connection-opening handshake sequence before opening the secure channel.*

client. The server-finish message includes a new session identifier, also encrypted with the server's private key.

Other SSL Options

SSL provides a mechanism for a client and server that have already initiated a connection to reconnect without having to renegotiate encryption options. This process starts with the client sending a client-hello message that refers to a previous session identifier. Both client and server maintain a cache of session identifiers which include encryption options received from the other system. If the server recognizes the client and the specified session ID, the SSL channel can be initiated without the need to resend any keys.

The connections described so far will authenticate the server to the client, but client authentication is also possible with SSL. The server can request authentication information with a "request-certificate" message after the server-verify message, which includes a different bit of challenge data. The client must encrypt this new data with its own private key, which the server will be able to decrypt using the client's declared public key, thus authenticating the client.

INTEGRATING SECURITY PROTOCOLS INTO THE WEB

Using SSL or S-HTTP is a matter of using special identifiers to indicate World Wide Web documents that require them. For example, a URL indicating a document defined with the Hypertext Transfer Protocol would look something like this:

```
http://www.mcompany.com/MAIN.html
```

The first part of the URL identifies the scheme which must be used to transmit that document. To require S-HTTP to transmit a document, its URL must be defined in the form

```
shttp://www.mcompany.com/SECURE.html
```

In this case, the scheme, shttp, is defined as Secure HTTP; any browser which supports Secure HTTP will respond appropriately to initiate a connection.

Documents requiring the browser to support SSL use a different scheme, https, with a resulting URL that looks like this:

```
https://www.mcompany.com/SECURE.html
```

It should be noted that browsers which have been written to the HTTP specification are supposed to gracefully handle schemes that they don't support. A browser that does not support S-HTTP would not be able to negotiate with the server to access a document defined with S-HTTP—but it should be able to access any HTTP document on the same server. The same goes for SSL, so merchants should be able to maintain secure information and insecure information on the same server.

SET

Several years ago, MasterCard and Visa, traditionally strong rivals, teamed together to create the Secure Electronic Transaction (SET) protocol.

Secure Electronic Transaction (SET) is an open specification for protecting payment card purchases on any type of network. The SET specification incorporates the use of public key cryptography to protect the privacy of personal and financial information over any open network. The specification calls for software to reside in the cardholder's (customer's) personal computer and in the merchant's network computer. In addition, there is technology residing at the acquirer's (the merchant's bank) location to decrypt the financial information, as well as at the certificate authorities location to issue digital certificates.

In early June 1997, SET 1.0 was published by MasterCard, Visa and a host of business partners including

- GTE
- IBM
- Microsoft
- Netscape
- SAIC
- Terisa Systems

- Verisign
- Visa

The SET specification is published in three parts:

- Book One: Business Specifications
- Book Two: Technical Specification
- Book Three: Formal Protocol Definition.

Although updated just prior to the publication of this book, the SET standard is subject to change over time. You can check for the latest versions of each document by visiting either the MasterCard or the Visa Web site.

```
http://www.mastercard.com
http://www.visa.com
```

Credit Card Business Basics

Before discussing SET, a few Credit Card processing definitions are in order. These terms are used throughout the SET document.

Cardholder:	The consumer, customer, you!
Issuer:	The bank who issued you a credit card.
Merchant:	The party from whom you are buying goods and services.
Acquirer:	The financial institution/bank who establishes an account with the merchant and processes payment authorizations and transactions for the merchant.
Payment Gateway:	A device operated by an acquirer (financial institution) that processes the merchant payment messages.
Brand:	Visa, MasterCard, Discover, etc.

It is also important to point out that MasterCard and Visa are associations with banks comprising the membership.

SET Requirements

According the SET Business Description of May 31, 1997 there are seven requirements for SET.

1. Provide confidentiality of payment information and enable confidentiality of order information that is transmitted along with the payment information.
2. Ensure the integrity of all transmitted data
3. Provide authentication that a cardholder is a legitimate user of a branded payment card account.
4. Provide authentication that a merchant can accept branded payment card transactions through its relationship with an acquiring financial institution.
5. Ensure the use of the best security practices and system design techniques to protect all legitimate parties in an electronic commerce transaction.
6. Create a protocol that neither depends on transport security mechanisms nor prevents their use.
7. Facilitate and encourage interoperability among software and network providers

EARLY SET TRIALS

Visa

On April 29, 1997 the world's first Internet purchases involving a Visacard and Secure Electronic Transaction (SET) technology from multiple vendors began in Singapore. The transactions involved SET technology developed by two different manufacturers. IBM developed the payment gateway linking Citibank to the Internet. VeriSign, using the SET Pilot Root, produced the digital certificates which make it possible for sensitive financial information to be used safely on the Internet.

American Express

At approximately 3:32 a.m. on June 2, 1997 a tiny bit of history occurred when an American Express Cardmember purchased a drill press from Wal-Mart's Web site located at www.wal-mart.com. This event will not get the attention generated by man walking on the moon or Alexander Grahm Bell making the first phone call, but it is very significant as the first Internet transaction in which actual goods were purchased using the Secure Electronic Transaction (SET) protocol. This is also the first demonstration of interoperability between different software implementations of the SET protocol. GlobeSet, Inc. provided the SET software used by the American Express Cardmember and Wal-Mart in making the transaction secure, and American express used its own SET software to receive and authorize the Card transaction.

As more trials occur, news will be posted on the respective companies web sites.

In Chapter 2 we discussed the issue of private and public encryption, message authentication and key certification. These are the building blocks of the SET standard.

An entire book could be dedicated to the entire SET process. However, with the root of the issue being *security,* we use the balance of this chapter to discuss the cryptography methods employed by the SET standard.

SET Business Specifications Document

The following text is an excerpt from section 3 of the SET Business Specifications document. The entire SET specification is included on the attached CD-ROM.[1]

---

[1] REPRINTED WITH PERMISSION FROM MASTERCARD INTERNATIONAL. © 1997.

CERTIFICATE ISSUANCE

PROTECTION OF SENSITIVE INFORMATION. Cryptography has been used for centuries to protect sensitive information as it is transmitted from one location to another. In a cryptographic system, a message is encrypted using a key. The resulting ciphertext is then transmitted to the recipient where it is decrypted using a key to produce the original message. There are two primary encryption methods in use today: secret-key cryptography and public-key cryptography. SET uses both methods in its encryption process.

SECRET-KEY CRYPTOGRAPHY. SECRET-KEY CRYPTOGRAPHY, also known as symmetric cryptography, uses the same key to encrypt and decrypt the message. Therefore, the sender and the recipient of a message must share a secret, namely the key. A well known secret-key cryptography algorithm is the Data Encryption Standard (DES), which is used by financial institutions to encrypt PINs (personal identification numbers).

FIGURE 4-5   *Secret-Key Cryptography*

PUBLIC-KEY CRYPTOGRAPHY. Public-key cryptography, also known as asymmetric cryptography, uses two keys: one key to encrypt the message and the other key to decrypt the message. The two keys are mathematically related so that data encrypted with either key can only be decrypted using the other. Each user has two keys: a PUBLIC KEY and a PRIVATE KEY. The user distributes the public key. Because of the

relationship between the two keys, the user and anyone receiving the public key can be assured that data encrypted with the public key and sent to the user can only be decrypted when the user uses the private key. THIS ASSURANCE IS ONLY MAINTAINED IF THE USER ENSURES THAT THE PRIVATE KEY IS NOT DISCLOSED TO ANYONE ELSE. Therefore, the key pair should be generated by the user. The best known public-key cryptography algorithm is RSA (named after its inventors Rivest, Shamir, and Adleman).

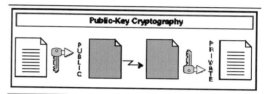

FIGURE 4-6   *Public-Key Cryptography*

Secret-key cryptography is impractical for exchanging messages with a large group of previously unknown correspondents over a public network. For a merchant to conduct transactions securely with millions of Internet subscribers, each consumer would need a distinct key assigned by that merchant and transmitted over a separate secure channel. On the other hand, by using public-key cryptography, that same merchant could create a public/private key pair and publish the public key, allowing any consumer to send a secure message to that merchant.

ENCRYPTION. Confidentiality is ensured by the use of message encryption.

RELATIONSHIP OF KEYS. When two users want to exchange messages securely, each of them transmits one component of their key pair, designated the public key, to the other and keeps secret the other component, designated the private key. Because messages encrypted with the public key can only be decrypted using the private key, these messages can be transmitted over an insecure network without fear that an eavesdropper could use the key to read encrypted transmissions.

For example, Bob can transmit a confidential message to Alice by encrypting the message using Alice's public key. As long as Alice ensures that no one else has access to her private key, both she and Bob will know that only Alice can read the message.

USE OF SYMMETRIC KEY. SET will rely on cryptography to ensure message confidentiality. In SET, message data will be encrypted using a randomly generated symmetric encryption key. This key, in turn, will be encrypted using the message recipient's public key. This is referred to as the "digital envelope" of the message and is sent to the recipient along with the encrypted message itself. After receiving the digital envelope, the recipient decrypts it using his or her private key to obtain the randomly generated symmetric key and then uses the symmetric key to unlock the original message.

NOTE. To provide the highest degree of protection, it is essential that the programming methods and random number generation algorithms generate keys in a way that ensures that the keys cannot be easily reproduced using information about either the algorithms or the environment in which the keys are generated.

DIGITAL SIGNATURES. Integrity and authentication are ensured by the use of digital signatures.

RELATIONSHIP OF KEYS. Because of the mathematical relationship between the public and private keys, data encrypted with either key can only be decrypted with the other. This allows the sender of a message to encrypt it using the sender's private key. Any recipient can determine that the message came from the sender by decrypting the message using the sender's public key.

For example, Alice can encrypt a known piece of data, such as her telephone number, with her private key and transmit it to Bob. When Bob decrypts the message using Alice's public key and compares the result to the known data, he can be sure that that the message could only have been encrypted using Alice's private key.

USING MESSAGE DIGESTS. When combined with MESSAGE DIGESTS, encryption using the private key allows users to digitally sign messages. A message digest is a value generated for a message (or document) that is unique to that message.[1] A message digest is generated by passing the message through a one-way cryptographic function; that is, one that cannot be reversed. When the digest of a message is encrypted using the sender's private key and is appended to the original message, the result is known as the digital signature of the message.

The recipient of the digital signature can be sure that the message really came from the sender. And, because changing even one character in the message changes the message digest in an unpredictable way, the recipient can be sure that the message was not changed after the message digest was generated.

EXAMPLE OF THE USE OF A DIGITAL SIGNATURE. For example, Alice computes the message digest of a property description and encrypts it with

---

[1] The algorithm used by SET generates 160-bit message digests. The algorithm is such that changing a single bit in the message will change, on average, half of the bits in the message digest. Roughly, the odds of two messages having the same message digest are one in 1,000,000,000,000, 000,000,000,000,000,000,000,000,000,000. It is computationally unfeasible to generate two different messages that have the same message digest.

her private key yielding a digital signature for the message. She transmits both the message and the digital signature to Bob. When Bob receives the message, he computes the message digest of the property description and decrypts the digital signature with Alice's public key. If the two values match, Bob knows that the message was signed using Alice's private key and that it has not changed since it was signed.

TWO KEY PAIRS. SET uses a distinct public/private key pair to create the digital signature. Thus, each SET participant will possess two asymmetric key pairs: a "key exchange" pair, which is used in the process of encryption and decryption, and a "signature" pair for the creation and verification of digital signatures. Note that the roles of the public and private keys are reversed in the digital signature process where the private key is used to encrypt (sign) and the public key is used to decrypt (verify the signature).

CERTIFICATES. Authentication is further strengthened by the use of certificates.

NEED FOR AUTHENTICATION. Before two parties use public-key cryptography to conduct business, each wants to be sure that the other party is authenticated. Before Bob accepts a message with Alice's digital signature, he wants to be sure that the public key belongs to Alice and not to someone masquerading as Alice on an open network. One way to be sure that the public key belongs to Alice is to receive it over a secure channel directly from Alice. However, in most circumstances this solution is not practical.

NEED FOR A TRUSTED THIRD PARTY. An alternative to secure transmission of the key is to use a trusted third party to authenticate that the public key belongs to Alice. Such a party is known as a CERTIFICATE AUTHORITY (CA). The Certificate Authority authenticates Alice's claims according to its published policies. For example, a Certificate Authority could supply certificates that offer a high assurance of personal identity, which may be required for conducting business transactions; this Certificate Authority may require Alice to present a driver's license or passport to a notary public before it will issue a certificate. Once Alice has provided proof of her identity, the Certificate Authority creates a message containing Alice's name and her public key. This message, known as a CERTIFICATE, is digitally signed by the Certificate Authority. It contains owner identification information, as well as a copy of one of the owner's public keys ("key exchange" or "signature"). To get the most benefit, the public key of the Certificate Authority should be known to as many people as possible. Thus, by trusting a single key, an entire hierarchy can be established in which one can have a high degree of trust.

Because SET participants have two key pairs, they also have two certificates. Both certificates are created and signed at the same time by the Certificate Authority.

SET AUTHENTICATION. The means that a financial institution uses to authenticate a cardholder or merchant is not defined by this specification. Each payment card brand and financial institution will select an appropriate method.

ENCRYPTION SUMMARY. This diagram provides an overview of the entire encryption process when Alice wishes to sign, for example, a property description and send it in an encrypted message to Bob. The numbered steps in the diagram are explained on the following pages.

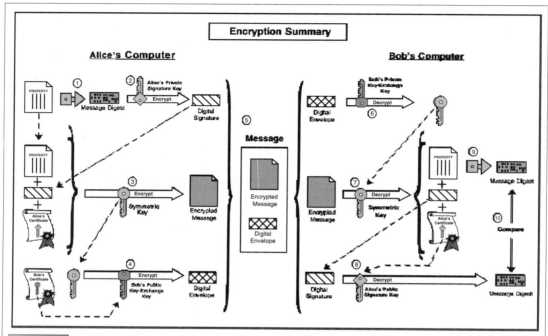

FIGURE 4-7 *Encryption Overview*

ENCRYPTION. The encryption process in Figure 4-7 consists of the following steps:

Step	Description
1	Alice runs the property description through a one-way algorithm to produce a unique value known as the message digest. This is a kind of digital fingerprint of the property description and will be used later to test the integrity of the message.
2	She then encrypts the message digest with her private signature key to produce the digital signature.
3	Next, she generates a random symmetric key and uses it to encrypt the property description, her signature and a copy of her certificate, which contains her public signature

key. To decrypt the property description, Bob will require a secure copy of this random symmetric key.

Step	Description
4	Bob's certificate, which Alice must have obtained prior to initiating secure communication with him, contains a copy of his public key–exchange key. To ensure secure transmission of the symmetric key, Alice encrypts it using Bob's public key–exchange key. The encrypted key, referred to as the digital envelope, is sent to Bob along with the encrypted message itself.
5	Alice sends a message to Bob consisting of the following: the symmetrically encrypted property description, signature and certificate, as well as the asymmetrically encrypted symmetric key (the digital envelope).

DECRYPTION. Likewise, the decryption process consists of the following steps:

Step	Description
6	Bob receives the message from Alice and decrypts the digital envelope with his private key–exchange key to retrieve the symmetric key.
7	He uses the symmetric key to decrypt the property description, Alice's signature, and her certificate.
8	He decrypts Alice's digital signature with her public signature key, which he acquires from her certificate. This recovers the original message digest of the property description.
9	He runs the property description through the same one-way algorithm used by Alice and produces a new message digest of the decrypted property description.
10	Finally, he compares his message digest to the one obtained from Alice's digital signature. If they are exactly the same, he confirms that the message content has not been altered during transmission and that it was signed using Alice's private signature key. If they are not the same, then the message either originated somewhere else or was altered after it was signed. In that case, Bob takes some appropriate action such as notifying Alice or discarding the message.

DUAL SIGNATURE. SET introduces a new application of digital signatures, namely the concept of dual signatures. To understand the need for this new concept, consider the following scenario: Bob wants to send Alice an offer to purchase a piece of property and an authorization to his bank to transfer the money if Alice accepts the offer, but Bob doesn't want the bank to see the terms of the offer nor does he want Alice to see his account information. Further, Bob wants to link the offer to the transfer so that the money is only transferred if Alice accepts his offer. He accomplishes all of this by digitally signing both messages with a single signature operation that creates a dual signature.

GENERATING A DUAL SIGNATURE. A dual signature is generated by creating the message digest of both messages, concatenating the two digests together, computing the message digest of the result and encrypting this digest with the signer's private signature key. The signer must include the message digest of the other message in order for the recipient to verify the dual signature. A recipient of either message can check its authenticity by generating the message digest on its copy of the message, concatenating it with the message digest of the other message (as provided by the sender) and computing the message digest of the result. If the newly generated digest matches the decrypted dual signature, the recipient can trust the authenticity of the message.

EXAMPLE. If Alice accepts Bob's offer, she can send a message to the bank indicating her acceptance and including the message digest of the offer. The bank can verify the authenticity of Bob's transfer authorization and ensure that the acceptance is for the same offer by using its digest of the authorization and the message digest presented by Alice of the offer to validate the dual signature. Thus the bank can check the authenticity of the offer against the dual signature, but the bank cannot see the terms of the offer.

USE OF DUAL SIGNATURES. Within SET, dual signatures are used to link an order message sent to the merchant with the payment instructions containing account information sent to the Acquirer. When the merchant sends an authorization request to the Acquirer, it includes the payment instructions sent to it by the cardholder and the message digest of the order information. The Acquirer uses the message digest from the merchant and computes the message digest of the payment instructions to check the dual signature.

IMPORT/EXPORT ISSUES. A number of governments have regulations regarding the import or export of cryptography. As a general rule, these governments allow cryptography to be used when:

- the data being encrypted is of a financial nature;
- the content of the data is well-defined;
- the length of the data is limited; and
- the cryptography cannot easily be used for other purposes.

The SET protocol is limited to the financial portion of shopping and the content of the SET messages has been carefully reviewed to satisfy the concerns of governments. As long as software vendors can demonstrate that the cryptography used for SET cannot easily be put to other purposes, import and export licenses should be obtainable.

CARDHOLDER CERTIFICATES. Cardholder certificates function as an electronic representation of the payment card. Because they are digitally signed by a financial institution, they cannot be altered by a third party and and can only be generated by a financial institution. A cardholder certificate does not contain the account number and expiration date. Instead the account information and a secret value known only to the cardholder's software are encoded using a one-way hashing algorithm. If the account number, expiration date, and the secret value are known, the link to the certificate can be proven, but the information cannot be derived by looking at the certificate. Within the SET

protocol, the cardholder supplies the account information and the secret value to the payment gateway where the link is verified.

A certificate is only issued to the cardholder when the cardholder's issuing financial institution approves it. By requesting a certificate, a cardholder has indicated the intent to perform commerce via electronic means. This certificate is transmitted to merchants with purchase requests and encrypted payment instructions. Upon receipt of the cardholder's certificate, a merchant can be assured, at a minimum, that the account number has been validated by the card-issuing financial institution or its agent.

In this specification, cardholder certificates are optional at the payment card brand's discretion.

MERCHANT CERTIFICATES. Merchant certificates function as an electronic substitute for the payment brand decal that appears in the store window — the decal itself is a representation that the merchant has a relationship with a financial institution allowing it to accept the payment card brand. Because they are digitally signed by the merchant's financial institution, merchant certificates cannot be altered by a third party and can only be generated by a financial institution.

These certificates are approved by the acquiring financial institution and provide assurance that the merchant holds a valid agreement with an Acquirer. A merchant must have at least one pair of certificates to participate in the SET environment, but there may be multiple certificate pairs per merchant. A merchant will have a pair of certificates for each payment card brand that it accepts.

PAYMENT GATEWAY CERTIFICATES. Payment gateway certificates are obtained by Acquirers or their processors for the systems that process authorization and capture messages. The gateway's encryption key, which the cardholder gets from this certificate, is used to protect the cardholder's account information.

Payment gateway certificates are issued to the Acquirer by the payment brand.

ACQUIRER CERTIFICATES. An Acquirer must have certificates in order to operate a Certificate Authority that can accept and process certificate requests directly from merchants over public and private networks. Those Acquirers that choose to have the payment card brand process certificate requests on their behalf will not require certificates because they are not processing SET messages. Acquirers receive their certificates from the payment card brand.

ISSUER CERTIFICATES. An Issuer must have certificates in order to operate a Certificate Authority that can accept and process certificate requests directly from cardholders over public and private networks. Those Issuers that choose to have the payment card brand process certificate requests on their behalf will not require certificates because they are not processing SET messages. Issuers receive their certificates from the payment card brand.

HIERARCHY OF TRUST. SET certificates are verified through a hierarchy of trust. Each certificate is linked to the signature certificate of the entity that digitally signed it. By following the trust tree to a known trusted party, one can be assured that the certificate is valid. For example, a cardholder certificate is linked to the certificate of the Issuer (or the Brand on behalf of the Issuer). The Issuer's certificate is linked back to a root key through the Brand's certificate. The public signature key of the root is known to all SET software and may be used to verify each of the certificates in turn. The following diagram ilustrates the hierarchy of trust.

The number of levels shown in this diagram is illustrative. A payment card brand may not always operate a geopolitical Certificate Authority between itself and the financial institutions.

ROOT KEY DISTRIBUTION. The root key will be distributed in a self-signed certificate. This root key certificate will be available to software vendors to include with their software.

ROOT KEY VALIDATION. Software can confirm that it has a valid root key by sending an initiate request to the Certificate Authority that contains the hash of the root certificate. In the event that the software does not have a valid root certificate, the Certificate Authority will send one in the response.

NOTE: In this extremely unusual case where the software's root key is invalid, the user (cardholder or merchant) will have to enter a string that corresponds to the hash of the certificate.

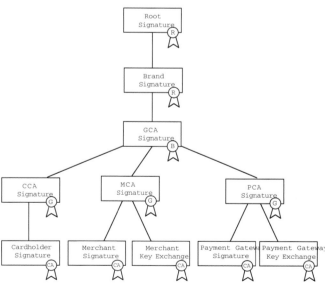

FIGURE 4-8 *Hierarchy of Trust*

This

confirmation hash must be obtained from a reliable source, such as the cardholder's financial institution.

ROOT KEY REPLACEMENT. When the root key is generated, a replacement key is also generated. The replacement key is stored securely until it is needed.

The self-signed root certificate and the hash of the replacement key are distributed together.

Software will be notified of the replacement through a message that contains a self-signed certificate of the replacement root and the hash of the next replacement root key.

Software validates the replacement root key by calculating its hash and comparing it with the hash of the replacement key contained in the root certificate.

Kinds of Shopping

VARIETY OF EXPERIENCES. Cardholders will shop in many different ways, including the use of online catalogs and electronic catalogs. The SET protocol supports each of these shopping experiences and should support others as they are defined.

ONLINE CATALOGS. The growth of electronic commerce is attributed largely to the popularity of the World Wide Web. Merchants can tap into this popularity by creating virtual storefronts on the Web that contain online catalogs. They can quickly update these catalogs as their product offerings change for seasonal promotions or other reasons.

A cardholder can visit these Web pages and select items to order. When the cardholder fin-ishes shopping and submits a request, the merchant's Web server can send the cardholder a completed order form to review and approve.

Once the cardholder approves the order and designates a payment card, the SET protocol enables the cardholder to transmit payment instructions by a secure means, while enabling the merchant to obtain authorization and receive payment.

ELECTRONIC CATALOGS. A growing number of merchants are distributing their catalogs via electronic media such as diskette or CD-ROM. This approach allows the cardholder to browse through merchandise off-line. With an on-line catalogue, the merchant has to be concerned about bandwidth and may choose to include fewer graphics or reduce the resolution of the graphics. By providing an off-line catalogue, such constraints are significantly reduced.

In addition, the merchant may provide a custom shopping application tailored to the merchandise in the electronic catalogue. Cardholders will shop by browsing through the catalogue and selecting items to include on an order.

Once the cardholder approves the order and chooses to use a payment card, an electronic message using the SET protocol can be sent to the merchant with the order and payment instructions. This message can be delivered on-line, such as to the merchant's Web page, or sent via a store-and-forward mechanism, such as electronic mail.

NONTECHNICAL CONSIDERATIONS

In addition to the technical considerations when preparing to process online credit card transactions, there are several nontechnical issues.

Banks establish deposit accounts for the money collected by the merchant in the form of credit card transactions. As discussed earlier, when a merchant is set up by the bank to accept credit card transactions, the merchant is issued a merchant number. The credit card issuing banks charge merchants a percentage of each credit card transaction. Depending on the merchant's financial profile (length of time in business, assets, etc.) and previous credit card transaction history, the percentage or fee can vary.

The fee is determined by several factors, including raw transaction processing costs, profit for the bank, and risk. Fraud is a huge issue with traditional credit card transactions. Newly established merchants, merchants with a certain business profile, or those with previous fraud experience pay a higher per-transaction fee.

The traditional credit card transaction fee is based on the transaction occurring in-person at the merchant's store or place of business. "MOTO," or mail order, telephone order, merchants pay a higher fee in most cases, as the merchant does not see the customer. As a consumer, you may notice this, as many MOTO merchants do not ship to an address different from the billing address on the credit card.

Many start-up mail order companies, if they can get a bank to issue them a merchant number, are charged high fees until the merchant builds a good processing track record.

This affects the online ordering and processing of credit cards, as the fee for a new business where no one sees or even speaks with the customer at the time of the sale is going to be high—even for companies with a strong credit card processing history. The bottom line is, you can build the most advanced Web site with the greatest graphics and the hottest products, but if you can't get a merchant number, you cannot accept credit card transactions. Additionally, if you do get a merchant number, but do not have a strong credit card processing track record, you will need to consider the impact processing fees will have on your bottom line.

FIVE

ELECTRONIC COMMERCE PROVIDERS

> "I have called this principle, by which each slight variation, if useful, is preserved, by the term Natural Selection."
>
> —CHARLES DARWIN, THE ORIGIN OF THE SPECIES.

O ver the past few years, a small handful of companies have been working furiously to crawl up onto dry land by producing acceptable Internet commerce products. Now scores of firms with "electronic commerce" as their middle name are competing, each with slightly different variations on the major themes spelled out in preceding chapters. Although there is an expectation that some of the largest companies—Visa and MasterCard, for example—will set standards for the electronic commerce field in short order, brash young newcomers can never be counted out.

By looking at a relatively broad cross-section of the products now available, and examining similarities and differences, it becomes possible to better understand the context in which they are being developed and offered to the public. It remains to be seen which technologies will be most successful as they adapt to the Internet business environment. In the long run, of course, only the fittest will survive.

WHAT TO LOOK FOR, WHAT TO LOOK OUT FOR

Attempting to publish an overview of all electronic commerce companies in 1997 is as ludicrous as compiling a directory of all major automobile manufacturers in 1895. Although the dominant players for the short term are already pretty obvious, there is no telling what will happen five years down the road.

Online Commerce Options

Ideally, online consumers should not have to make any choices or any special arrangements to order products electronically. Merchants have a much greater responsibility to implement a specific product or set of products, ranging from the use of secure Web servers to getting set up to accept payment through different payment mechanisms.

Banks are moving quickly to examine and evaluate electronic banking and electronic transactions. Banks and other financial institutions are working with companies like CyberCash, First Virtual, Netscape, Microsoft, and others in an effort to produce seamless payment systems for consumers and merchants alike.

Consumer Choices

Consumers can opt to do nothing beyond getting a Web browser that supports the secure exchange of transaction information using either the Secure Sockets Layer (SSL) or Secure HTTP (S-HTTP) protocols. Doing so may prove sufficient for many consumer needs: It lets the consumer pay for goods and services by credit card, and it protects the transaction from being intercepted. However, it doesn't protect the consumer from dishonest merchants, who could set up enticing deals on the World Wide Web to trick consumers into sending them their credit card numbers. This possibility can be avoided by educating consumers to exercise the same caution in doing business online that they would use in dealing with telemarketers.

Consumers willing to get more involved have more options, but they can only use these methods with merchants that accept them. As with credit cards, wide acceptance is key: You may like to use your Diners Club or Carte Blanche cards, but you're more likely to find a gas station that accepts MasterCard or Visa. The facts of life dictate that if you only want to use one credit card, you're better off with the card that will be accepted by the most merchants.

Of course, some cards may be accepted at more places, but not at the places you want to shop. If your local gas station only takes its own charge card, a truckload of gold cards will not help you. The same goes for online payment methods — so far, there is no single solution, and it is likely there will always be some degree of choice for the consumer.

Registering with a third-party organization that acts as a go-between for merchants and consumers can provide an extra level of security for consumers. The third party can act on behalf of both the merchant and the consumer, taking the payment information from the consumer and settling transactions for the merchant. This means the consumer does not have to trust the merchant with payment information, because the intermediary company never passes that on to the merchant. This also means that the consumer can make purchases (relatively) anonymously.

For consumers willing to set up special bank accounts, electronic checking or digital cash products may be a good option. These schemes can also work anonymously. A consumer can encrypt payment settlement information and send it to the merchant — who has to pass it along to the consumer's bank, where it is decrypted, and payment is forwarded to the merchant.

Merchant Choices

The Internet merchant must take greater care in setting up to accept electronic payments. The simplest option is to have someone else manage a secure Web server and set up shop there. This could mean setting up a store on an electronic mall or paying an Internet service provider to manage your Web site for you.

But there are many choices at this level. There are literally hundreds of "electronic malls" active on the Internet, on which a merchant can set up shop. On the other hand, large businesses may be willing to spend a lot to get a commercial environment that securely accepts orders, processes and settles the payment information, and can be integrated into a corporate fulfillment system.

There are other options, too. In addition to secure or commerce servers, which support credit card payment, the merchant can also elect to support some of the less familiar payment methods. Merchants can accept digital cash or electronic checks, or use other systems. Other systems take care of sensitive payment information offline. For example, you can set up as a First Virtual merchant if you want to sell a digital product that can be delivered over the Internet.

Choosing Functions and Features

For consumers, the most important aspects of an electronic commerce provider will probably be these:

- Reliability
- Security
- Simplicity
- Acceptability

Consumers have come to rely on their credit and charge card companies not just to extend credit, but to extend protection against unscrupulous vendors (providing recourse when improper charges are made), thieves (minimizing liability when a card is lost or stolen), and the vicissitudes of daily life (offering protection plans which replace lost or stolen goods). Likewise, these companies are also relied on to bill correctly, and to credit payments promptly. The same kind of reliability will be expected of electronic commerce service providers.

The security issue is one that will never go away. Even if the strongest possible encryption is used to send payment information, there are still many security holes. A security chain is only as strong as its weakest link, and companies engaging in this business can be exposed through any number of non-Internet attacks:

- The disgruntled employee with access to payment information
- Storage of payment information with insufficient security (unlocked file cabinets, unsecured terminals)
- Improper disposal of printed material (thieves could steal unshredded reports)

Although the general reader may suspect me of paranoia, experienced systems and network engineers are likely to come up with half a dozen more possibilities.

Electronic commerce schemes must be simple to achieve widespread appeal. Consumers prefer to use a single, multipurpose credit card such as Visa or MasterCard rather than set up credit accounts with every different retailer they purchase from. Many consumers prefer to pay for groceries by credit card rather than go through the process of getting a check-cashing identification card for a particular supermarket. And if you are in a hurry, cash can't be beat. The same goes for electronic commerce schemes: If they can be made to be simple, painless, and even more easy than transacting business in person, then they will be successful.

Finally, electronic commerce schemes should offer widespread acceptability. A scheme that is accepted only by a few merchants will not be attractive to consumers who don't do business with those merchants; a scheme that few consumers have chosen will be one that few merchants seek out.

What Lies Ahead

This industry is still in the very earliest phase of its infancy and is undergoing rapid change every day. What is current in the middle of 1997 may not be by the end of the year; however, the fundamental mechanisms are likely to remain in place for longer. This chapter provides overviews of about a dozen companies involved in the Internet commerce arena. Some of them are working together, while others are competing; the only certainty is that things will change.

The descriptions in this chapter and in the rest of this book should be used more as indicators of the way electronic commerce works than as exact descriptions of current offerings.

COMPANY PROFILES

The company profiles that follow should not be considered in any way comprehensive or exhaustive, but merely indicative of the types of organizations that are offering tools or products for electronic commerce.

By the time this book gets to the copy editor, not to mention you, the reader, another company will undoubtedly have come to the market with a new electronic commerce product or service. Fortunately, the Internet provides a way to stay current with search engines. Chances are you have seen one of the popular search engines listed below.

```
http://www.yahoo.com/
http://www.altavista.digital.com/
http://guide-p.infoseek.com/
http://www.lycos.com/
http://query.webcrawler.com/
```

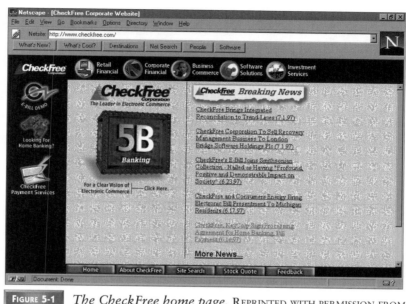

CheckFree Corporation

P.O. Box 2168
Columbus, Ohio 43216-2168
E-mail: billpay-info@checkfree.com
Telephone: 1-800-882-5280
www: http://www.checkfree.com

Checkfree Corporation was founded in 1981 and is a privately held company headquartered in Columbus, Ohio. Checkfree is a leading provider of bill payment and online banking payment disbursement services. According to Checkfree, it processes more than 54 million transactions and $6 billion annually through electronic funds transfer methods with CompuServe, GEnie, Delphi, and other online services.

FIGURE 5-2 *The CommerceNet home page.* REPRINTED WITH PERMISSION FROM COMMERCENET. © 1997.

CommerceNet, Inc.

East Coast Office:
  3209-A Corporate Court
  Ellicott City, MD 21042
  Telephone: (410) 203 2707
  Fax: (410) 203 2709

West Coast Office:
  4005 Miranda Avenue, Suite 175
  Palo Alto, CA 94304
  Telephone: (415) 858 1930
  Fax: (415) 858 1936
  E-mail: feedback@commerce.net
  www::   http://www.commerce.net/

CommerceNet, Inc., is an Internet commerce consortium of approximately 150 members, including many of the companies profiled here — as well as many others involved in providing Internet services, software and information publishers, online sales organizations, and more. CommerceNet is a not-for-profit corporation whose purpose is to help define and create the electronic marketplace on the Internet. See Chapter 9 for more details about this organization.

FIGURE 5-3 *The CyberCash home page.* REPRINTED WITH PERMISSION FROM CYBERCASH, INC. © 1997.

CyberCash, Inc.

2100 Reston Parkway
Reston, VA 22091
Telephone: (703) 620-4200
Fax: (703) 620-4215
E-mail: info@cybercash.com
www: http://www.cybercash.com

CyberCash, Inc., was founded in 1994. It offers an online payment service for the Internet. The CyberCash Secure Internet Payment Service carries information about credit card transactions across the Internet using public key cryptography to provide security and reliability. Debit card and electronic cash services have been announced, as well. The CyberCash payment system is described in greater detail in Chapter 6.

DigiCash bv

World headquarters:
    Kruislaan 419
    1098 VA Amsterdam
    The Netherlands
    Telephone: +31 20-592 9999
    Fax: +31 20-665 1126
    E-mail: info@digicash.nl
    www: http://www.digicash.nl/
    Anonymous ftp to ftp.digicash.nl

New York office, USA
    55 East 52nd street, 39th Floor
    New York, NY 10055-0186

Telephone: +1 212-909-4092
+1 800-410-ECASH (+1 800-410-32274)
Fax: +1 212-318-1222
E-mail: office.ny@digicash.com
www: http://www.digicash.com/
Anonymous ftp to ftp.digicash.com

Founded in April 1990, DigiCash produces electronic payment technology products, including hardware-only chip cards, software-only products, and hybrid products. The DigiCash payment system allows private and secure electronic transfers of cash, using public key cryptographic tools to reliably encode values into "digital coins" which cannot be counterfeited and which, when spent, are credited to the appropriate account anonymously.

This method will be discussed at greater length in Chapter 8.

FIGURE 5-5 *The FSTC home page.* REPRINTED WITH PERMISSION FROM

Financial Services Technology Consortium

http://www.fstc.org

Electronic checking requires cooperation of banks and other financial institutions, as well as the development of the software to support it. The Financial Services Technology Consortium (FSTC) was formed late in 1995 in support of just such cooperation. Its sixty-five founding member organizations include major banks as well as government agencies, high-technology companies, and others. Summaries of projects undertaken by consortium members are posted on the home page.

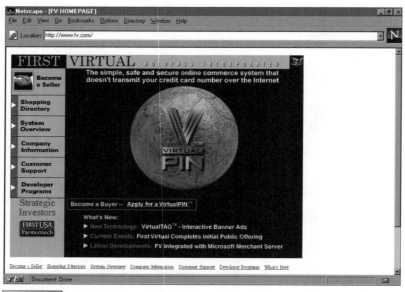

FIGURE 5-6   *The First Virtual home page.* THIS INFORMATION IS BEING PRINTED WITH-
OUT THE REVIEW OF FIRST VIRTUAL HOLDINGS INCORPORATED, AND MAY NOT
BE CURRENT AS OF THIS DATE. FIRST VIRTUAL, VIRTUALTAG AND VIRTUALPIN
ARE MARKS OF FIRST VIRTUAL HOLDINGS INCORPORATED. © 1997

First Virtual Holdings Incorporated

11975 El Camino Real, Suite 200
San Diego, CA 92130
Telephone: (619) 793-2700
Fax: (619) 793-2950
www: http://www.fv.com
E-mail addresses:
    Information: info@fv.com
    Application: apply@fv.com
    FAQ: help@fv.com

First Virtual actually began selling online on the Internet in October,
1994, making it one of the earliest companies offering electronic commerce offering including full services for transactions as well as a place to
sell digital products. First Virtual uses a "kinder and gentler" approach to
online sales. This method will be described at greater length in Chapter 6.

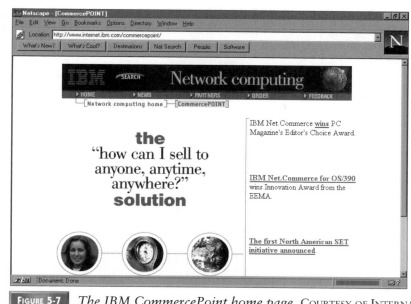

FIGURE 5-7 *The IBM CommercePoint home page.* COURTESY OF INTERNATIONAL BUSINESS MACHINES CORPORATION. © 1997.

IBM Corporation

IBM North America
1133 Westchester Avenue
White Plains NY 10604
Toll-free number (U.S.): 1-800-IBM-3333
E-mail: ibm_direct@vnet.ibm.com
www: http://www.internet.ibm.com/commercepoint/

IBM has developed the CommercePOINT series of products and services to offer business-to-business and traditional consumer selling opportunities on the Web. One of IBM's strongest assets is the private data network they can offer their customers for secure communications off the Internet.

FIGURE 5-8 *The Internet Shopping Network home page.* REPRINTED WITH PERMISSION FROM INTERNET SHOPPING NETWORK. © 1997.

Internet Shopping Network

3475 Deer Creek Road
Palo Alto, CA 94304
Telephone: 1-800-677-7467
          1-415-842-7400
E-mail: info@internet.net
www: http://www.internet.net

The Internet Shopping Network (ISN), a division of the billion-dollar television retailer Home Shopping Network, Inc., has been marketing computer hardware and software, among many other items, on the Internet since 1994.

ISN is one of the largest retailing and mall operations on the Internet, offering online shoppers access to a broad range of products, including more than 35,000 computer products from more than 1100 major companies.

ISN uses the Netscape Secure Commerce Server, though it started out requiring customers to call in to a special telephone line to provide credit card and delivery information. It still uses this as an option.

It is included in this list as a representative of the type of online "store" that is becoming more common. ISN does not use any special techniques for transacting business online, other than the Netscape Commerce Server and, of course, its own methods for creating and presenting product descriptions — which cannot be discounted, but which are beyond the scope of this book.

MasterCard International

2000 Purchase St.
Purchase, NY 10577
Telephone: 914-249-2000
E-mail:
www: http://www.mastercard.com

MasterCard International is an association composed of member banks. MasterCard along with Visa is jointly developing the Secure Electronic Transaction specification (SET).

MasterCard International is also heavily involved in the development of smart card technology, discussed in Chapter 8.

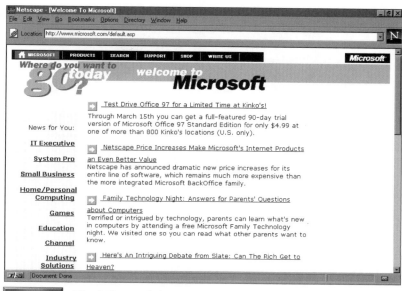

FIGURE 5-10 *The Microsoft home page.* REPRINTED WITH PERMISSION FROM MICROSOFT CORPORATION. © 1997.

Microsoft Corp.

1 Microsoft Way
Redmond, WA 98052
Telephone: (206) 882-8080
www: http://www.microsoft.com

Although it was not one of the first companies to develop products and services for the Internet, today Microsoft is a dominant player. Microsoft offers both an Internet browser for the end user and several commerce and information servers with which to build Electronic Commerce applications.

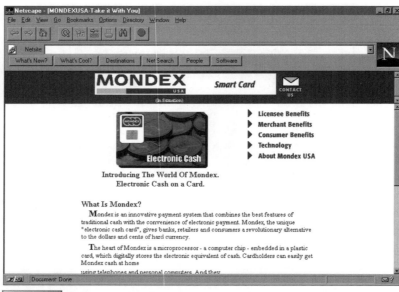

FIGURE 5-11 *The Mondex home page.* REPRINTED WITH PERMISSION FROM MONDEX USA SERVICES. © 1997.

Mondex International

1st Floor, Podium
Drapers Gardens
12 Throgmorton Avenue
London EC2N 2DL
England
Fax: +44 (0) 171-920 5505
E-mail: news@int.mondex.com
www: http://www.mondex.com/mondex/home.htm

Work on the Mondex scheme started in the United Kingdom in 1990 and has resulted in a major test in Swindon (a large town in southwest England, 70 miles from London) begun in 1995; the scheme has also been tested in Australia and the United States. Essentially, Mondex implements digitally signed electronic cash encoded in smart cards. This electronic cash can be exchanged between individuals or between consumers and merchants, provided all are equipped with the Mondex cards or devices. The cards can also be used in ATMs, as well as any number of Mondex devices.

Some of the special features include the ability to do the following:

- "Load" the card with various different currencies
- Institute a reward system so that lost cards will be returned (although if a card is truly lost, the value on it is also lost)
- Use a personal password on the card to prevent anyone but the owner from accessing values on it

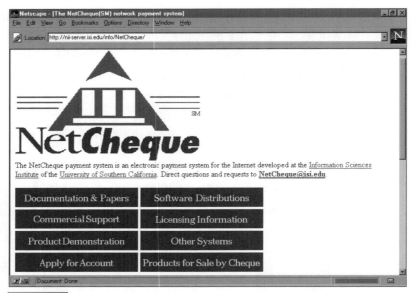

FIGURE 5-12   *The NetCash home page.* REPRINTED WITH PERMISSION FROM
http://www.netcheque.org/info/netcheque. NETCHEQUE IS A
REGISTERED SERVICES MARK OF THE UNIVERSITY OF SOUTHERN
CALIFORNIA. © 1997.

NetCash/NetCheque

NetCheque Project
USC Information Sciences Institute
4676 Admiralty Way
Marina del Rey, CA 90292-6695
Fax: (310) 823-6714
E-mail: NetCheque@isi.edu
www: http://nii.isi.edu/info/NetCheque

The University of Southern California, like other universities, is
sponsoring an initiative to contribute to the Internet commerce

environment. USC is doing so through its Information Sciences Institute, which is developing NetCheque and NetCash.

NetCash is intended to be a basis for an electronic currency to be used to pay for product purchased through the Internet in real time. Stated NetCash properties include the following:

- Security
- Anonymity
- Scalability
- Acceptability
- Interoperability

NetCheque has been developed as a related instrument for transferring funds between participating entities, in a manner similar to the way bank checks are used. Together, the two schemes offer a full range of payment options to users, moving from non-anonymous payment by check to completely anonymous transactions.

The NetMarket Company

The American Twine Building
155 Second Street
Cambridge, MA 02141-2125
Telephone: 1-800-867-3777
Fax: 1-617-441-5099
E-mail: info@netmarket.com
www: http://www.netmarket.com/sa/pages/home

The NetMarket Company was founded in August of 1993. NetMarket offers online World Wide Web transaction encryption. NetMarket's transaction encryption is based on the Pretty Good Privacy (PGP) program. PGP implements public key digital signature transactions.

Netscape Communications Corporation

501 East Middlefield Road
Mountain View, CA 94043
Telephone: 1-415-254-1900
Fax: 1-415-528-4124
E-mail: info@netscape.com
www: http://home.netscape.com

Started in April, 1994, Netscape's first products have been Netscape Navigator, a widely distributed World Wide Web browser, and the Netscape server line, including the first secure World Wide Web commerce server.

Netscape developed a secure protocol, Secure Sockets Layer (SSL), to encrypt and decrypt World Wide Web data as it is sent and received by underlying Internet software, rather than using the Secure HTTP protocol to provide security enhancements within the World Wide Web applications themselves. This protocol has been made available to the public and has been proposed as an Internet standard.

Netscape's secure servers are discussed at greater length in Chapter 7, and their protocols are discussed at greater length in Chapter 4.

FIGURE 5-14   *The Open Market home page.* REPRINTED WITH PERMISSION
FROM OPEN MARKET, INC. © 1997.

Open Market, Inc.

> 245 First Street
> Cambridge, MA 02142
> Telephone: 1-800-801-8504
>   1-617-949-7000
> Fax: 1-617-621-1703
> E-mail: info@openmarket.com
> www: http://www.openmarket.com

Founded in 1994, Open Market offers software, services, and customer solutions for electronic commerce on the Internet and the World
Wide Web. These include Web servers, both secured and not, World
Wide Web authoring and site management tools, and tools to manage
transaction services. Open Market's Integrated Commerce Environment
is an infrastructure for Internet commerce and is described in greater
detail in Chapter 7.

FIGURE 5-15 *The RSADSI home page.* REPRINTED WITH PERMISSION FROM RSA DATA SECURITY. © 1997.

RSA Data Security, Inc.

100 Marine Parkway, Suite 500
Redwood City, CA 94065-1031
Telephone: (415) 595-8782
Fax:　　　(415) 595-1873
E-mail:　　info@rsa.com
www:　　　http://www.rsa.com

The owner of all the important patents relating to public key cryptography, RSADSI is an important player in the development of secure electronic commerce. In fact, all major proposed standards, specifications, and schemes supporting secured and encrypted online transactions refer to or rely on algorithms and technologies licensed by RSADSI. RSADSI is discussed in more detail in Chapter 2.

FIGURE 5-16 *The Secure Computing home page.* REPRINTED WITH
PERMISSION FROM SECURE COMPUTING. © 1997.

Secure Computing

2675 Long Lake Road
Roseville, MN 55113
Telephone: 1-800-692-5625
E-mail: sales@sctc.com
www: http://www.sctc.com

Secure Computing Corporation has a long history of supporting
government and corporate security needs with firewalls and related
products. In late 1996, Secure Computing added identification and
authentication products to their product mix.

FIGURE 5-17   *The Surety Technologies home page.* REPRINTED WITH PERMISSION FROM SURETY TECHNOLOGIES. © 1997.

Surety Technologies

One Main St.
Chatham, NJ 07928
Telephone: (201) 701-0600
Fax: (201) 701-0601
E-mail: info@surety.com
www: http://www.surety.com

Starting in 1993, Surety Technologies, Inc., began marketing an electronic notary service called Digital Notary. Its purpose is to give corporations and individual users a method of proving authenticity and integrity of electronic records — in other words, to act as an electronic notary service. Surety provides the software as well as acting as a trusted third-party certifier. Digital Notary includes client software and a license to notarize a certain number of documents, depending on the product. Surety's 1997 pricing schedule is as follows:

Monthly Service Fees

	Price Plan A	Price Plan B
Initial Server Site and Server ID	$500	$1,500
Additional Server Sites	$100	$100
Additional Server ID's	$100	$100

Monthly Transactions[1]

Plan A	Transaction Price	Plan B	Transaction Price
Zero–2,000	Included	Zero–10,000	Included
2,001 and above	$0.20	10,000–20,000	0.14
		20,001–40,000	0.13
		40,001–80,000	0.13
		80,001–200,000	0.13
		200,001–400,000	0.13
		400,001–600,000	0.13
		600,001–800,000	0.13
		800,001–100,000	0.13
		1,000,001–1,500,000	0.13
		1,500,001–200,000	0.13
		Above 2,000,000[2]	0.04

REPRINTED WITH PERMISSION FROM SURETY TECHNOLOGIES. © 1997.

It is included here as an example of a company offering a service which reproduces digitally what has traditionally been thought of as a face-to-face transaction: notarizing a document.

---

[1] A transaction constitutes *creation* or *validation* of a Surety Digital Notary™ "Certificate"
[2] Transaction 2,000,000 and below = $.05
 Transactions above 2,000,000 = $.04
 • Software, documentation and maintenance included.
 • Integration/development services at Surety's standard T & M Rates
 • Technical phone support: $35 per 15 minute increment

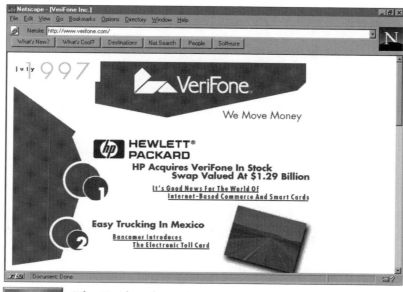

FIGURE 5-18 *The Verifone home page.* REPRINTED WITH PERMISSION FROM VERIFONE, INC. © 1997.

Verifone

Three Lagoon Drive
Redwood City, CA 94065-1561
Telephone: (415) 591-6500
Fax: (415) 598-5504
www: http://www.verifone.com

Chances are if you have used a credit card lately, the little box the merchant used to get an authorization was made by Verifone. Verifone has a very strong POS (point of sale) business for processing credit card transactions. Verifone is leveraging their POS and credit card experience into the smart-card and smart-card device business.

Verifone has also created these levels of electronic commerce products:

- Vgate
- Vpos

FIGURE 5-19 *The VeriSign home page.* REPRINTED WITH PERMISSION FROM
VERISIGN, INC. © 1997.

VeriSign, Inc.

100 Marine Parkway, Suite 525
Redwood City, CA 94065
Telephone: (415) 508-1151
Fax: (415) 508-1121
E-mail: info@verisign.com
www: http://www.verisign.com

Spun off by RSADSI to act as the certificate authority for Netscape
Commerce Server customers, VeriSign is the "trusted third party"
responsible for maintaining records of public keys and their owners.
In fact, it is necessary for an online merchant to register with VeriSign
before the Netscape Commerce Server can be used.

Registering a Netscape Commerce Server includes submitting
paperwork identifying and certifying the site, the server name, and the
webmaster of the site; generating and submitting a public/secret key
pair to VeriSign; and receiving acknowledgment; and paying for the
service. There is an up-front fee plus an ongoing maintenance fee.

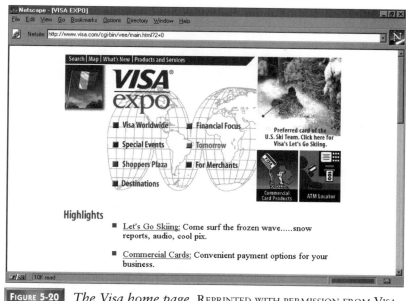

Visa

900 Metro Center Blvd
Foster City, CA 94404
Telephone: (415) 432-3200
www: http://www.visa.com

Visa is an association of member banks. Along with MasterCard International, Visa is developing the Secure Electronic Transaction specification (SET).

VISA is also heavily involved in the development of smart card technology, discussed in Chapter 8.

A Host of Others...

These companies are among the more interesting, and in many cases, more likely to succeed in the long run. There are many, many more companies that are providing Internet commerce services in one form or another, as described in the section on services in Chapter 3. There are various associations, research groups, agencies, and consortia, all providing some kind of service or support to the issues of electronic commerce. There are also less formal proposals: for example, individuals or groups offering to start their own electronic currencies, possibly based on barter of products or services. Others include payment systems instituted by online malls for use only at those malls, using telephone, fax, or other methods for collecting credit card information, and user IDs and passwords for making purchases.

To get more information about all these companies (and all the new ones which have surely sprung up since this book went to press), the best place to start is with an online search engine such as Yahoo,

```
http://www.yahoo.com
```

The pointers provided in the companion CD-ROM should also be useful to anyone wishing to get more complete information and, in particular, the latest news and developments from participating organizations.

SIX

ELECTRONIC PAYMENT SYSTEMS

In God we trust — all others pay cash

— FROM THE SIGN OVER THE CASH REGISTER AT THE STORE
AROUND THE CORNER

Anything that makes it possible for a consumer to spend money online can be construed as an electronic payment system. As discussed in earlier chapters, these payment systems can be electronic checking systems, third-party systems, or electronic currency systems. All of these provide for the exchange of values between individuals. Some require prior arrangements by all participants, although this is changing. This chapter describes in greater detail how two representative payment systems work on the Internet.

DIGITAL PAYMENT SYSTEMS

Digital payment systems, unlike electronic commerce environments, focus on getting a payment from a customer to a merchant. The emphasis is on the customer: At least so far, the customer is required to make some kind of commitment to the payment system in question in order to use it. For example, the customer may need to acquire and install some software, or make some kind of contact with the digital payment system provider in order to register as a user of that service. Merchants also must make a specific commitment to one or more providers of digital payment services.

Neither customer nor merchant is bound by any single commitment, however. Just as the average consumer in a typical suburban mall may have a pocketful of credit cards (as well as a checkbook and cash), so the typical online consumer may very well use several different methods to pay for products purchased on the Internet. The same goes for merchants, who both online and offline are usually willing to accept a variety of different payment options.

Although digital payment systems require a higher level of activity and commitment from both consumers and merchants, the reward to providers of such systems is very attractive. Software publishers offering secure World Wide Web servers earn a profit on each sale of their server software, but companies offering a digital payment system are able to earn a profit on each sale made using the service itself.

This chapter examines two very different digital payment systems. CyberCash uses a straightforward interpretation of digital commerce, basing its service on the need for secure, private, and reliable transactions. CyberCash offers a digital payment mechanism that uses modern cryptographic technologies, including public and private key encryption and digital signatures, implemented through special client and server software.

Consumers store their payment information in an encrypted digital wallet, and they can make credit card payments as well as digital cash transfers through CyberCash. CyberCash can be accepted for virtually any type of transaction, from small to large purchases, although peer-to-peer digital cash transfers may be preferable for most smaller purchases. Consumers need special free client software to set up a "digital wallet," while merchants must install free server software. Although the end-user application can be installed and configured in a few minutes, installing and configuring a merchant's World Wide Web server to accept CyberCash payments is more complicated.

First Virtual, on the other hand, approaches digital commerce using different assumptions about the sale of information over the Internet. First Virtual's founders created the Green Commerce model, which works from the assumptions that people are basically willing to pay for valuable information, as long as they don't have to pay up front for a pig in a poke. Up through the early 1990s, the Internet culture largely encouraged and rewarded people who shared information, and tended to discourage the use of the Internet for profit taking and profit-oriented activities. By offering a method of buying and selling information products over the Internet, First Virtual allows information merchants the opportunity to offer their information for a fair price, while still giving information consumers the opportunity to take products for a "test drive."

First Virtual is for buying and selling information only; it is not to be used to sell products or services, although it can be used for subscriptions, memberships, and charitable contributions.

Using no encryption or digital signatures, First Virtual relies on personal identification and e-mail confirmations to make sure no one is charged improperly. Perhaps most startling (to some people) is the attitude that consumers can be trusted to be willing to pay for information which they believe is useful, and that they should not be required to pay for information which they don't feel meets their needs. However, this is essentially the same approach taken by many bookstores and magazine stands: You can browse and read all you want, as long as you don't abuse the privilege.

The First Virtual payment system can be implemented by sellers, and used by customers, on World Wide Web servers, on file transfer (ftp) servers, and even in e-mail. For the entry-level information merchant, First Virtual offers a virtual mall, called InfoHaus, through which just about anyone can sell information on which commissions and fees are paid to First Virtual. First Virtual also provides, through their Internet servers, sample HTML code, an application programming interface, and source code for implementing the system on existing server and client software.

This chapter examines both First Virtual and CyberCash, describing them and their products, and explaining how they work.

FIRST VIRTUAL INTERNET PAYMENT SYSTEM

The First Virtual organization includes some of the most respected names in Internet circles: Marshall Rose is responsible for seminal work in electronic mail and Internet network management protocols, Nathaniel Borenstein is the primary author of the MIME protocol for multimedia and multilingual e-mail, and Einar Stefferud has been a key contributor to the development of the Internet since 1975. By considering the issues of digital commerce as it applies to the Internet, the First Virtual solution comes up with a novel approach that takes advantage of the nature of open networks.

First Virtual has created a payment system, the Internet Payment System, to be used exclusively for the sale of information over the Internet, rather than for products or services. Using an automated telephone system to collect payment information about the participant, First Virtual eschews cryptographic methods (encryption or digital signatures), preferring to rely instead on close monitoring of sales and purchases to reduce fraud.

The definition of "information" ranges from the familiar, such as recipes, a marketing report, or a novel, to virtually anything that can be digitized, such as software, photographs, music, or electronic performance art. Likewise, donations to charities, memberships in organizations, and subscriptions to publications can also be charged through First Virtual. Not permitted for sale are products with a physical presence or services.

Fundamental Assumptions

The First Virtual Internet Payment System is based on three fundamental assumptions. First, electronic information merchants can produce as many or as few copies of any information product at no incremental cost per copy because once the information has been developed and offered for sale once, the cost of selling it again is virtually zero.

This is why physical products or services are not to be sold through First Virtual. If a copy of a digital newsletter is delivered but not paid for, there is no cost to the merchant, but if a crystal vase is delivered but not paid for, the merchant loses real money: the cost of the vase.

Although the merchant takes on the risk that customers will decide not to pay after taking a look at the information being sold through First Virtual, there is no actual financial loss, because a copy of the product that is not paid for still doesn't cost the merchant anything. There is no opportunity cost to the lost sale, because the person perusing the information would not have purchased it, and the information is still available for sale to someone else at the same time.

Next, information buyers, like buyers of any other product, need some way to examine products before they buy. For digital sales, this means they need to be able to download it and check it out before deciding if it is worth the money. Customers almost always want to test-drive a car, or skim through a book, or rap on a melon, before deciding to buy. Digital information consumers have little or no opportunity to test-drive information, other than actually downloading it and taking a look at it.

Finally, buying and selling should be simple and have as low an entry cost in time, money, and effort as possible. The objective is to create a system through which it is possible to buy information with a minimum of fuss or special preparation. At the same time, selling information should be simple and inexpensive—and a possibility for virtually all individuals.

These assumptions lead to certain conclusions, which produce a different view of the information marketplace than that taken by most other commerce providers:

- Because there is no cost (or negligible cost) associated with sending out a copy of the information being sold, "returns" or "stolen goods" don't, in fact, cost the merchant anything.
- Information products are sold "on approval" with the customer required to explicitly reply either yes or no to a request for payment, but only after having received a copy of the information.
- Information products can be sold through virtually any Internet application and do not require vendors or buyers to buy special software. More important, First Virtual offers facilities (see the later section of this chapter on the First Virtual InfoHaus) to individuals to sell information online for very minimal cost.

The First Virtual Internet Payment System is more formally defined by the Green Commerce model and the Simple Green Commerce Protocol (SGCP), which are included on the companion CD-ROM to this book.

Automation and First Virtual

One assumption about online commerce that is not stated explicitly, but which becomes clear after a short exposure to First Virtual, is that the system depends to a huge degree on automation of processes. The First Virtual system is intended to work exclusively through automated e-mail responders, through forms used on the World Wide Web, and through automated terminal sessions. It is possible to use this system as both a buyer and seller without ever speaking or corresponding with an actual human representative.

First Virtual is able to keep its support structure small by relying on documentation and automated systems. As a result, the documentation has to be complete and comprehensive. Even so, the basic First

Virtual operations are all very straightforward as long as one follows the directions. Throughout the documentation are gentle and diplomatically phrased suggestions that before attempting to contact a human being at First Virtual, the user should take a deep breath and try reading the manuals.

The only telephone number listed in the documentation is the account application number, and getting help from a person requires sending e-mail to a special address. However, it is entirely possible to happily buy and sell through First Virtual without ever speaking or corresponding with a human.

By relying on automation to such a great extent, First Virtual is able to provide services to a large customer population without requiring a large infrastructure. By automating customer service as well as the actual transaction, First Virtual is able to better apply its human resources.

Account Setup and Costs

There are two ways to set up as a seller on the First Virtual Internet Payment System: Pioneer and Express. The *Pioneer* sellers' program is designed for people who want to start selling their information over the Internet without establishing themselves as traditional sellers requiring a credit check or other bureaucracy.

The Pioneer application process is rather simple, starting with an online application. After the application is received and processed, First Virtual will e-mail a 12-digit application number and instructions to the seller on how to send bank account information to First Virtual via postal mail. Monies due to the seller are deposited into the seller's account via the US ACH direct-deposit system. The Pioneer application fee and annual renewal is US$10.

The *Express* seller program is for those sellers who already have a credit card merchant number available to accept credit card payments. The application fee is US$350 and the annual renewal is US$250.

Becoming a buyer is very easy, with an online application fee of US$2 per year, and you must use a credit card to pay for the items you purchase.

At the very least, each seller and buyer must have an e-mail connection to the Internet, but transactions can be completed through the First Virtual World Wide Web site or through a remote terminal session (telnet) with their system.

Beyond the account initiation charges, purchasers pay no costs other than the price of any information they decide to buy. Sellers pay a transaction fee ($0.29), as well as 2% of the selling price on each transaction. A $1.00 processing charge for depositing funds in the seller's account is also levied.

Opening a First Virtual Account

Becoming a buyer of information requires nothing more than an electronic mail link to the Internet and a credit card. Although buyers were initially required to transact business in United States dollars, currency exchange is currently being handled at the credit card level, meaning no matter what country your Visa or MasterCard is issued in, the credit card company will convert from your home currency to U.S. dollars.

Initiating a First Virtual account is a two-step process for consumers, and a three-step process for sellers of information. All participants must register first as information buyers; sellers then send a check for

Connecting to First Virtual by the World Wide Web, the applicant first fills out the form on the Web page displayed in Figure 6-1. Information provided by the applicant online is limited to contact information, including name, electronic and postal mail addresses, telephone number, an optional additional e-mail address to send copies of transaction notifications, and a First Virtual ID choice.

The ID phrase is selected by the applicant. First Virtual modifies this phrase (up to 24 letters or numbers) slightly and uses it to create the First Virtual account identifier.

Sending e-mail to the address

apply@card.com

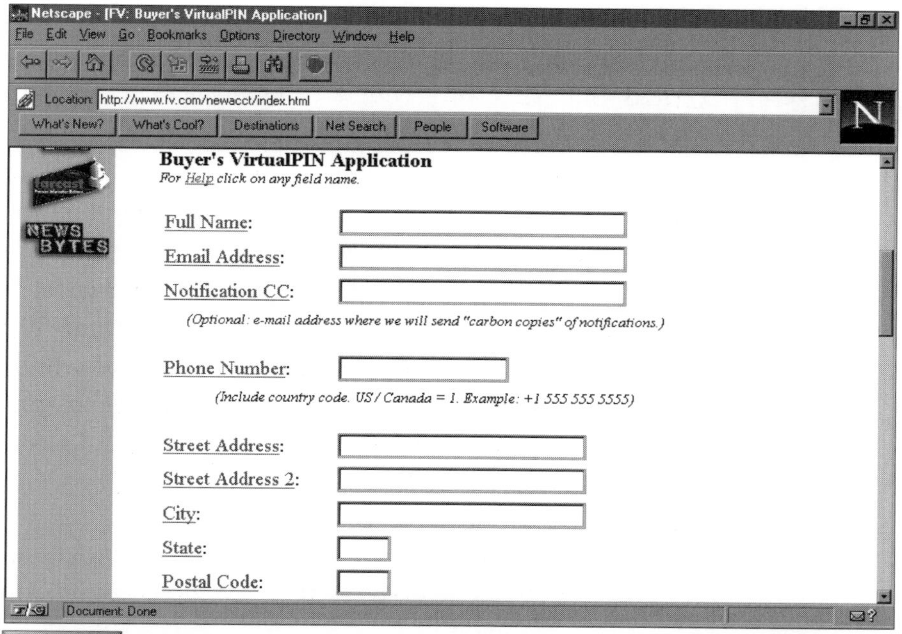

FIGURE 6-1 *The First Virtual account application on the World Wide Web.*
THIS INFORMATION IS BEING PRINTED WITHOUT THE REVIEW OF FIRST VIRTUAL
HOLDINGS INCORPORATED, AND MAY NOT BE CURRENT AS OF THIS DATE. FIRST
VIRUTAL, VIRTUALTAG AND VIRTUALPIN ARE MARKS OF FIRST VIRTUAL
HOLDINGS INCORPORATED. © 1997

returns an electronic copy of an application form. Likewise, applicants
can initiate a telnet session with the host

```
telnet.card.com
```

to provide this information interactively and directly to First Virtual's
application system.

In all cases, this is the only information the applicant provides
online. Once the form has been filled out it must be returned to First
Virtual—automatically through the terminal session, or by pressing
the APPLY button in the World Wide Web server, or by sending back a
copy of the completed application through e-mail.

The next step is to wait for an e-mail message from First Virtual
confirming that the new account application has been received and

containing the account identifier and an application number. The applicant then makes a telephone call to a toll-free number (in the United States; a direct dial number is provided for international users) to supply credit card information to First Virtual. The caller keys the application number and credit card account information into an automatic response system. First Virtual will then respond by e-mail message with completed account information, assuming that the application has been approved; a $2.00 charge against the credit card will be made to defray the cost of setting up the account. The response includes the modified account ID, as well as information about how to register as an information seller through First Virtual.

Figure 6-2 shows the e-mail message received after completing the online application.

```
Subj:  newacct-result — 97021471***
Date:  97-02-14 17:05:18 EST
From:  sgcs-server@card.com (FV Commerce Server)
Resent-from:  sgcs-server@card.com
Reply-to:     support-newacct@card.com
To: stlmurph@aol.com

We have received the First Virtual account application for
Paul A. Murphy (with PIN-Choice, **********).

Your account is almost ready to use.  This message tells you how to
activate it so that you can use it to buy or sell over the Internet.

ACTIVATING YOUR ACCOUNT FOR BUYING:

  1) Call the toll-free, 800 number to register your credit card
     number. (This is necessary to avoid sending your credit
     card information over the Internet.)

        From inside the US: +1 800 383-8332

        From outside the US: +1 770 333-0500

  2) Follow the recorded instructions and enter your 12 digit
     application number.  Your application number is:

        9702-1471-****
```

FIGURE 6-2 *First Virtual Account Application Email Summary and Instructions (continued on following page).*

(continued from previous page)

> This application number is used for activation purposes only.
> This application number is NOT your VirtualPIN (account
> identifier). It can not be used for buying. You may wish
> however to keep this number in case you forget your VirtualPIN.
>
> 3) Next, enter your Visa or MasterCard credit card number and
>   expiration date.
>
>   We will charge your credit card the annual fee of $2.00 (two US
>   dollars) at this time and each year thereafter.
>
> 4) After your call, you will receive e-mail from us, most likely
>   within two hours, containing your activated VirtualPIN. You
>   will then be ready to buy!
>
>   Due to technical factors beyond our control, account activation
>   can take as long as 24 hours. We are working on reducing this
>   delay — please be patient.
>
> NOTE: If you do not receive an e-mail confirmation within 24
> hours, you may check the status of your application by sending an
> e-mail message to "findappl@card.com" with your
> application number, 9702-1471-3319, in the subject
> heading. If you continue to have problems, send an e-mail message
> to "support@fv.com" with details of when you called the 800
> number and your application number. A help operator will assist you.
>
> ALSO NOTE: We have observed that some customers have difficulty
> interacting with our telephone response unit. If you are unable
> to complete the telephone-based portion of the application, you
> may send us your credit card information by fax. On a single
> page, please type your:
>
> - Name
> - VISA or MasterCard number and expiration date
> - Application number, 9702-1471-****
> - E-mail address
> - Phone number (in case we need to contact you)
> Please fax this information to +1 619 793 8133. We will enter your
> information into our system during our normal business hours.
>
> To also activate your account for selling over the Internet, please
> see below.
>
> Welcome to First Virtual!
>
> ACTIVATING YOUR ACCOUNT FOR SELLING:

FIGURE 6-2 *First Virtual Account Application Email Summary and
Instructions (continued on following page).*

(continued from previous page)

```
If you would like to sell using your First Virtual account, follow
these steps to activate your account for selling:

  1) Choose the bank account you would like us
     to direct-deposit your funds into (via the US ACH system).

  2) Write a check on that account for $10.00 (ten US dollars), made
     payable to:

         First Virtual Holdings Incorporated

     The routing/transit numbers and account information on this
     check should tell us where to deposit your funds. Please verify
     this with your bank. If the information necessary to make a
     direct deposit into your account is not on the check, please
     attach a note your check giving the correct numbers.

  3) Write your application number in the "memo" section of
     the check. This ensures that the correct First Virtual account
     is linked to your bank account.  Your application number is:

         9702-1471-****

  4) Then, mail the check to:

         First Virtual Holdings Incorporated
         Attn: Merchant Support
         P.O. Box 500224
         San Diego, CA 92150-0224

  5) Within 10 business days, you will receive an e-mail message
     from us indicating your account is operational. If you do not
     receive a message within 10 business days, you may check the
     status of your application by sending an e-mail message to
     "findappl@card.com"
     with your application number,
         9702-1471-****,
     in the subject heading.

Welcome to First Virtual as an Internet Seller!

----------------------------------------

IF YOU DO NOT KNOW WHY YOU ARE RECEIVING THIS MESSAGE,
someone else probably applied for a First Virtual account and used
an incorrect e-mail address.  Please ignore this message; you will be
```

FIGURE 6-2 *First Virtual Account Application Email Summary and Instructions (continued on following page).*

(continued from previous page)

```
sent three automated reminders, and then the application will be deleted
and no account will be opened.

IF YOU DECIDE NOT TO ACTIVATE YOUR ACCOUNT,
please ignore this message.  You will be sent three automated reminders,
and then the application will be deleted and no account will be opened.

NOTE:  Based on your application, we believe that your mail system
does not handle structured Internet e-mail messages.  Therefore, we will
send only text messages to you, rather than structured messages.  If you
wish to receive structured messages instead, please send e-mail to
support-newacct@card.com for further information.

Use of the First Virtual Internet Payment System is governed by our
Terms and Conditions effective 25 October 1996, as may be amended from
time to time. To receive a current copy of our TACs pertaining to your
use of our system, send a blank e-mail message to one or more of the
following addresses:

     Buyer Terms and Conditions:              "tacs-buyer@fv.com"
     Pioneer Seller Terms and Conditions:     "tacs-pioneer@fv.com"
     Express Seller Terms and Conditions:     "tacs-express@fv.com"
     InfoHaus Terms and Conditions:           "tacs-infohaus@fv.com"

     Operating Rules for Buyers, Pioneer Sellers,
     Express Sellers, and InfoHaus Merchants:    "op-rules@fv.com"

First Virtual is a servicemark of First Virtual Holdings Incorporated.

For your information, here is the account profile we received from you:
street-address: **************
city:                 Ballwin
full-name:            Paul A. Murphy
newacct-id:           <MwThZ5o3OQcBAAA@infohaus.com>
x-user-agent:         Mozilla/3.0 (Win95; U)
x-remote-host:        pn1-ppp-06.primary.net
email-address:        STLMURPH%aol.com@mime.challenged.card.com
country:              US
phone-number:         +1-3143942116
pin-choice:           *************
state:                MO
postal-code:          63011
preferred-language:   EN
preferred-currency:   usd us dollars
address-redistribution: Y
html-capable:         N
```

FIGURE 6-2   *First Virtual Account Application Email Summary and Instructions.*

Setting Up as a Seller

Although credit cards are great for paying for products, they are not intended as two-way instruments. First Virtual sellers must set up a checking account (or use an existing one) to accept payments credited through the system. Sellers simply send a check for $10.00 to First Virtual, noting their application number in the memo field on the check.

This is all that is necessary, at least administratively. The information merchant must have some method of distributing information products on the Internet, which will be discussed in greater detail next.

The First Virtual Transaction Process

The First Virtual information merchant offers a product online, making it available through a First-Virtual compatible server on the Internet, and including product pricing and description. The First Virtual Internet Payment System transaction process goes something like this:

- A customer attempts to download the offered information from the server, at which point the server requests a First Virtual account identifier.
- The merchant has the option of verifying, through First Virtual, that the account identifier is valid. The server sends a query to First Virtual, which responds by confirming that the account ID is valid.
- The offered information is sent to the buyer directly from the merchant's server.
- The merchant's server sends an e-mail message to First Virtual, detailing the transaction: the buyer and seller account ID, the item purchased, and the item price.
- First Virtual sends an e-mail message to the customer, asking whether he or she wishes to pay for the item.
- If the customer replies with "yes," the merchant's account will be credited (minus transaction fees) for that sale; if the customer replies "no," no further action is taken. If no response is received,

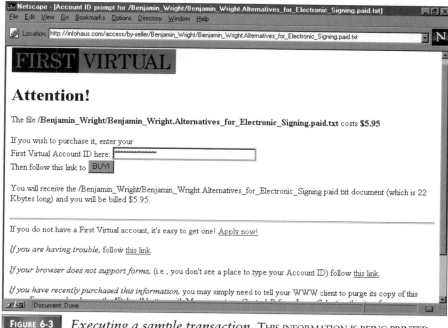

further attempts are made. The merchant is kept apprised of the result of each transaction.

- A third option, "fraud," is available to the customer and is used to indicate that the customer did not initiate the transaction. This invalidates the transaction, and the customer's account ID is canceled to avoid further attempts to use it.

Confirming Transactions

Customers are notified by e-mail of any transaction made with their account ID. Part of the agreement between participants and First Virtual mandates that the participant supply an e-mail address used frequently and exclusively by the participant. This assures that customers can respond to First Virtual with their purchase decisions in a timely fashion, and will be able to notify First Virtual of unauthorized use of their account ID.

Once a transaction has been made—a customer downloads a file containing information being sold by a merchant—and once the merchant sends a message to First Virtual indicating a sale is pending, First Virtual sends out an e-mail confirmation to the customer. The message includes customer name, the item being purchased, the merchant, and the price, and asks whether the customer wishes to authorize payment for the product.

The following is a sample email confirming a purchase.

```
Subj:   <19970216.08974001307@card.com> — transfer-query
Date:   97-02-16 12:41:49 EST
From:   sgcs-server@card.com (FV Commerce Server)
Resent-from: sgcs-server@card.com
Reply-to:    response@card.com
To: stlmurph@aol.com

Transaction: Alternatives_for_Electronic_Signing
Cost:      5.95 usd us dollars
Seller-Name: Benjamin Wright
Transfer-ID: <4383658.10615.0@buyers.infohaus.com>
Server-ID:  <19970216.08974001307@card.com>

Benjamin Wright has requested that
Paul A. Murphy should be charged 5.95 (in usd us dollars)
for "Alternatives_for_Electronic_Signing".


Please reply to this message with ONE word,
either YES, NO, or FRAUD.

Your message should be addressed to "response@card.com" and
the Subject should contain your Server ID,
    <19970216.08974001307@card.com>.
The Body of your reply should contain only one word.

— The Definitions of Yes, No, and Fraud are as follows: —

1) "Yes" - You authorize us to charge your
           credit card 5.95 usd us dollars.

    This confirms your order. For "try before you buy"
    products, "yes" means you received the product, examined it, and
    feel it is worth paying for.
```

2) "No" - You decline this request for payment.

A "No" response cancels your sale. For "try before you buy" products, "No" means you did not receive a satisfactory product.

3) "Fraud" - You authorize your VirtualPIN to be IMMEDIATELY cancelled because you believe it was STOLEN.

A "Fraud" response means you were unaware of this transaction and did NOT request to purchase this product.

************** PLEASE NOTE **************
If you do say "Fraud", we will PERMANENTLY cancel your VirtualPIN. Just like reporting a credit/debit card stolen, this action closes your account. You will need to apply for a new VirtualPIN to make any future purchases through First Virtual.

NEED HELP?

If your situation does not fit any of the three options above, you can respond with the word "Help", followed by a description of your problem. The text that follows the word "Help" will be forwarded to a Customer Support Representative and personally responded to.

IF YOUR MAIL SYSTEM CANNOT CONSTRUCT SUFFICIENTLY LONG SUBJECT LINES:

Please send a message to response-challenged@card.com with the first (and only) lines in the message being the following two lines:

Server-ID: <19970216.08974001307@card.com>
Authorization: yes (or no or fraud)

Use of the First Virtual Internet Payment System is governed by our Terms and Conditions effective 25 October 1996, as may be amended from time to time. To receive a current copy of our TACs pertaining to your use of our system, send a blank e-mail message to one or more of the following addresses:

Buyer Terms and Conditions: "tacs-buyer@fv.com"
Pioneer Seller Terms and Conditions: "tacs-pioneer@fv.com"
Express Seller Terms and Conditions: "tacs-express@fv.com"
InfoHaus Terms and Conditions: "tacs-infohaus@fv.com"

Operating Rules for Buyers, Pioneer Sellers,
Express Sellers, and InfoHaus Merchants: "op-rules@fv.com"

FIRST VIRTUAL is a servicemark of First Virtual Holdings Incorporated.

The customer then simply replies to that message, using the "reply" feature of his or her e-mail program, with the body of the message containing only a single word:

- "Yes" authorizes the payment of the stated amount. This means you received the information product, it was what you wanted and expected, and that the price was what you intended to pay for it.
- "No" declines payment of the stated amount, and means that you attempted to download the information but never received it, you received a corrupted file, or you received it but it was not what you expected. If you believe the bill was the result of a simple mistake (like an accidental or duplicate billing), you can also answer "no."
- "Fraud" indicates you suspect a fraudulent use of your account. This response will immediately cause your account to be suspended, and you will have to open a new account to use First Virtual again.

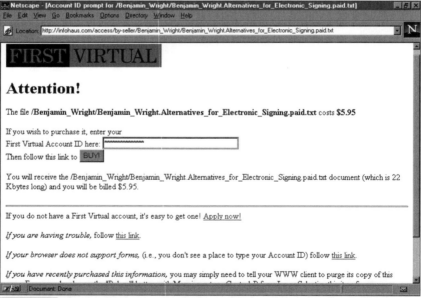

FIGURE 6-4 *A sample purchase confirmation.* THIS INFORMATION IS BEING PRINTED WITHOUT THE REVIEW OF FIRST VIRTUAL HOLDINGS INCORPORATED, AND MAY NOT BE CURRENT AS OF THIS DATE. FIRST VIRUTAL, VIRTUALTAG AND VIRTUALPIN ARE MARKS OF FIRST VIRTUAL HOLDINGS INCORPORATED. © 1997

If no response is received, further attempts will be made to contact the customer; ultimately, if confirmation messages are ignored, First Virtual will take appropriate steps. This may include canceling the account, since part of the agreement between the account holder and First Virtual stipulates that the account holder checks e-mail on a regular basis.

Reducing Merchant Risk

First Virtual acknowledges that the information merchant is at risk of having unscrupulous customers download information and use it, or even copy and redistribute it, without paying for it. This, First Virtual asserts, is a risk of selling any kind of information product, whether it is a book, a music recording, or a shrink-wrap software package, since anyone can photocopy, tape, or make disk copies of these products. However, the risk is much higher with files downloaded through the Internet, since it is trivially easy to resend these files as e-mail enclosures.

In any case, the merchant is not entirely at the mercy of the customer. First Virtual scrutinizes transactions, looking for customers who abuse the privilege of trying out information first before paying for it. Customers who consistently download information and consistently refuse payment will eventually be warned, and ultimately terminated as First Virtual account holders.

Some merchants will have higher sales completion rates than others, if they offer "good stuff" that has a high perceived value to consumers, as opposed to material that customers are routinely disappointed by. This information is also taken into account when evaluating whether a customer seems to be taking advantage of the ability to download information without paying in advance.

InfoHaus

Selling online can be an expensive proposition; maintaining an online presence through an Internet World Wide Web (or other application) server has always required a significant investment of money and time.

FIGURE 6-5 *Individuals can use the InfoHaus server to sell information products with the First Virtual Internet Payment System.*
THIS INFORMATION IS BEING PRINTED WITHOUT THE REVIEW OF FIRST VIRTUAL HOLDINGS INCORPORATED, AND MAY NOT BE CURRENT AS OF THIS DATE. FIRST VIRUTAL, VIRTUALTAG AND VIRTUALPIN ARE MARKS OF FIRST VIRTUAL HOLDINGS INCORPORATED. © 1997

As part of its effort to keep the Internet open to individuals as well as large companies, First Virtual opened a public access information warehouse to be used in conjunction with the First Virtual payment system. Figure 6-5 shows the opening page from the InfoHaus World Wide Web server.

First Virtual provides the Internet server, offering participants' information to browsers and buyers on the Internet through World Wide Web, file transfer (ftp), or e-mail distribution. The fees to participate are minimal, with costs including a percentage of each transaction and small transaction fees.

The result is a service that permits talented (or not) individuals to sell the fruits of their labor online. Representative information merchandise cited in examples includes recipes, limericks, prose, poetry, photographs, drawings, software, and instructions for installing software packages. The idea is that anyone who has something interesting or useful to express can sell that expression online as long as it is digitizable. By pricing the product attractively and attracting sufficient interest, First Virtual's Web site suggests, it is possible to make a decent living from providing information not available elsewhere for less.

InfoHaus Services

Information merchants can exhibit and sell their wares through the InfoHaus service simply by downloading their products and product descriptions to the InfoHaus server. The normal information seller fee structure (transaction fee of $0.29 plus 2% of the sale price) remains in place and is augmented by an additional 8% charge on all sales. There is also a storage fee of $1.50 per megabyte (or fraction thereof) of information stored on the InfoHaus server.

For example, if a piece of software is sold for $25.00, the regular First Virtual fee would be $0.29 plus $0.50 (2% of $25.00), or $0.89. If that were the only sale for the billing period, you would pay an extra $1.00 processing fee and receive a credit of $23.11 for that period.

This assumes you are using your own Internet server to distribute the software (which could easily cost hundreds of dollars per month to support — or it could be practically free). However, should you choose to distribute through the InfoHaus, you would be charged an additional 8%, or $2.00, on the $25.00 sale, and a storage fee of $1.50 per month (assuming the software is less than 1 megabyte), for a net credit of $19.61.

Using InfoHaus, your software (or other information product) is made available on a professionally maintained Internet server, and the proceeds are deposited directly to your account. Keep in mind, too, that this assumes only a single sale — sell the same software 100 times in a month, and the net proceeds are $2,218.50; sell it 1000 times in a month and you net $22,207.50. At that point, the extra 8% bite InfoHaus takes becomes $2000, so you would begin thinking about setting up your own server then.

The InfoHaus deep appeal comes from the thought that once you've written the software, or novel, or cure for the common cold, you can put it up on the server. While you are off at the beach, or at work, or wherever, all you need is just a tiny fraction of the tens of millions of people connected to the Internet to take a look at your product and decide that it's worth it. For example, if you can interest one in ten thousand of the people connected to the Internet to pay you a dollar each for your story about your trip to Antarctica, you've made a few thousand dollars.

Installing an InfoHaus Store

First Virtual offers step-by-step instructions that walk potential merchants through the process of setting up a shop and downloading information to be sold. However, because no assumptions are made about the type of software used to connect through the Internet, the process uses the lowest-common-denominator Internet tools: e-mail, telnet (terminal emulation), and ftp (file transfer). The result is that although there are no fancy graphics or online forms, the process is still surprisingly simple — particularly when considering the alternative, which is setting up your own Internet connection and configuring your own server.

A merchant can set up an InfoHaus shop even before being activated as a First Virtual seller, but obviously cannot be paid until after being activated as a seller. Communicating with the InfoHaus server, through a telnet connection or by e-mail, is straightforward: The entire process is intended to be navigated without human interaction, including any hand-holding from First Virtual.

To become a merchant, you start by providing the InfoHaus with the following information:

- Business name — the name under which your information products will be sold
- First Virtual account identifier, required for settling transactions
- The e-mail address linked to your First Virtual account, so transaction notifications can be sent

- Your preferred currency; this defaults to United States dollars, which so far is the only option available
- Preferred language, which also is so far limited to English (EN)
- A brief description of your business, which will appear beneath your business name on the InfoHaus main page

The simplest way to set up a shop is to connect by telnet (an Internet application) to the system

```
telnet.infohaus.com
```

Log in as user "ih" and respond appropriately to the system prompts. Figure 6-6 shows what the opening of the session looks like.

The first steps continue after the user indicates whether or not the X11 window server is running (a workstation graphics terminal

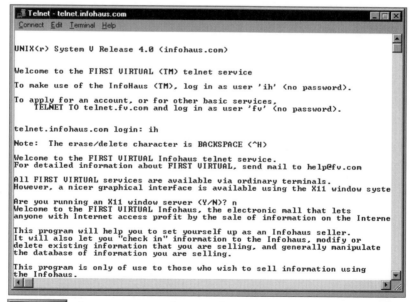

```
Telnet - telnet.infohaus.com
Connect  Edit  Terminal  Help

UNIX(r) System V Release 4.0 (infohaus.com)

Welcome to the FIRST VIRTUAL (TM) telnet service

To make use of the InfoHaus (TM), log in as user 'ih' (no password).

To apply for an account, or for other basic services,
     TELNET TO telnet.fv.com and log in as user 'fv' (no password).

telnet.infohaus.com login: ih

Note:  The erase/delete character is BACKSPACE (^H)

Welcome to the FIRST VIRTUAL Infohaus telnet service.
For detailed information about FIRST VIRTUAL, send mail to help@fv.com

All FIRST VIRTUAL services are available via ordinary terminals.
However, a nicer graphical interface is available using the X11 window syste

Are you running an X11 window server (Y/N)? n
Welcome to the FIRST VIRTUAL Infohaus, the electronic mall that lets
anyone with Internet access profit by the sale of information on the Interne

This program will help you to set yourself up as an Infohaus seller.
It will also let you "check in" information to the Infohaus, modify or
delete existing information that you are selling, and generally manipulate
the database of information you are selling.

This program is only of use to those who wish to sell information using
the Infohaus.
```

FIGURE 6-6 *Setting up an InfoHaus shop through the telnet interface simply requires following the prompts.* THIS INFORMATION IS BEING PRINTED WITHOUT THE REVIEW OF FIRST VIRTUAL HOLDINGS INCORPORATED, AND MAY NOT BE CURRENT AS OF THIS DATE. FIRST VIRUTAL, VIRTUALTAG AND VIRTUALPIN ARE MARKS OF FIRST VIRTUAL HOLDINGS INCORPORATED. © 1997

```
Welcome to the FIRST VIRTUAL Infohaus, the electronic mall
that lets anyone with Internet access profit by the sale of
information on the Internet.

This program will help you to set yourself up as an Infohaus
seller.  It will also let you "check in" information to the
Infohaus, modify or delete existing information that you are
selling, and generally manipulate the database of information
you are selling.

This program is only of use to those who wish to sell
information using the Infohaus.

Type 'N' to register as a new Infohaus merchant.
Type 'C' to check in a new item to be sold individually.
Type 'M' to set up a new magazine (subscription on a
       'per volume' basis)
Type 'B' to set up a new 'boxed set' (for purchasing a set of
       items as they become available)
Type 'Q' to quit.

Newseller/Checkin/Magazine/Boxset/Quit?
n
```

FIGURE 6-7   *The InfoHaus welcome and opening options.* THIS INFORMATION IS
BEING PRINTED WITHOUT THE REVIEW OF FIRST VIRTUAL HOLDINGS INCORPORATED,
AND MAY NOT BE CURRENT AS OF THIS DATE. FIRST VIRUTAL, VIRTUALTAG AND
VIRTUALPIN ARE MARKS OF FIRST VIRTUAL HOLDINGS INCORPORATED. © 1997

system). As a first step, the system welcomes the user, explains the
purpose of the program, and asks the user to indicate which function
is desired, as shown in Figure 6-7. Answers to prompts are displayed
in boldface.

When first setting up an InfoHaus shop, you enter the letter "n"
(for "New Seller"), and the program continues by explaining a bit
about the service, and prompting for more information, as shown in
Figure 6-8.

Once the basic First Virtual account information has been entered,
the business information is requested, as shown in Figure 6-9.

At this point the system recaps what you have already entered, and
you have the option of accepting it as displayed, going back and editing it, or quitting the system, as shown in Figure 6-10.

```
FIRST VIRTUAL is happy to invite you to register yourself to
sell information in our "Infohaus" — the electronic mall that
allows anyone to profit by selling information on the Internet.
In order to be an Infohaus seller, you must first have an
account with FIRST VIRTUAL.
If you do not already have an account, you may get one by
sending email to apply@card.com or by using telnet to
telnet.fv.com.

Assuming that you already have a FIRST VIRTUAL account, please
answer the questions that follow.
Please enter your First Virtual account ID:
kale-miracle of networking
Please enter your email address:
    Stlmurph@aol.com
Please enter your currency name:
Enter a blank line to use the default answer, USD US Dollar

Please enter your language name:
Enter a blank line to use the default answer, EN English
```

FIGURE 6-8 *The InfoHaus welcome and opening options.*

```
Each Infohaus seller is made known to buyers by a
"doing-business-as" name rather than by First Virtual
Account-ID.  This name constitutes your identity as an
Infohaus seller, and allows you to publicize your seller
account without publishing your actual Account-ID.
Please enter the name under which you want to do business
on the Infohaus:
Murphy & Company
Please enter a brief (<60 character) description of your
Infohaus business
Providing the finest in information products
Please enter a short textual description of yourself and
your service, to be browsed by potential buyers.
(Enter your answer and then type a period (".") alone
on a line.)
Type a period alone immediately to use the default answer,

Paul A. Murphy, author and electronic commerce consultant, answers all your
    questions about online banking and secure electronic commerce.
```

FIGURE 6-9 *Entering InfoHaus shop business name and descriptions to be used to identify yourself and your products.* THIS INFORMATION IS BEING PRINTED WITHOUT THE REVIEW OF FIRST VIRTUAL HOLDINGS INCORPORATED, AND MAY NOT BE CURRENT AS OF THIS DATE. FIRST VIRUTAL, VIRTUALTAG AND VIRTUALPIN ARE MARKS OF FIRST VIRTUAL HOLDINGS INCORPORATED. © 1997

```
Your newseller-request now looks like this:

Account-ID: kale-miracle of networking
Email-Address: stlmurph@aol.com
Preferred-Currency: USD US Dollar
Preferred-Language: EN English
Doing-Business-As: Murphy & Company
Brief-Description: Providing the finest in information products

Paul A. Murphy, author and electronic commerce consultant, answers all your
     questions about connectivity and the Internet.

Please check over the information displayed above to make sure
it is correct.
     Type 'S' to send in the newseller-request,
          'E' to edit the information,
      or 'Q' to quit without applying.
Send/Edit/Quit?
```

FIGURE 6-10 *New shop registrants can modify their entry, accept it, or quit.*

The process continues similarly to add new products to the new shop.

Using e-mail to set up a new InfoHaus shop is a little more complicated, as it requires first addressing your message

```
mimeserver@infohaus.com
```

and including as a header (or as the very first line of the message, if your e-mail program doesn't allow that) the line

```
Content-Type: application/fv-infohaus;
          transaction=newseller-request
```

This can be all on a single line, or it can be broken (as shown), as long as at least one space precedes the second half to indicate it is a continuation of the line above. Next, include the following lines, filled in appropriately:

```
Doing-Business-As: (your business name)
Preferred-Currency: USD
Account-ID: (Your First Virtual account ID)
EMail-Address: (your e-mail address)
```

With a blank line after this, the rest of the message will be treated as the shop description.

Whether you've used telnet or e-mail, after submitting this information, you must wait for a confirmation message from First Virtual indicating the store has been set up. The next step is to send the information product to the InfoHaus server. The information must be prepared and packaged for sale, and products must be registered. Sending the files to InfoHaus is easiest to do using ftp (file transfer protocol), but can also be done with e-mail. However, to use ftp, connect to the system

```
ftp.infohaus.com
```

Log in as user "ftp" and enter your e-mail address as your password. Switch to the directory

```
/infohaus/incoming
```

and transfer the product and product description files.

This is a simplified version of the procedures; the merchant must be sure to register, name, and refer product files correctly, and doing this all via e-mail requires a process similar to that described earlier for registering a shop by e-mail.

Security Considerations

Although users are urged to keep their account IDs private, the ID is readily accessible to merchants and is transmitted in the clear across the Internet, making it accessible to eavesdroppers. The account ID is also the basic unit of identification between buyer and seller, so, theoretically, an unscrupulous merchant could attempt fraud using customer account IDs.

Although it might seem that First Virtual is an unsecure method of selling, it should be remembered that all sensitive information is maintained securely by First Virtual entirely offline. The only risks involved are that customers may take advantage of merchants and steal information (which is inherent in any information sale), and that someone may make unauthorized use of an account ID.

Encryption and Cryptography

First Virtual eschews encryption and digital signatures. Some of the reasons include the following:

- Encryption and digital signatures are considered cumbersome and difficult, and add extra steps to the process.
- Cryptographic methods such as encryption and digital signatures are complicated, and if not used correctly they can yield a false sense of security.
- Cryptographic methods are subject to patents and export controls, and may also require certification authorities (for authentication of public keys, for instance) to be used correctly, which increases their cost and limits their distribution.
- Keeping payment information offline reduces the need to encrypt and sign transactions.

This last reason may be the strongest argument. First Virtual participants never send any sensitive payment information on the Internet, but rather use an account identifier for both buying and selling information online.

The Security Situation

It may be worthwhile examining the information components of the Internet Payment System, the information that is exposed, and the risks involved.

First, the information components break out into two categories: data which is transmitted across the Internet, and data which is not. The original account application includes name, contact information (physical and electronic mail addresses), and telephone number. E-mail address, application number, and account ID are transmitted across the Internet — but credit card information is never transmitted across the Internet, nor is it ever stored on a system accessible via the Internet.

The conclusion, therefore, is that credit card information is not at risk in this scheme. However, information about individual transactions, as well as information about new accounts, *may* itself be accessible to thieves monitoring the Internet or intercepting e-mail.

Next, consider the Internet Payment System procedures. No payment is made until a notification has been sent by e-mail to the customer and an affirmative response has been received from that customer indicating that payment should be made. As soon as the legitimate customer receives notification of an improper transaction attempt using the customer's account ID, a response indicating that it is a result of fraud will invalidate all future attempts with that account ID.

The conclusion is that simply intercepting an account ID will yield a thief access to Internet Payment System information for a limited time. First Virtual recommends that customers provide an e-mail account address that is checked regularly.

The next step is to consider what happens if a thief were able to subvert a First Virtual customer's e-mail account. This can happen in two general ways: through carelessness on the part of the customer, or through cleverness on the part of the perpetrator. A customer who does not properly protect the e-mail system or account risks having the e-mail account hijacked or subverted. Leaving a workstation while still logged in to the e-mail account, using an unsuitable password (or no password) to protect the account, or leaving the e-mail gateway system unprotected are all easy ways to lose control over e-mail.

The other possibility, of a thief capable of intercepting e-mail and responding to it as the customer without gaining access to anyone's systems, is much less likely. Although forging e-mail in someone else's name is considered to be relatively easy, diverting e-mail in transit takes more resources.

However, in the event that the account ID is captured and e-mail responses can be forged, the fraud would not be discovered until the customer receives his or her credit card bill. At that point, the fraud can be reported and accounts can be corrected. In fact, First Virtual holds approved transactions for a period of up to 91 days to avoid paying out for just such a fraudulent transaction.

In no case is there anything at risk beyond a certain degree of aggravation. When the information being offered online is "stolen," nothing of value is actually taken away from the merchant—the theft does not prevent the merchant from selling that same information to any honest buyer at any time.

First Virtual's documentation addresses this topic at length, since it is an important issue to both merchants and customers. They observe that intercepting an e-mail stream and forging responses is quite hard to do and would undoubtedly leave sufficient traces to expose the thief to apprehension. Also interesting is the comment that someone with the ability to do this may have more attractive and rewarding targets than information providers selling through First Virtual.

Comparison is also made to the prevalence of credit card fraud in the nondigital world, and the fact that there may be more efficient methods of stealing credit cards than hijacking First Virtual Internet Payment System accounts.

Less compelling are the suggestions that someone intercepting a First Virtual account ID might not be able to correlate it with its e-mail address, or that someone intercepting transactions might not be familiar with the First Virtual protocols or how to use them. Although First Virtual may not provide any link between account ID and e-mail address, that information is linked in the original e-mail account confirmation. More importantly, the First Virtual protocols are readily and freely available online—and First Virtual is hard at work to promote the use of those protocols—so it would be ingenuous to believe First Virtual transactions would be protected by obscurity.

Security Conclusions

Ultimately, there is no question that the First Virtual Internet Payment System may have some vulnerabilities—as any payment system does. Wherever values are being exchanged or transported, there are risks due to greedy and unscrupulous individuals, who will attempt to steal whenever they can. The fact is that the risks involved in using First Virtual's Internet Payment System are balanced by the stakes involved, which are kept at an acceptable level by limiting sales only to data or intangibles and withholding payment until the sale has been confirmed by the customer.

First Virtual leaves pricing issues entirely to the merchant, while suggesting that a lower price will invite more interest from prospective customers than a high price. Moreover, customers tend to be less critical of less expensive information than they may be of pricier products. As a result, many of the vendors found in the InfoHaus price their information quite reasonably. The fact that the products are relatively inexpensive may also help add to the security of the system, if only by reducing the amount of risk taken by the seller — stealing a copy of a photograph of a sunset, priced at a dollar, may not tempt too many thieves.

More important, and more admirable, is the fact that First Virtual depends to some extent on the essential goodness, or at least law-abidingness, of most citizens. The fact is, most people are able to restrain themselves from walking away with whatever is not bolted down, whether they are visiting someone else's home or browsing through a store. When these people find an information product that gives them a few dollars' worth of use, they are glad to pay for it.

Summing Up the First Virtual Internet Payment System

Inasmuch as it can only be used for information and intangibles, First Virtual's Internet Payment System cannot be expected to be a complete answer for electronic commerce — particularly if you are a merchant selling physical products. However, it is likely to remain a very important mechanism for the transfer of digital products among individuals, small companies, and companies just entering the Internet marketplace.

CYBERCASH

Starting out in August, 1994, its founders set for CyberCash the goal of working with financial institutions and merchants to provide an accessible and acceptable payment system for the Internet. CyberCash offers a secure conduit to deliver payments between customers, merchants, and banks. CyberCash has been described as the Federal Express of the Internet payment business, since it offers safe, efficient, and inexpensive delivery of payments across the Internet—practically instantaneously.

CyberCash makes available the software and services needed to exchange payments securely across the Internet with its Secure Internet Payment Service. Using a procedure that incorporates encryption and digital signatures, CyberCash gives consumers a "digital wallet," and merchants a conduit to Internet payment processing through their own banks. Customers are able to authorize payments out of their digital wallets. The payments are signed and encrypted, then sent through the merchant back to CyberCash, which in turn passes the transaction to the merchant's bank for processing. The digital wallet initially supported only credit cards, but now supports digital cash transfers for small dollar amounts for products and services that are too inexpensive to justify using a credit card.

CyberCash makes its software available at no charge, both for the client and the server applications. Neither the customer nor the merchant is charged directly for transactions: CyberCash charges participating banks and credit card processors fees similar to those charged by traditional methods. These fees are covered by the banks' or processors' standard service charges to merchants.

The CyberCash Model

Very simply, CyberCash acts as a conduit for transactions among the Internet, merchants, consumers, and banking networks. Merchants wishing to use CyberCash to securely process credit card transactions must establish a merchant account with a bank offering CyberCash to its merchants, and modify their servers to include the CyberCash PAY button. Customers wishing to use CyberCash have several options for obtaining the client software. Customers can initialize their CyberCash identity by linking at least one credit card or checking account to the service — there is no charge to consumers for this service.

CyberCash client software is available from several sources, including CyberCash's World Wide Web site; some Internet browser software programs will include the CyberCash wallet, and select banks have begun offering CyberCash client software to their customers.

When the customer completes a purchase and begins a CyberCash transaction by clicking on the CyberCash PAY button of a merchant's World Wide Web site, the merchant receives information about the customer's order, as well as an encrypted message from the customer's CyberCash client. The encrypted data includes the customer's payment information. The merchant's CyberCash software verifies that neither the order nor the encrypted payment information has been modified during transmission, and then forwards the encrypted message to CyberCash.

Once CyberCash receives the encrypted payment message and verifies that no modifications have been made to it in transit, CyberCash determines if the transaction is a CyberCash credit-card-based transaction or CyberCoin transaction. With CyberCash (credit card) transactions, CyberCash decrypts that message, reformats it, and forwards it to the merchant's designated bank or credit card processor. The bank or processor responds almost immediately to CyberCash, which in turn forwards the approval (or refusal) to the merchant's server. Once approval is received by the merchant's server, it notifies the customer. The whole process, from the customer initiating the payment to getting approval, takes less than 20 seconds.

With CyberCash, the wallet is used to manage your credit cards. In a sense, the CyberCash process electronically presents your credit card payment to the merchant in the process described above, just like the last time you physically pulled the card out of your wallet and presented it to a merchant.

With CyberCoin, your electronic wallet essentially holds digital money, which can be added to your wallet using the credit card used for other transactions or your checking, which can be linked to your wallet. Once one of these accounts is linked to your wallet, you can request dollars to be transferred to your CyberCoin wallet in US$20 increments.

Your CyberCoin money is placed into an account at CyberCash, and as you make CyberCoin transactions, money is pulled from your wallet and sent to the CyberCoin merchant's wallet.

The CyberCash client software manages all of this for the consumer, including setting up an identity, or CyberCash Persona, linking credit cards to that persona, and keeping track of CyberCash transactions through a transaction log. In addition, the software includes other administrative and configuration options for customizing and managing the CyberCash service, for backing up the CyberCash persona information, and for downloading the latest version of the client.

The CyberCash merchant server must be properly set up before the merchant can accept CyberCash transactions. This process includes installing the CyberCash software, as well as embedding the CyberCash PAY button into the ordering pages on the World Wide Web server. Once tests have been successfully completed, the merchant can begin accepting CyberCash. The entire process can be completed as quickly as a few days, if the merchant's bank is already a participant; if the merchant's bank is new to CyberCash, the process may take a month or two.

CyberCash Security Considerations

CyberCash uses a combination of RSA public key and DES secret key technologies to protect and guarantee data through encryption and digital signatures. The CyberCash software has been approved for export from the United States, even though it employs a very strong version, using 768-bit RSADSI keys. This high level of encryption is intended to protect the sensitive portions of commercial transactions.

The CyberCash software uses the strongest encryption approved so far by the U.S. Government for worldwide use. It uses full 768-bit RSA as well as 56-bit DES encryption of messages. All transactions are authenticated with MD5 (a message digest procedure) and RSA digital signatures.

Customer Protection

With the use of digital signatures and encryption, CyberCash is able to keep transmissions secure for all practical purposes, as discussed in Chapter 2. It can be asserted that CyberCash is free from any danger of hackers intercepting or modifying transmissions between the merchant and the customer, or between the merchant and CyberCash. However, since the customer must provide his or her own password, attacks on individual accounts are possible, just as they are in any system that uses passwords for access. This exposure is limited to the systems on which the customer has installed the CyberCash client software — sensitive customer information is not stored on servers from which the customer has made purchases.

Using CyberCash

CyberCash offers significant advantages to both the customer and the merchant. For the customer, there is no need to register each time he or she first shops with a merchant, mall, or payment system. Unlike secure Web browser/Web server combinations, CyberCash does not require the customer to reenter credit card information for transmission to the merchant—and the customer does not have to worry about possible security issues with the merchant's own server, since the payment information is not decrypted until it arrives at the CyberCash payment server.

The CyberCash-enabled merchant gets the benefit of offering a convenient payment method to customers, without limiting the customers' choice of Internet browser. Also, the merchant can install CyberCash on any existing World Wide Web server system, without having to purchase a new server program. In addition, CyberCash transaction approvals are virtually instantaneous.

CyberCash Availability

Starting with a single participating bank, Wells Fargo & Co. in 1995, CyberCash has lengthened their list of banks to several dozen. CyberCash is also working directly with third-party services and expects to serve several hundred banks.

The number of merchants offering CyberCash is also growing. During its first few months of operation only a handful of places would accept CyberCash, but that is changing rapidly. With the addition of the CyberCoin feature, merchants of digital information such as software, images, and computer-based information that are traditionally smaller items are able to offer their products online. CyberCoin is offered primarily for items of less than $10 where using a credit card would not make sense for the merchant or shopper. The term "micropayment" is often used to describe CyberCoin transactions.

CyberCash Client Application

Before you can use CyberCash, you must install and configure the CyberCash Client Application. This program is actually an Internet application, capable of communicating with merchants and with CyberCash over your TCP/IP connection to the Internet. This is the piece of software that manages your "electronic wallet," keeping track of your credit cards, electronic cash, and tracking transactions. This is also the piece of software that applies all the cryptographic tools necessary to encrypt transaction information and transmit it securely.

Getting the Software

CyberCash distributes its client software in several ways. It has been bundled with Internet startup kits and browser software. Recently, large banks began not only providing back-end support for CyberCash merchants, but also distributing the CyberCash client for consumers. We have also included the CyberCash client on the CD-ROM accompanying this book.

And of course, you can download the software from the CyberCash World Wide Web site with the following address:

```
http://www.cybercash.com
```

Once the software is installed, consumers can use the CyberCash PAY buttons, which participating merchants include in their World Wide Web documents, to pay for selected items.

Installing the Software

The Windows version of the Client Application is a single, compressed, and self-extracting program: executing the program causes it to uncompress the component files. One of these files is a setup program, which takes the customer through the process of installing and initializing the software.

Running the setup program should be routine to anyone who has installed software before. Under Windows, the routine first asks the user where to install the CyberCash client: The default is the directory C:\CYBER. The files are then copied to the indicated directory.

As the next step, the CyberCash application offers to search the system for Internet browsers so it can add CyberCash functionality to them. This is why at the start of the process the user is cautioned to exit any Internet browser that may be running on the desktop, since the following lines are added to the browser INI file:

```
[Viewers]
Type0=application/x-cybercash
application/x-cybercash=C:\Cyber\cyber.exe
Type1=application/cybercash
application/cybercash=C:\Cyber\cyber.exe
```

```
[Suffixes]
application/x-cybercash=cym
application/cybercash=cym
```

These lines ensure that when the customer is browsing a CyberCash-enabled Web page, the browser will do the right thing whenever a CyberCash PAY button is clicked. When the customer clicks on the CyberCash PAY button, the browser needs to be able to interpret the data that will be sent from the server. It also needs to be aware that that data must be handled by calling up the CyberCash application. The original INI file is saved with the file extension CYB.

Running the Software for the First Time

Keeping with the popular trend among software vendors of using wizards, organized programs within a program, CyberCash has created several wizards to walk users through the installation process.

The first wizard presented is the welcome wizard, which helps you indicate whether the network you are using to connect to the Internet has a proxy-based server. A proxy-based server can be several things, but is traditionally a firewall. Most Internet service providers do not use proxy-based servers, and most large corporate networks should. If you have questions, contact your ISP or system administrator. The second question is whether you are creating your first wallet or are wishing to a reinstall a previously established wallet.

At this point the software will connect to the CyberCash administration server via the Internet and will start the New Wallet wizard, which will let you create your persona and attach at least one credit card to your wallet.

Figure 6-11 shows the screen for you to request a wallet ID (i.e., name) and tell CyberCash what your e-mail address is.[1]

The next two screens prompt you to enter and confirm both a password for use when using the wallet and a verification ID you can supply now so that CyberCash customer service employees can con-

---

[1] FIGURES ON PAGES 177–188 ARE REPRINTED WITH PERMISSION FROM CYBERCASH, INC. © 1997.

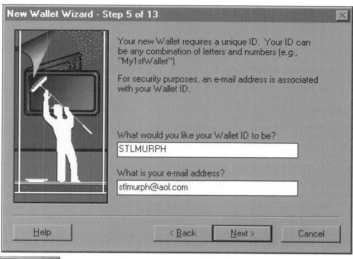

FIGURE 6-11 *New Wallet setup screen 5.*

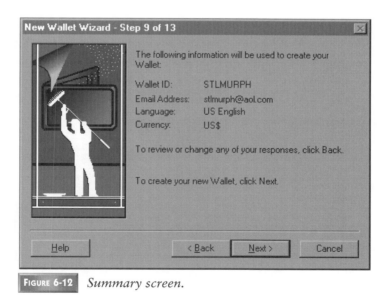

FIGURE 6-12 *Summary screen.*

firm who you are should you need to call for assistance. With other products and services, your mother's maiden name is commonly used as a verification ID. The next screen will prompt you for the currency you would like with your wallet. At the time this edition of the book

was written, despite plans to add others, only the U.S. dollar is supported with the CyberCash wallet. Figure 6-12 shows you a summary
screen of your selections to this point in the process and offers you a
chance to make any changes.

The next thing you will see is a CyberCash screen informing you
that the Security keys are being generated (Figure 6-13). Once the keys
are established, they will be used to encrypt your data and send if off
to CyberCash.

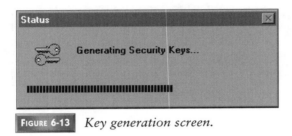

FIGURE 6-13 *Key generation screen.*

CyberCash will respond with a screen similar to Figure 6-14, confirming that your information has been received and what your new
wallet ID is.

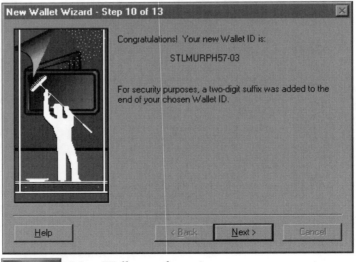

FIGURE 6-14 *New Wallet confirmation.*

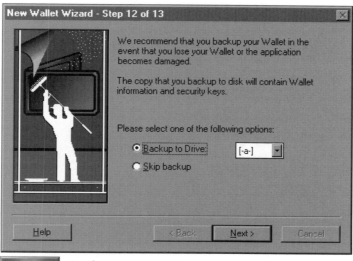

FIGURE 6-15 *Backup screen.*

There are two more tasks before completing the new wallet process. First, CyberCash allows for a confirmation message with all transactions. If you are going to make a lot of small transactions and do not want to be bothered with confirmations below a certain transaction total, you can set that threshold as well. Of course, all transactions appear in the transaction log.

The final task with this first wizard is to make a backup of your CyberCash persona information (Figure 6-15). This is very important in case you have a computer failure and cannot retrieve the keys and information in your digital wallet.

Linking Payment Information

Now that you have established your account or persona with CyberCash and your wallet is in place, the next thing to do is attach a credit card and or a checking account to pay for the goods you purchase online.

With the credit card you can pay for goods paid for with CyberCash and add money to your CyberCoin wallet. You can also add money to your CyberCoin wallet by linking a checking account to your CyberCash persona.

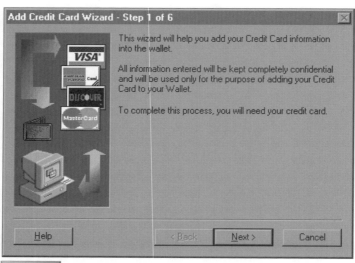

FIGURE 6-16 *Add Credit Card screen 1 of 6.*

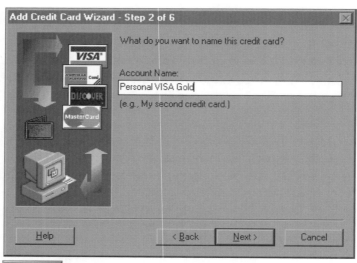

FIGURE 6-17 *Name Credit Card screen.*

Attaching a credit card or checking account to your CyberCash persona is very easy. The process of adding the credit card begins with the Add Credit Card wizard (Figure 6-16).

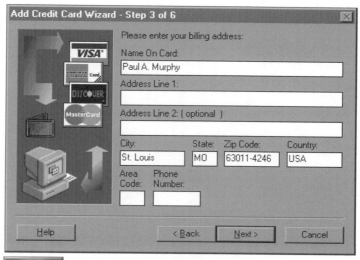

FIGURE 6-18   *Credit Card Billing information screen.*

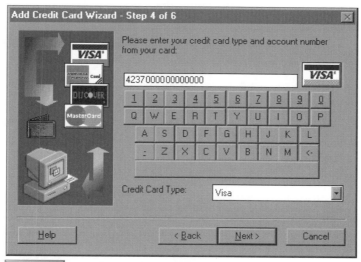

FIGURE 6-19   *Credit Card Number Entry screen.*

The next step is to name the credit card to be used, in Figure 6-17, and enter your credit card billing information as it appears on your monthly credit card statement (Figure 6-18).

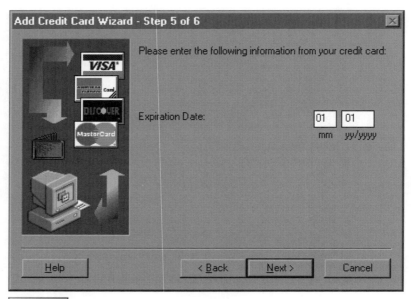

FIGURE 6-20   *Credit Card Expiration Date Entry screen.*

In Figures 6-19 and 6-20, we enter the actual credit card number and expiration date.

When the process of adding the credit card to your wallet is complete, CyberCash will reply with a confirmation, and you will be ready to utilize the service at any merchant offering CyberCash as a payment mechanism.

CyberCoin

With your wallet established, and at least one credit card attached to it, you can also set up the CyberCoin portion of your wallet by simply adding money. The process begins with Figure 6-21.

The next step is to chose the amount of money you would like to place in your CyberCoin wallet. Transfers can occur in US$20 increments (Figure 6-22).

In Figure 6-23 you can chose either credit card or checking account as the source for the money.

You finally see a confirmation, Figure 6-24 where you double-check your request and then press FINISH.

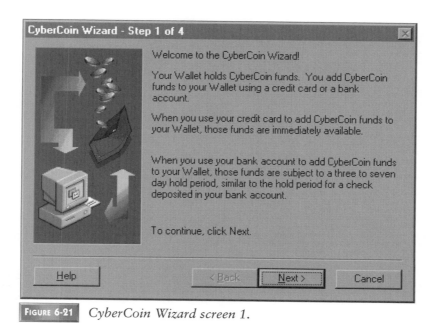

FIGURE 6-21 *CyberCoin Wizard screen 1.*

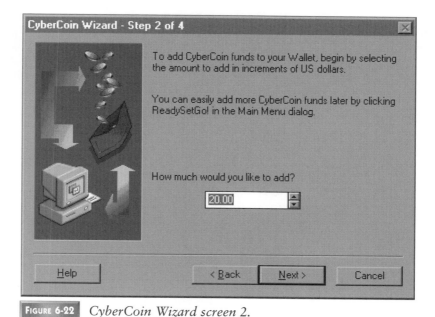

FIGURE 6-22 *CyberCoin Wizard screen 2.*

FIGURE 6-23 *CyberCoin Wizard screen 3.*

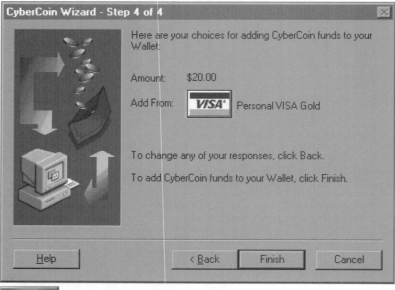

FIGURE 6-24 *CyberCoin Wizard screen 4.*

Configuration and Administration

The CyberCash client application allows the user to manage credit card information and links, so new cards can be added or old ones removed. Administration functions include everything from modifying persona information, to backing up or restoring CyberCash data, to getting the latest version of the application. Figure 6-25 shows the choices available.

More important, the client keeps track of transactions in a transaction log. Information about each transaction is maintained in a log and can be printed or canceled if desired. The transaction log shown in Figure 6-26 simply shows a record of linking credit cards to a persona.

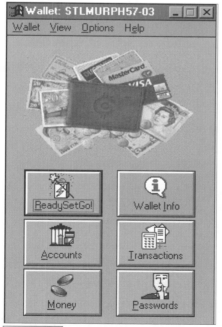

FIGURE 6-25 *The CyberCash Client Application administration panel.*

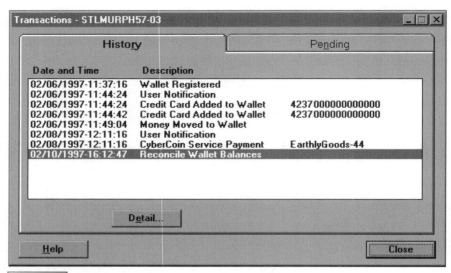

FIGURE 6-26   *A CyberCash Client Application transaction log.*

Making a Purchase

CyberCash customers can purchase products over the Internet by browsing the World Wide Web sites of merchants displaying the CyberCash logo. CyberCash merchants range from Virtual Vineyards (the first CyberCash merchant), offering premium wines and food, to alternative music vendors, and scores of companies in between.

The customer selects items for purchase, proceeds to the merchant's payment page, which is frequently referred to as the shopping cart, and clicks on the CyberCash PAY button. This initiates a transmission of information about the transaction from the merchant's server to the customer's system. The CyberCash Client Application is started. It responds by displaying a payment request summary, including an order number, the merchant's CyberCash ID, and the purchase amount, as shown in Figure 6-27. The customer can also chose the payment method, which in the case of Figure 6-27 is a Visa card.

The customer at this point can still decline the sale by clicking on CANCEL or proceed with the transaction by pressing PAY. At this

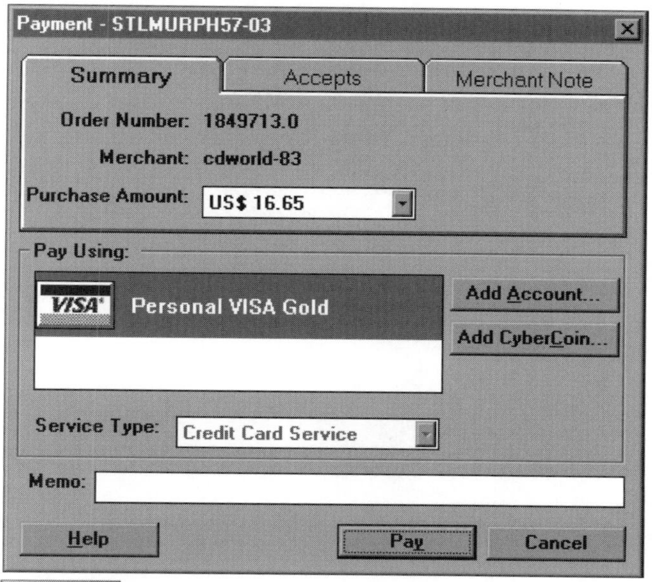

FIGURE 6-27 *CyberCash payment request summary.*

moment the transaction occurs and can take up to 20 seconds for an authorization. As is clear from the example, this panel displays an order number, as well as the credit cards that may be accepted for the order. Note that only cards that are acceptable are displayed.

When the customer chooses to continue, the CyberCash application software puts together all the information received from the merchant (price, credit cards accepted) with the customer's payment information, and the transaction occurs.

Once a credit card is chosen, the software encrypts and signs that information and sends it on to the merchant.

The merchant receives a signed message indicating what products are to be purchased, as well as an encrypted and signed copy of the payment information. Both are verified, and the (still-encrypted) payment information is forwarded to the CyberCash payment server. At that point, the process of credit card authorization is almost the same as if the customer were presenting the credit card at a shop:

FIGURE 6-28   *Transaction authorization notification from the CyberCash Secure Internet Payment Service includes purchase and payment summary information.*

The same information is sent on to the bank by CyberCash, and the merchant receives an authorization within seconds. As shown in Figure 6-28, successful completion of the transaction is reported back to the client, with a transaction summary. Besides the obvious difference that the transaction between customer and merchant takes place entirely online, another important difference to note is that the merchant does not have access to the customer's actual credit card account information.

Selling through CyberCash

Although the CyberCash client application is quite simple to install and use, even for early implementers, the first CyberCash merchants did not have it quite as easy. The first version of the CyberCash merchant server software was for UNIX systems only. Current releases include support for Solaris, BSDI, SGI Irix, NT, SunOS, Digital UNIX, SCO, and Linux. The CyberCash World Wide Web site is very complete with merchant software and installation information.

CyberCash is supporting the VIP (Value-added Integration Provider) program, which brings together prospective merchants with companies that have already developed sites with CyberCash functionality and are offering related services to other merchants. Another option for merchants is to purchase an integrated package from one of the systems integrators working with CyberCash to include CyberCash functionality in a ready-to-use, integrated server.

Merchants setting up to accept CyberCash payments have to take care of three general tasks:

- Open an account with a bank offering CyberCash services
- Modify server home pages to include the CyberCash PAY button
- Install the related CyberCash software on the server

CyberCash Merchant Code

The merchant code functions in support of both shopping and administration. This code is invoked only when a customer makes a purchase decision. When the customer initiates the purchase payment process, the merchant code responds by sending an encrypted message to the customer's system to begin. The process, as has been described earlier, moves information between the customer, the merchant, and the CyberCash payment server.

The merchant software includes administrative functions, allowing merchants do the following:

- Check on an order data base to review orders
- Process supporting transactions such as voids, credits, and authorizations
- Perform merchant-originated transactions, as when the merchant has received a telephone order

Other parts of the software perform the cryptographic functions necessary for encryption, decryption, digital signatures, and verification. Also included are information files, test software, a database program that can log orders, and sample merchant shopping pages.

The process of getting a merchant site online with CyberCash can take as little as a few days, as long as the merchant's bank is already set up to provide CyberCash services. As the merchant software becomes available for more platforms, the process could become even simpler.

Summing Up the CyberCash System

CyberCash offers some real values to the consumer:

- It keeps payment information private, even from the merchant.
- It offers a convenient electronic wallet to store payment information, so the information need not be reentered every time a purchase is made.
- It maintains a transaction log to handle, track, and document every transaction.

Likewise, CyberCash is attractive to merchants:

- There is no extra charge for using CyberCash.
- It is a convenience for customers, who may prefer not to have to reenter credit card numbers on the Internet.
- It offers merchants useful tools for tracking and transacting business on the Internet.
- It is soon to be widely supported by banks and credit card companies.

Most important, CyberCash is committed to complying with the Visa/MasterCard standards for credit card transactions across the Internet. All in all, CyberCash is committed to providing a secure, simple, and accepted solution for Internet commerce.

HOT off the Presses: PayNow

With the Cybercash model we have seen how to establish a digital wallet or secure channel for sending instructions to a third party and securely send funds to a merchant at the time of a sale. We have also seen a way to securely designate a checking account and/or a credit card as the source of the money sent on our behalf.

So what else can we do with this technology? That is exactly what the folks at CyberCash and Princeton Technologies were thinking when they created PayNow, an electronic bill-payment process.

On the consumer side of the electronic commerce equation, online banking and bill payment for consumers is a growing trend in North America. The online bill payment process begins with the creation of a relationship between a consumer, or a business for that matter, and a financial institution (i.e., bank, S&L, credit union) for the purpose of paying bills.

With online banking, you can use either your computer or telephone to instruct the bank to send money to just about anyone you would normally pay with a check, after a relatively painless enrollment and setup process. The benefit for the consumer is convenience, as there are no checks to buy or write, no postage to pay, and greater control over when your payments are processed.

The PayNow concept is that once you have established your relationship with CyberCash and have attached a checking account to your CyberCash wallet, there is no reason CyberCash can't be used to execute an electronic payment to a participating PayNow merchant. For example, suppose your electric company signs up for this program and installs the CyberCash merchant server on the company Web site. Either through the traditional bill you would receive in the mail or through online bill presentment (a financial e-mail, if you will), you make your payment with your CyberCash wallet instead of by writing a traditional check.

Your payment would be protected with all of the software-based encryption, which is at the heart of the CyberCash wallet, to complete the transaction.

The PayNow Secure Electronic Check Service reduces costs for companies like the electric company by eliminating paper check processing costs. You will enjoy lower mailing fees, and PayNow increases the accuracy of bill remittance.

For the current or future online merchant, CyberCash now offers a complete online payment suite of digital cash (CyberCoin), use of existing credit cards (CyberCash), and now secure checks (PayNow).

Princeton Technologies, based in Princeton, NJ, is a large processor of online banking transactions for several large banks and has teamed with CyberCash for this program.

Although the first trials are just getting underway as the second edition of this book goes to press, the process holds great potential and is a great example of several technologies coming together to create new applications.

SEVEN

ONLINE COMMERCE ENVIRONMENTS

He who pays the piper calls the tune.

— TRADITIONAL PROVERB

Since it is the online merchant who pays the Internet marketing piper, the merchant gets to call the electronic commerce tune. The merchant decides what products to offer online, how those products will be described and depicted, and what options for payment are available to customers.

An online commerce environment is differentiated from an electronic payment system most notably by the use of a secure server. The secure server provides a secure channel between customer and merchant, over which business can be securely and reliably transacted. The merchant may also choose to accept other types of electronic payment, as well as offer support for mail orders and telephone orders, but by setting up a secure World Wide Web server, the merchant makes it possible for anyone with a credit card to place an order immediately and directly over an Internet link.

In a sense, the online commerce environment is an invention of the industry, offering a method of packaging all the products necessary to sell online. Rather than starting and stopping at the point of taking an order in exchange for payment information, the online commerce environment can include much more. Online commerce integrators may be able to supply the hardware, software, and network connection for the merchant's World Wide Web server, the labor and programming involved in creating the digital storefront, and the payment and settlement mechanisms, as well as programming to link online transactions into existing organizational systems. This chapter examines some secure World Wide Web browser and server offerings.

If you had to pick one word to describe the electronic commerce server market circa 1997, it is competition.

To begin with, there is tremendous competition for Internet servers in general. Regardless of the need for secure transactions, companies such as Microsoft and Netscape are developing and supporting entire categories of new software products and development tools. All share the same goal of helping companies and individuals place their information on a computer accessible by the Internet.

In addition to offering the Internet browser software, they offer Internet server software, including secure servers, and a host of development tools equipping armies of software developers to create end-user applications.

Although they do not offer an Internet browser software program, Open Market is an example of the many companies offering a line of Internet commerce products, including a secure World Wide Web server and other supplemental tools and services.

This chapter examines the secure server and browser offerings from Netscape Communications and Microsoft and takes a look at the Open Market softgoods transaction model to demonstrate how a commercial environment can handle online transactions.

SERVERS AND COMMERCIAL ENVIRONMENTS

Although it is the centerpiece of an online commercial environment, the secure World Wide Web server cannot stand alone. It must be implemented on a secure and reliable hardware platform and connected to the Internet securely and reliably, and orders must be processed securely and reliably once the merchant receives them. However, without a secure server, secure transactions would require some other secured mechanism, either electronic payment systems like First Virtual or CyberCash (Chapter 6) or digital money (Chapter 8).

Choosing Payment Methods

Merchants have traditionally allowed their customers to use a variety of payment methods: cash, credit card, personal check, travelers' check, or store credit account are all common. Limiting customers to one or two payment methods would likely cost a merchant some business. The same goes for the online shop: Limiting shoppers to a single method will also limit the number of sales possible online.

Many online merchants offer at least a telephone number to call in an order and a fax number or postal address where customers can send a copy of an order form. Those willing to accept orders online may be using one or more payment systems as well as a secure server. This gives the customer a range of options: offline ordering by phone, fax, or mail; online ordering with a payment system; or online ordering through the secure channel provided by a secure server.

The advantage of a secure server is that it serves the casual Internet consumer who has a new World Wide Web browser and a credit card, but has never set up to use any electronic payment or digital money system. Since software publishers are continuing to incorporate SSL and S-HTTP and other secure protocols (Chapter 4) into their World Wide Web browser products, secure servers supporting those protocols are also growing in the marketplace.

At the same time, merchants are free to offer other payment methods: electronic payment systems or digital money systems generally operate in any transmission medium. The result is that a merchant can offer the simplest payment method, entering credit card information directly into a form maintained on a secure server, while still allowing the more serious Internet consumer to do business wielding an electronic wallet.

Server Market Orientation

World Wide Web server software comes in all shapes and sizes, particularly since any server product must conform to a well-known set of rules — HTTP.

Web browsers that support S-HTTP can be used with servers that support S-HTTP to produce a secure channel; browsers and servers that support SSL can also produce a secure channel. Microsoft and Netscape have incorporated roughly equivalent support for S-HTTP and SSL into their browsers. If you want to conduct secure business with the vast majority of Web-browser users on the Internet, your server must implement SSL.

Since these two browsers are the current de facto standard for the Web browser market, and are so widely available, they outnumber other browsers in general use.

Although there are other World Wide Web servers that support S-HTTP, or that secure commercial transactions by implementing PGP (Pretty Good Privacy, an implementation of public key encryption and digital signature technology) between consumer and merchant, they are not as compelling to merchants because they are not perceived as being as widely and broadly implemented either in servers or in browsers.

NETSCAPE

With an incredibly successful initial public offering in the summer of 1995, Netscape's shares rocketed from an original estimated offering price of $13 for 3.5 million shares to be offered, to an actual offering price of $28 for a total of 5 million shares. On the first day of trading, the shares opened at over $70, finally settling down to the mid-50s.

Netscape's attractions include their highly acclaimed Navigator World Wide Web browser, and their history in the commerce server area.

Netscape has organized their commerce server strategy around three basic components: Netscape Client Products, the Netscape Commerce Platform, and Netscape Commercial Applications. These three elements piece together a commerce model, including everything needed to begin an Internet commerce site. This model leaves the door open for new technologies in Internet commerce from Netscape as well as other Internet vendors.

The Netscape Client Products include the Netscape Navigator Client Products, also referred to as the browsers. To develop commercial Web sites, Netscape offers the Netscape Commerce Platform, a set of servers. This includes a family of integrated software applications that enable you to bring up a full-scale commerce site quickly. These applications can be used individually or together to create different online businesses. The two basic applications systems include the Netscape Publishing System and the Netscape Merchant System.

By distributing their browser over the Internet at no charge for evaluation or educational purposes, Netscape helped ensure its wide distribution. Server products are also available for a limited evaluation period, which also helps to secure market share. Netscape delivers to merchants shopping for a World Wide Web server a broad installed base of potential customers using browsers supporting the SSL security protocol.

Netscape produced SSL, a method of obtaining a secure channel between client and server, at a time when others were working on a different solution: S-HTTP. Rather than wait for customers and merchants to start installing S-HTTP servers and clients, Netscape implemented SSL in their products and made them widely and easily available.

Netscape's Approach to Building Business

Netscape's approach to developing its business as an Internet commerce environment provider has so far proven successful: actively put client and server applications into the hands of online consumers and merchants, and actively develop standards and contribute them to the industry. The Netscape browser is easily accessible from their World Wide Web site, as is a fully functional evaluation version of their secure server. This ensures that their products are widely distributed and installed — which makes the final sale that much more likely.

As mentioned before, by making public their security protocol specifications, Netscape guarantees that anyone can create a browser that will be compatible with the Netscape secure servers. It also guarantees that anyone can create a server that will be compatible with Netscape secure browsers — and many have. Netscape retains a head start in developing software, while allowing potential buyers the freedom to choose other products. Making the protocols public and allowing other software developers to produce Netscape-compatible browsers and servers has been good for Netscape and the industry in general.

Netscape has generated sufficient interest in their products for individual users to make their name synonymous with World Wide Web browsers. At the same time, Netscape has defined the protocols needed to do business with all the people who use the Netscape browser, so merchants looking for a way to sell to them will naturally consider Netscape, too.

The next section examines the Netscape product line, looking first at the features, particularly security and commerce options, of the Netscape Navigator World Wide Web browser. The features and use of the Netscape Commerce Server are discussed next, followed by an overview of some of Netscape's other Internet products.

NETSCAPE PRODUCT LINE

This section will look at the Netscape Navigator browser, particularly at the way it implements secure commercial transactions, and will briefly describe the Netscape Commerce Server, again focusing on secure commercial transactions.

A great source for ongoing information on Netscape is to frequently visit their World Wide Web site:

```
http://home.netscape.com/
```

Netscape Navigator

To recap the discussion from Chapter 3, a World Wide Web browser must be capable of sending requests for documents and services residing on World Wide Web servers, and of interpreting and displaying those documents appropriately. As discussed earlier, the most basic Web browser must be able to handle three protocols:

- Uniform Resource Locator (URL). This is the format defining a syntax for pointing at Internet and World Wide Web resources. Most URLs point at resources with three parts, the scheme or protocol (for example, HTTP or ftp); the server offering the resource (an Internet host name, or less often an Internet Protocol numerical address); and the resource itself (often a specific file, or simply the root of the specified Web server).

- Hypertext Transfer Protocol (HTTP). This is the protocol that defines the interaction between Web browser and server. Based on the protocols that define electronic mail, it basically defines a set of queries and responses between the browser (client) and the server. The client makes a connection and requests a document or resource; the server responds either by sending the requested resource or by sending an error message indicating why the resource is not available.

- Hypertext Markup Language (HTML). This is the protocol that defines the way Web documents are expected to be displayed; HTML consists of tags that are used to define different functional parts of the resource. The browser must be able to interpret the different tags in an appropriate way and then display the resource to reflect the different tags' values: A block of text defined as a paragraph is displayed as a paragraph using the default text display font, and a block of text defined as a heading is displayed using the font defined for use as a heading.

The Netscape Navigator browser fulfills all these functions, just as any other World Wide Web browser does.

In addition to these features, Netscape Navigator supports numerous software add-ons for everything from spell-checking your e-mail, to running small applications called applets, to playing music files from the Internet. New add-ons are being introduced all the time, and those already in distribution are undergoing constant development and updates. Properly describing some add-ons can fill an entire book and is outside the scope of this one. The use of online information resources such as newsgroups and mailing lists is one of the best ways to learn more and stay current in this changing business.

Navigator's most important value-added feature, however, is the ability to support secure transactions with SSL encryption of sensitive information. More important to users, securing the transmission of sensitive information is done automatically, with the browser being alerted to the need for SSL by a URL with the scheme type HTTPS instead of HTTP. The browser and the server negotiate keys for secure transmissions, without involving the user.

Getting Netscape Navigator

The Netscape Navigator software is available through Netscape's own World Wide Web server and at various other FTP sites around the Internet. Although the product is increasingly available as a shrink-wrapped software package from retailers and as software preloaded when you purchase a new computer, the entire group of Navigator software is available for sale online. According to the Netscape Navigator Web page:[1]

Netscape Navigator is the world's leading Internet client. Netscape Navigator 3.0 adds fully integrated video, audio, 3D, and Internet telephone communications capabilities.

- Netscape Navigator Gold is the premium of Netscape Navigator, adding an easy-to-use editor that lets you create and publish live, online Web pages.
- Netscape Navigator Personal Edition has all the capabilities of the world's most popular Internet navigation software and adds easy, automatic dial-up connection to your choice of Internet service providers.
- Netscape Navigator Subscription Program lets you download Netscape client software upgrades for one year. It is the most convenient way to stay current with the latest versions.

- Netscape Navigator Dial-Up Kit enables service providers (ISPs) and corporations to get users online quickly and reliably. Dial-Up Kit combines an account wizard for easy installation with the flexibility to customize configurations and packaging to your requirements.
- Netscape Power Pack is a suite of companion utilities for Navigator and Navigator Gold for Windows. Included in the suite are tools for virus protection, spell checking, site monitoring, chat capabilities, and plug-ins.
- International customers can now take of Netscape Navigator 3.0 in French, German, and Japanese, as well as Navigator 3.0 beta versions in Danish, Dutch, Italian, Korean, Portuguese, Spanish, and Swedish.

Netscape also supports a program to distribute the software through Web sites run by Netscape server products, called "Netscape Now." Netscape servers can support special features such as tables, backgrounds, and dynamic documents (for graphics that can be changing over time, like weather maps), but these may only be viewed with the Netscape browser (or with some other browser that supports Netscape's extensions).

The Netscape Now program allows merchants (or other Web site sponsors) to add a button to their Web documents that, when clicked on, will allow the person browsing the document to retrieve a copy of Navigator. A special graphic button is made available to these sites, which allows visitors to the site to download the latest version of Navigator directly.

---

[1] REPRINTED WITH PERMISSION FROM NETSCAPE COMMUNICATIONS CORPORATION. © 1997.

Clicking on a Netscape Now! button results in a sequence of screens that walk you through the process of selecting and downloading the software, starting by indicating which Netscape product you want to download. Next, you are prompted to indicate which operating system you are using, your desired language, and what continent you are connecting from. This helps point you to the nearest ftp sites. These sites all store copies of the distribution file, which is a self-extracting executable file. Execute the file, and it uncompresses the Navigator program and related files. Finally, you are pointed to a text file that contains some installation instructions and program notes.

Using Netscape Navigator

The Netscape Navigator program works roughly like any other World Wide Web browser. Under Windows, it requires that Internet connectivity be established by some means, whether a LAN connection or a telephone (SLIP or PPP; see the glossary in Appendix A) connection through an Internet service provider. Once connectivity has been established, starting Navigator initially will connect the user directly to the Netscape URL noted earlier.

Figure 7-1 shows the Netscape Navigator version 3.0 using the default configuration. Starting from the top of the display, the user can manage the session using the pull-down menu bar options (File, Edit, View, Go, and so on). Directly below the menu bar is the toolbar, which includes icons that represent some of the most commonly used functions (Back and Forward, to move between Web pages, return to the Home page, and so on). The menu-bar and toolbar functions will be described in greater detail later.

Beneath the toolbar is the Location field or window, containing the URL of the currently displayed resource. To the right is a large "N" that displays shooting stars when the browser is in the process of retrieving a resource; clicking on this "N" will return the user to the Netscape home page. Finally, just above the actual browser display is a series of directory buttons, which connect to areas of the Netscape Web site that correspond to the directory button title ("What's New!" refers to new World Wide Web sites; "Net Search" points to resources for searching the World Wide

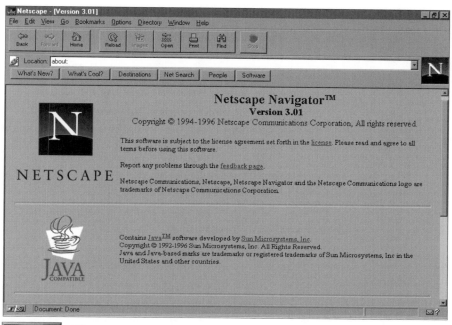

FIGURE 7-1 *The Netscape Navigator browser display is, on the surface, much like other browsers, displaying World Wide Web resources with supporting functions.* REPRINTED WITH PERMISSION FROM NETSCAPE COMMUNICATIONS CORPORATION. © 1997.

Web for resources). Displaying the toolbar, location, and directory buttons are options, although the default is to display all of them.

Navigator users can browse the Internet immediately, simply by clicking on links highlighted in the display on the home page. The user can also double-click on the Location box, enter a new URL, and press the Enter key to connect. Clicking on one of the directory buttons connects the user to the appropriate page on Netscape's Web site.

Toolbar tools include the following:

- Back, for moving backward to the previous Web document retrieved
- Forward, for moving forward along a path already taken (this button is active only when a forward path is possible)
- Home, for returning to the default home page

- Reload, to load a fresh copy of the current document (to reflect changes made between the time the document was originally loaded and the current time)
- Images, to cause graphics to be loaded (in particular when the user has opted not to load graphics by default)
- Open, to have the browser open a Web document by entering its URL (this is similar to simply entering the URL in the Location box)
- Print, for printing the current document
- Find, for locating a word or text string in the current document
- Stop, for terminating a query in progress

It is not unusual for users to be able to use any type of browser with little or no instruction or documentation. This is a tribute to browser designers, who have managed to make most World Wide Web functions sufficiently graphical and intuitive, and to the designers of World Wide Web pages, who have made the documents themselves sufficiently intuitive and graphical by using HTML to create them.

There are quite a few more functions, accessible through the menu bar. Very briefly, they include functions listed under the File menu:

- New Window opens a new instance of the browser, so more than one Web document can be displayed at once.
- Open Location has the same function as the Open button (or as typing a URL into the Location box) — it retrieves the designated resource.
- Open File points the browser at a file on the same system, and is functionally the same as entering the filename as a URL (using the scheme "file:").
- Save As saves the current Web document as a file on the local computer.
- Mail Document allows the user to send the current Web document either as an electronic mail message or as a posting to a newsgroup.
- Document Info, which will be discussed in greater detail in the next section, provides necessary information about the current Web resources, including security and encryption information.

- Page Setup lets you define how a Web resource is to appear if printed out by the local computer.
- Print sends the displayed Web resource to a printer.
- Print Preview lets you see how the Web resource would look if printed.
- Close simply closes the current window; if only one browser window is open, it exits Navigator.
- Exit ends the program and closes all windows.

The Edit pull-down menu includes the same editing functions you would normally find in a Windows application, including Undo, Cut, Copy, Paste, and Find.

The View pull-down menu includes Reload, which does the same thing as the Reload toolbar button, getting a fresh copy of the resource. Load Images is available to retrieve and display graphics when the default is to not load images; Refresh causes the browser to redraw the current resource; and the Source function causes the browser to display the actual HTML-tagged Web document in a window.

The Go pull-down menu includes many of the navigating functions of the toolbar tools: Back, Forward, Home, and Stop Loading are included. More important is the View History function, which displays the URLs of previously displayed resources. Clicking on one of them returns the viewer to that URL. Also displayed under the Go pull-down menu is a list of the most recent of the previously viewed documents, listed by number (the current one is "0" and the one before that is "1") and document title.

The Bookmarks pull-down menu is used either to view the current list of bookmarks, or to add to it. The Options pull-down menu is used to set preferences, as well as to turn on or off the display of different parts of the Navigator interface, such as the toolbar, the directory buttons, and other items. The Preferences panel allows the user to customize the browser — selecting different applications for viewing different types of files, for instance — as well as to optimize performance by setting cache sizes for RAM and disk caches of Web material (thus allowing data to be saved in case the user wishes to return to it without having to reload it all from the Internet). The user can also modify the way documents and styles are displayed on screen, and can set up the use of supporting applications such as e-mail, news, and other Internet applications.

The Directory pull-down menu points the browser to the same locations on the Netscape World Wide Web site as the directory buttons on the toolbar. Help provides access to help documents using the browser interface.

This is hardly an exhaustive set of instructions for using Navigator, but it briefly covers most of its functions — except for those relating to security and secure commerce.

Netscape Navigator Security Implementation

The underlying protocol implemented in the Netscape Navigator and the Netscape Commerce Server, SSL, is described in detail in Chapter 4. Its operation, however, is much simpler. When an SSL-enabled browser connects to a server offering SSL documents, the two programs negotiate the cryptographic terms of their connection, and if they are successful, the secure information is transmitted.

The Netscape Navigator handles secure transmissions in several ways. The first, and most obvious to the first-time Navigator user, is for the browser to notify the user about security issues under the following circumstances:

- When entering a secure server space
- When retrieving a secure document
- When transmitting information without encryption

Figure 7-2 shows the message that appears when a site is first accessed using a secure server.

These notices can be turned off through the Preferences panel under the Options pull-down menu.

Navigator notifies the user of security status of a Web document more graphically, and less obtrusively, by displaying a blue bar across the top of the Web display window and by showing the security key

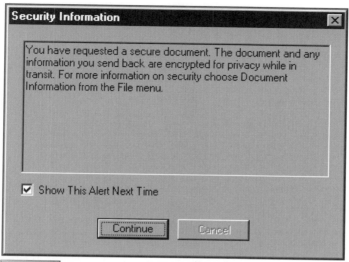

on a blue background in the lower left corner of the program display. Figure 7-3 illustrates the "unsecure" (left) and "secure" (right) document keys displayed depending on the status of the document. There is also a special "mixed" key symbol for documents that include both secure and unsecure information.

Finally, the user can check the security status of the current document by choosing the Document Info option from the File pull-down menu. The resulting general information, as shown in Figure 7-4, includes the document's title, its full URL, date and time of last modification, and what type of encoding is used.

Security information, as illustrated in Figure 7-5, shows the type of document (whether a secure or an unsecure document) and describes

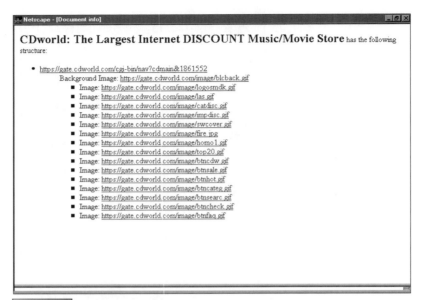

FIGURE 7-4 *General document information displayed by Netscape Navigator includes document URL and other basic data.* REPRINTED WITH PERMISSION FROM NETSCAPE COMMUNICATIONS CORPORATION. © 1997.

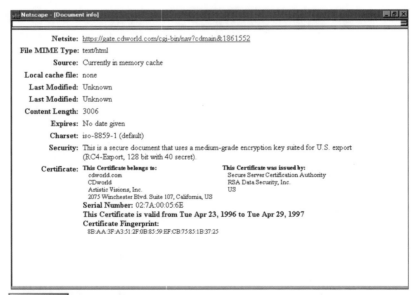

FIGURE 7-5 *Netscape Navigator displays the server certificate, along with an explanation of cryptographic protection of the current document.*

the type of encryption used to protect it. Also displayed are the contents of the server security certificate, which include identifying information such as the serial number of the server, who issued the certification, and who the certification was issued to.

These features help the user be aware of when security is being invoked, which is particularly useful because most security is implemented automatically using the merchant's server certificate to exchange session key information.

Most security passes from the merchant's server to the customer's browser; there is no reason why security cannot pass in both directions. This would require browsers to be configured with their own public key certificate, but it would allow customers an added level of control over their transactions.

Netscape Commerce Server

The Netscape Commerce Server is a piece of software that, when executed on the appropriate platform running Unix or Windows NT, permits publication of World Wide Web data to the Internet or other TCP/IP-based internetworks. This server supports publication of network resources created with the Hypertext Markup Language (HTML), using the Hypertext Transfer Protocol (HTTP) to respond to requests for resources over the Internet. In addition, it supports the use of the Common Gateway Interface (CGI) for collecting information from Web browsers and sending it to another application.

The Netscape Commerce Service was the first HTTP server implementation that supported the use of the Secure Sockets Layer (SSL) to provide security for Web transactions, as described in Chapter 4. Netscape also provides its own application programming interface, called NSAPI, to provide simpler integration of added server functions. Another important feature, according to Netscape, is much faster processing of resource requests from browsers. Finally, Netscape server management is done from the Netscape browser, which means the administrative interface is familiar as well as accessible across networks.

As with most Internet application servers, a World Wide Web server functions by "listening" to its Internet connection for requests from remote clients, which in the case of the Web are simply browsers trying to retrieve resources. Once a request has been received, the server software creates a separate process on the computer acting as server to handle that request. In this way, the server is able to respond to multiple concurrent requests from different clients, instead of making each one wait for the server program itself to handle each individual request.

Netscape's server permits the configuration of a prearranged number of active processes ready in memory to respond to browser requests. This saves time when a browser makes a request, because there is no waiting for a process to be created in response to that request.

Netscape's use of its own browser to perform administrative functions helps to make managing a World Wide Web server more manageable. Installation, configuration, and maintenance are performed

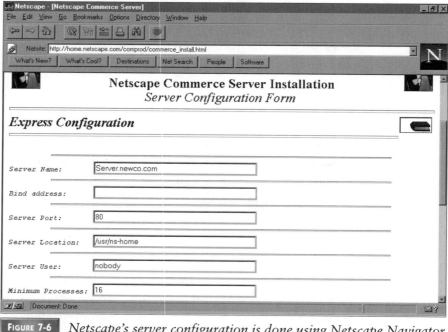

FIGURE 7-6 *Netscape's server configuration is done using Netscape Navigator as a management tool.* REPRINTED WITH PERMISSION FROM NETSCAPE COMMUNICATIONS CORPORATION. © 1997.

using CGI forms, making the process simpler than trying to configure a command-line UNIX implementation. Another benefit to using Netscape Navigator is that it enables secure communications between the browser and the server, so maintenance can be performed over the Internet with no worry that configuration commands or passwords can be stolen or modified. Figure 7-6 is the Netscape demonstration page, which shows what the server configuration looks like.

Netscape has compiled a list of clients demonstrating different applications at the following site:

```
http://home.netscape.com/comprod/business_solutions/commerce/casestudies/
    product.html
```

SSL Security Breaches

After only a single month as a public corporation, Netscape's SSL security protocol fell to at least three different groups. The first two were brute-force attacks, using networks of workstations to attempt every possible key combination. More alarming was the third attack, which circumvented the encryption algorithms and targeted Netscape's implementation of the algorithms.

Brute-Force Attacks

In August 1995, a graduate student in France announced that he had broken the SSL encryption on a sample transmission provided as a challenge in an Internet newsgroup dedicated to discussion of cryptography and its use. Approaching the encrypted text with the knowledge that it used a 40-bit encryption key approved for export from the United States, the student was able to program a simple brute-force attack on the ciphertext using spare computing cycles on over 100 systems accessible to him through his academic affiliations. After about 8 days, the plain text was achieved, revealing a fictional name and address as well as other online transaction information.

As it turned out, another amateur was later confirmed as having priority in this achievement, and subsequent attacks succeeded even more quickly, but after an initial flurry of interest everyone went back to what they were doing. The vulnerability of the 40-bit encryption has always been clear, at least to those who are informed about cryptography. The intention seems to have been to protect transaction information from determined criminals, while keeping it accessible to, say, government agencies. Although the rapid "breaking" of the encryption is troubling, several factors have been cited as mitigating what might be seen as weaknesses in the export encryption scheme:

- It took more than a week and an estimated $10,000 of computer time to break a single transmission. To decode another transmission requires a similar expenditure, since a different key would be used.
- Nonexport encryption uses 128-bit keys, so transactions made within the United States are fully protected against similar attacks: A similar brute-force attack on a 128-bit key ciphertext would be millions of times more difficult.
- There are easier ways to steal credit cards.

Even though a determined amateur can break the encryption, the difficulty of doing so make it an acceptable risk. After all, cardoor and ignition locks are sufficient in most cases to protect automobiles from casual thefts, even though a determined thief can defeat most car security systems.

Netscape SSL Implementation Flaw

In September 1995, two graduate students reported that they had succeeded in breaking SSL security in under a minute on a standard desktop workstation. They spent about two days analyzing the ways in which the Netscape software generated "random" keys for transmission encryption; they discovered that the key choices were related to the system's clock time and were fairly easily guessed.

By narrowing down the options for generating keys, the students were able to bypass breaking the encryption scheme. Netscape's implementation of a random-number generator was sufficiently weak to completely undermine the strength of its encryption algorithms. It should be noted that although the brute-force attacks against the 40-bit encryption noted in the previous section can be eliminated by increasing the size of the key, this attack is valid against any size key.

Netscape quickly implemented an improved random-key generator and included it in a scheduled upgrade. However, this attack demonstrates that encryption alone is not sufficient to provide complete security for transactions, and that the entire application implementation must be designed for security, not just some part of it.

MICROSOFT

This section will look at the Microsoft Internet Explorer browser, particularly at the way it implements secure commercial transactions, and will briefly describe the Microsoft Back Office series of servers and products focusing on secure commercial transactions.

A great source for updated Microsoft is their World Wide Web site:

```
http://www.home.microsoft.com
```

Microsoft Internet Explorer

There is a great deal of competition among Netscape and Microsoft in the battle for Internet market share. Microsoft, in their truly competitive form, has taken the precedents set by Netscape and has tried to build a better mousetrap. Like Netscape, Microsoft has developed both Internet browsers and servers.

The Microsoft Internet Explorer is an Internet browser that meets the same requirements for supporting the URL, HTTP, and HTML protocols described earlier in this chapter and in Chapter 3.

Microsoft Internet Explorer supports most if not all of the plug-ins, add-ons, and related functions offered in the Netscape browser software. Explorer also offers support for the SSL security protocol. For the average user, it can be hard to tell a functional difference between Navigator and Explorer.

Getting Microsoft Internet Explorer

Bill Gates once described Explorer as "priced to sell." This was a comical reference to underscore the fact that Internet Explorer comes with every copy of Windows 95 and is available as a free download from Microsoft at

```
http://home.microsoft.com/using/using.asp
```

Microsoft has a program for Web designers to add a button leading visitors to a Web page where they can download the software.

The process is very similar and begins at the "Using Microsoft" page. Select the Internet product, which in this case is the Internet Explorer. You can select one of the following versions: 3.01 for Windows 95 and NT, 3.0 for Mac, or 3.0 for Windows 3.1. You will then be given a choice of which products and add-ons you would like to receive. Your next choice is which language version (for example, U.S. English) you would like to receive. Finally, you are given a choice of servers around the world to download your file from.

The file you receive is a compressed program that will uncompress and install itself when you simply run the program.

Using Microsoft Internet Explorer

Explorer works like any other World Wide Web browser requiring a modem or local area network connection. Upon running Explorer for the first time, you will see the default configuration displayed in Figure 7-7.

Like other browsers, the user can immediately connect with other sites on the Internet by clicking on any available link. The user can also double-click on the Address box, enter a new URL, and press the Enter key to connect.

The Toolbar tools include the following:

FIGURE 7-7 *The Microsoft Internet Explorer browser.* REPRINTED WITH PERMISSION FROM MICROSOFT CORPORATION. © 1997.

- Back, for moving backward to the previous Web document retrieved
- Forward, for moving forward along a path already taken (this button is active only when a forward path is possible)
- Stop, for terminating a query in progress
- Refresh, to load a fresh copy of the current document (to reflect changes made between the time the document was originally loaded and the current time)
- Home, for returning to the default home page
- Search, a quick link to a Microsoft-prepared Web page providing a quick way to find material on the Internet through the use of one or many of the Internet search engines currently available
- Favorites, for access to a tool for creating and managing a list of your favorite Web sites; this is also referred to as bookmarks
- Print, for printing the current document
- Font, for changing the font of the displayed page
- Mail, for accessing the Internet mail and news readers
- Edit, for viewing and editing the Web-page source files

There are quite a few more functions accessible through the menu bar. Very briefly, they include functions listed under the File menu:

- New Window opens a new instance of the browser, so more than one Web document can be displayed at once.
- Open Location has the same function as the Open button (or as typing a URL into the Location box) — it retrieves the designated resource.
- Save and Save As saves the current Web document as a file on the local computer.
- New Message allows the user to immediately create an electronic mail message.
- Send allows the user to send a shortcut to someone else through several different means.
- Page Setup lets you define how the page is presented (for example, portrait versus landscape, height, width).
- Print sends the displayed Web resource to a printer.
- Create Shortcut allows the user to create a shortcut to the Web resource on the screen.
- Properties displays the properties for the document, including the security information.
- Close simply closes the current window; if only one browser window is open, it exits Explorer.

The Edit pull-down menu includes the same editing functions you would normally find in a Windows application, including Cut, Copy, Paste, and Find.

The View pull-down menu includes the ability to toggle on or off the toolbar or status bar. Fonts acts just like the icon on the toolbar, allowing the screen font to be changed. Stop, like the icon, will stop the query in process, and Refresh causes the browser to redraw the current resource. The Source function causes the browser to display the actual HTML-tagged Web document in a window. Options brings up a page of different settings and switches that will tailor the way the browser displays Web pages.

The Go pull-down menu includes the Back and Forward and Home functions. Search the Web and Best of the Web take you to Web pages developed by Microsoft to help you find information on the Web. Access to Internet mail and news readers is listed next, followed by a listing of the last few URLs you have visited. A very important feature is the History File function, which displays the URLs of previously displayed resources. Clicking on one of them returns the viewer to that URL.

The Favorites pull-down menu is used either to view the current list of bookmarks, or to add to it. Finally, Help provides access to help documents using the browser interface.

This is just a brief overview of Internet Explorer, briefly covering the major functions with the exception of those relating to security and secure commerce.

Sanity Check

If you are finding the overview of the Microsoft Internet Explorer to be very similar to the overview of Netscape's Navigator, you are on the right track. What was once a horse race that Netscape led by several lengths, the fight for market share in the browser business, is a very close race to call in early 1997. This is one of the strongest examples of the competition between Netscape and Microsoft.

Microsoft Internet Servers

Microsoft outlines their Internet Commerce Strategy on the web at http://www.microsoft.com/commerce.[2] A white paper detailing their strategy is also available from that site.

---

[2] REPRINTED WITH PERMISSION FROM MICROSOFT CORPORATION. © 1997.

MICROSOFT INTERNET COMMERCE STRATEGY

Microsoft is providing a comprehensive Internet Commerce offering to meet the demanding needs of businesses creating commerce solutions. This includes the delivery of best-of-breed commerce products — components, tools, APIs to enable extension — an open secure payment architecture, and complete solutions through partnerships with industry leaders.

Microsoft is currently delivering a server and tools commerce foundation based on Site Server, Enterprise Edition. Site Server, Enterprise Edition runs on the Windows NT Server operating system, and extends Microsoft's Active Server platform — Internet Information Server, Microsoft Transaction Server and the Component Object Model architecture. Site Server, Enterprise Edition integrates with the Microsoft Internet Security Framework and Windows NT security to ensure support for secured access, authentication, and non-repudia-

tion. Microsoft's commerce foundation is secure, scalable, and reliable.

To support secure and convenient Internet-based payment for consumers, Microsoft is currently delivering an open payment architecture based on Site Sever, Enterprise Edition and the Microsoft Wallet. The Wallet is available free on the Web and will be part of future releases of Microsoft Internet Explorer and Microsoft Windows. Microsoft's payment architecture enables exchange of products, information, and services for different forms of payment on the Internet. Microsoft will support standards, such as Secure Electronic Transaction (SET) and SSL, to ensure interoperability of secure payment systems between banks and financial institutions, businesses, and consumers.

The creation and ongoing management of Internet Commerce sites involves the efforts of multiple participants and the combination of several software offerings for a complete solution. Microsoft is working together with leading software companies, banks and financial institutions, systems integrators, site developers, and hosting service providers to make it easier for customers to build and manage complete Internet Commerce solutions.

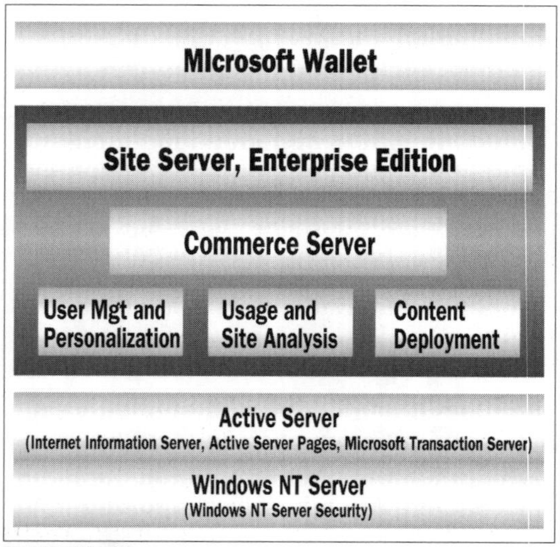

SERVER AND TOOLS FOUNDATION FOR COMMERCE

Site Server, Enterprise Edition

Microsoft Site Server, Enterprise Edition is a comprehensive Web site environment for the enhancement, deployment and advanced management of commerce-enabled Web sites on Windows NT Server and Internet Information Server.

Site Server, Enterprise Edition consists of tools and components to commerce-enable your site, deploy content reliably between staging and production environments, and manage and conduct data analysis of your site. Commerce Server,

FIGURE 7-8 *Microsoft Internet Commerce Products*

the follow-on release to Merchant Server 1.0, is a Site Server, Enterprise Edition feature that provides horizontal commerce functionality.

COMMERCE SERVER. Commerce Server provides the following key features:

- Server components for managing electronic catalogs, users and orders.
- Order Processing Pipeline to manage the order process workflow — more than 30 default components to allow price lookups, product and price promotions, inventory look-up, shipping and handling among other functions.
- Order Processing Pipeline API enabling integration of software from independent companies, such as commercial tax calculation, Enterprise Requirements Planning, accounting, payment, shipping modules and applications. More than 30 independent companies have delivered or are planning to deliver compatible components.
- Site creation and management tools, including the StoreBuilder Wizard, that enable easy, custom creation of commerce sites; these tools support remote creation and management for Hosting Service Providers.

Active Desktop		
Microsoft Wallet	Buy Now	Independent Applets
Site Creation and Management Tools				
Store Foundation Wizard	Store Builder	Pipeline Editor	Commerce Host Administrator	Independent Tools
Commerce Starter Sites			
Adventure Works	Clock Peddler	Volcano Coffee	Microsoft Press
Commerce Objects				
Catalog	User	Order	Order Pipeline	Independent Components
Windows NT Server and Active Server		

FIGURE 7-9 *Microsoft Internet Commerce Functional Components*

- Buy Now — new online selling technology that allows companies to embed product information and order forms in most any online context, such as online banner ads.

Figure 7-9 illustrates the functional elements of Commerce Server.

COMMERCE SERVER COMPONENTS. In conjunction with Active Server Pages, Commerce Server components provide the run-time environment for the presentation and operation of commerce Web sites. Commerce Server components are ActiveX Server components that supply the basic set of services for access to product information, access to user information, and creation of an order form for presentation to and processing by the order processing pipeline. In addition, there are Commerce Server components for traffic collection, message management, and site debugging. The Commerce Server Components allow developers to significantly shorten development time of sophisticated commerce sites.

ORDER PROCESSING PIPELINE. The Order Processing Pipeline (OPP) components are key to any commerce site. They allow businesses to enforce rules that direct the processing of orders through a specified sequence of stages and procedures. The OPP is a comprehensive data structure consisting of COM components that manage 14 stages in order processing.

Pipeline components included with Site Server, Enterprise Edition are optional and can be integrated with existing systems or replaced with components supplied by independent software companies, created to work with OPP interfaces. The interfaces of the Order Processing Pipeline are described in the Commerce Server Software Development Kit (SDK). The Order Processing Pipeline, by enforcing rules for a specified processing sequence, ensures component interoper-

Order Processing Pipeline	Product Information
	Merchant Information
	User Information
	Order Initialization
	Order Check
	Item Price Adjust
	Order Price Adjust
	Shipping
	Handling
	Tax
	Order Total
	Inventory
	Payment
	Accept

FIGURE 7-10 *Order Process Pipeline*

ability; this lets customers create a multitude of custom solutions with off-the-shelf add-ons.

TOOLS AND STARTER SITES. Commerce Server tools in Site Server, Enterprise Edition makes it easier to build and maintain online sites that use Commerce Server components and the Order Processing Pipeline. These tools integrate with other Site creation and management tools such as the FrontPage™ Web authoring and management tool, Visual InterDev™ Web development system, Internet Information Server Service Manager, and SQL Server™ Enterprise Manager. Together, these tools — Store Foundation Wizard, StoreBuilder Wizard, Commerce Host Administrator, and the Pipeline Editor — make it simpler for site developers to create and manage site virtual directories, site structure, database schema, and the Order Processing Pipeline configuration.

Starter Sites, Active Server Pages templates delivered with Site Server, Enterprise Edition, demonstrate the capabilities of the product to serve the needs of different businesses. Starter Sites are used as a tool for learning how to implement certain types of functionality in a commerce site. Future releases of Site Server, Enterprise Edition will support new starter sites to enable quick development of additional applications such as corporate purchasing, supply chain trading, and distribution of digital goods and services.

CLIENT COMPONENTS

Buy Now. Buy Now enables consumers to make quick purchases from any site on the Internet. When the shopper clicks an online banner ad, product name, or any other link, Buy Now opens a window within any browser window to facilitate purchasing. The user is left in the context of the current site or page to complete the purchasing process. Buy Now is integrated with the Microsoft Wallet on the client side and with the Site Server, Enterprise Edition Commerce Server database and Order Processing Pipeline on the server side.

Businesses can include links that initiate Buy Now from within their Commerce Server–based store or catalog (for featured products, for example) or from sites or Web pages other than their own.

Integration with Microsoft Wallet. Site Server, Enterprise Edition integrates with and uses the Microsoft Wallet. By providing this support out of the box, users of Site Server, Enterprise Edition can process transactions that are submitted by users of the Microsoft Wallet.

Site Server, Enterprise Edition for Business-to-Business Commerce

In order to meet the needs of businesses looking to lower the cost of creation of business-to-business commerce sites, Microsoft continues to invest heavily in developing enhanced business-to-business functionality. Future enhancements include:

- Corporate Purchasing and Supply Chain Trading Starter Sites, to support rapid creation of solutions.
- Business Document Pipeline for managing communication of structured business documents, such as ANSI x.12 transaction sets, between companies.
- Integration of business to business payment modules such as Electronic Funds Transfer (EFT) solutions, together with independent software companies, allowing businesses to execute payments through the Internet.
- Enhanced ERP integration for tying in online commerce with existing Enterprise Resource Planning systems.
- Configuration and advanced search support for management of complex electronic catalogs as well as support for dedicated configuration management solutions from independent companies.

BUSINESS DOCUMENT PIPELINE. The Business Document Pipeline (BDP) is a workflow system similar in concept to the Order Processing Pipeline but designed to simplify the integration of structured business document communication into Internet commerce sites. The Business Document Pipeline is schema and transport-independent. This gives developers of commerce sites a choice in the use of message formats — EDI or other — and transports — S/MIME, DCOM, EDI or other transports. BDP will support document translation, including a plug-in interface for independent company EDI translation software; data encryption for transmission over the internet; document authentication via digital signatures; and

transport independence to allow sending and receiving of documents over the Internet, VANs, or other networks.

The Business Document Pipeline, business-to-business starter sites, improved facilities for managing complex electronic catalogs, and simpler ERP integration will combine to form a powerful business-to-business commerce platform. Most important of all, businesses will develop sites more quickly and at less expense.

Microsoft Windows NT Server and Active Server

INTERNET INFORMATION SERVER AND ACTIVE SERVER PAGES. Microsoft Internet Information Server (IIS) is the only Web server integrated with the Microsoft Windows NT server operating system, providing a powerful platform for Web-based line of business applications. By optimizing around the Windows NT Server platform, Internet Information Server delivers high performance, excellent security, ease of management, and is up and running in minutes.

With IIS 3.0, Microsoft introduced Active Server Pages, an open, compile-free scripting environment in which you can combine HTML, scripts and server components to create dynamic HTML and to enable powerful web-based business solutions. Active Server Pages support virtually any scripting or component language, and provides the easiest way for Web developers to create powerful, dynamic Web sites on Windows NT Server.

Site Server, Enterprise Edition runs on top of Internet Information Server and extends Active Server Pages. The starter sites that ship with Commerce Server are a collection of Active Server Pages that call into commerce specific ActiveX server components.

MICROSOFT INTERNET SECURITY FRAMEWORK AND WINDOWS NT SECURITY. The Microsoft Internet

Security Framework (MISF) is a comprehensive set of cross-platform, interoperable security technologies that support Internet security standards. Developers and Webmasters can use this set of technologies for a variety of applications, including secure communications, Internet Commerce, and controlled access to information or resources. MISF technologies support existing Internet security standards. Applications using MISF technologies will be able to interoperate with other standards-based software. Microsoft is also actively participating in standards bodies to ensure continued interoperability.

MISF technologies implemented to date include: Authenticode technology, CryptoAPI 1.0 and CryptoAPI 2.0, support for client authentication, support for SSL 3.0, and PCT-secure channel protocols. MISF technologies will soon include a certificate server and Personal Information Exchange (PFX) 1.0 protocol. Support will also be incorporated for Transport Layer Security (TLS), the follow-on specification of SSL, currently near final specification by the Internet Engineering Task Force (IETF).

Microsoft Windows NT Server offers excellent security services for account management and enterprise-wide network authentication. Large organizations need flexibility to delegate account administration and manage complex domains. Internet security concerns are driving the development of public, key security technology that must be integrated with Windows NT security. To meet these expanding needs, Microsoft is developing the Distributed Security Services Technology preview, a related white paper is available at http://www.microsoft.com/ntserver/info/aasecurwp.htm. This white paper examines the components of the Windows NT Server Distributed Services Technology preview and provides details on its implementation.

For user authentication, Commerce Server integrates security mechanisms provided within Windows NT security and MISF:

• Windows NT Challenge/Response
• Hypertext Transfer Protocol (HTTP) basic authentication
• Personal certificates

Commerce Server limits browser-based access to store management pages to users with Windows NT accounts that have been defined as administrators or store managers. In addition, Commerce Server has the capability of requiring account authentication for access to the store's file system, for users of the Windows NT file system (NTFS). It is recommended that customers use the Secure Sockets Layer support in IIS for the security of transactions between the client and the server.

MICROSOFT TRANSACTION SERVER. Microsoft Transaction Server is designed to simplify the development of infrastructure needed to execute business logic. It provides services that make it easy for developers to handle security, directory, process and thread management, and database connection management. In addition, Microsoft Transaction Server provides a transaction monitor that enables transactional integrity across business components. Future versions of Site Server, Enterprise Edition will take advantage of Microsoft Transaction Server to enable transactional integrity as part of the Order Processing Pipeline.

MARBLE. "Marble" is the code name for commerce extensions for banks and financial institutions that need to create Web sites for the purpose of supporting financial transactions. Marble will enable financial institutions to execute and complete banking and brokerage transactions in a more secure manner through the support of Open Financial Exchange (OFX), a financial transaction protocol backed by Microsoft, Intuit, and CheckFree. Although the initial release of "Marble" is available separately, it is fully compatible with — and relies on — BackOffice and Site Server, Enterprise Edition components.

OPEN PAYMENT ARCHITECTURE

Microsoft provides an open and extensible payment architecture on the client and server. For the server, the Site Server, Enterprise Edition APIs, or Order Processing Pipeline APIs, enable commerce site payment integration. For the client, the Microsoft Wallet and Wallet Payment Modules architecture serve as the point of integration. Leading payment software companies around the world are supporting this architecture with a diverse set of payment methods.

Support for SET and SSL

Microsoft's payment architecture not only supports multiple payment methods but multiple secure payment protocols as well, including SSL and Secure Electronic Transaction (SET). SET, a standard driven by a number of leading industry companies including Visa and Mastercard, is a powerful secure payment alternative. SET is a three-way protocol and manages the interfacing of consumer, merchant, and financial institution in one single message. A number of independent payment software companies are delivering SET payment solutions based on the Microsoft Wallet and Site Server, Enterprise Edition API.

Microsoft Wallet Description

The Microsoft Wallet is a cross-server payment front-end solution. It can be integrated into any commerce site, even sites that are not based on Site Server, Enterprise Edition. The Microsoft Wallet is available as an ActiveX control for Internet Explorer users and as a Netscape plug-in.

The Microsoft Wallet consists of the Payment Selector control and the Address Selector control. The Payment Selector control provides for the entry, secure storage, and use of various types of payment methods for paying for online purchases. The Address Selector control provides for the entry, storage, and use of addresses that can be referenced for shipping and billing during online order entry. The Payment Selector control also provides a programmatic interface for Wallet Payment Modules, plug-in modules created by independent payment software companies. In addition to open credit card solutions, Payment Modules will be created to support digital cash, private-label credit cards, check payment, and other methods.

Additional information regarding Microsoft's open payment architecture and the Wallet can be found at www.microsoft.com/commerce/wallet.

CREATION OF COMPLETE SOLUTIONS WITH MICROSOFT COMMERCE PARTNERS

The creation and ongoing management of Internet Commerce sites involves the efforts of multiple participants and the combination of several software offerings for a complete solution. Depending on the depth of any given solution, businesses may need to add order processing extensions, integrate with existing systems, and interface with payment systems and financial institutions. Microsoft's commerce partners enable customers to create custom solutions. They provide payment solutions, software extensions, hosting services, and integration and consulting expertise.

Payment Solutions from Independent Software Companies, Banks, and Financial Institutions

Leading suppliers of payment software, credit processors, banks, and financial institutions from around the world are working with Microsoft to make it easy for customers to incorporate their payment solutions into the Microsoft Wallet and Site Server, Enterprise Edition.

MICROSOFT INTERNET COMMERCE STRATEGY SOLUTIONS

Microsoft's Internet Commerce Strategy meets the demanding needs of businesses creating commerce solutions. The following table provides a summary of solutions to critical requirements identified above.

Requirement	Microsoft Internet Commerce Strategy Solution
1. Lower cost deployment and management of custom Internet commerce sites	• Site Server, Enterprise Edition Commerce Server Components. • Tools: StoreBuilder Wizard, Pipeline Editor. • Starter Sites. • Support for remote Hosting by Internet Service Providers, allowing low-cost creation of commerce sites.
2. Simpler integration with existing systems	• Components offered by Microsoft Commerce Partner solutions that integrate with and extend Site Server, Enterprise Edition, including those from Enterprise Requirements Planning and accounting vendors: SAP, Baan, Great Plains et al. • Site Server, Enterprise Edition Order Processing Pipeline API, enabling custom integration.
3. Flexible support for payment	• Open payment architecture and multiple Microsoft Commerce Partners offering payment solutions (listed above).
4. Secure access	• Integration with Microsoft Internet Security Framework and Windows NT security; Site Server, Enterprise Edition Commerce Server supports Windows NT Challenge/Response, HTTP authentication, and personal certificates.
5. Simpler, lower cost business document processing, EDI-compatible	• Planned enhancements including the Business Document Pipeline. • Leading independent EDI and electronic commerce software vendors providing solutions that will integrate with the Business Document Pipeline.
6. Dynamic, promotional, searchable content management	• Site Server, Enterprise Edition electronic catalog support. • Independent configuration management software companies that offer solutions that integrate with Site Server, Enterprise Edition.
7. Contextual transactions for online direct marketing	• Site Server, Enterprise Edition Buy Now feature.
8. Standards-based solutions	• Support for TCP/IP, HTML, HTTP, COM / DCOM, Java, and ANSI X.12, SET, SSL, S/MIME.

For the Balance of This Century

As we discuss Internet specific server issues, it is important to high-light Microsoft's role in offering servers for all types of client–server computing applications — not just Internet servers. This includes products such as Microsoft NT, a very popular solution for companies to manage their internal computer networks. These servers include functionality for sharing files, e-mail, and databases. Microsoft is also the leading maker of desktop applications such as word processors, spreadsheets, and databases.

As we complete the second edition of this book in the spring of 1997, Internet trends are pointing to a future where the Internet is not just a novel toy or game but a growing business application at the office and appliance in the home.

As this happens, the Internet will most probably follow a path like that of e-mail. At first, it was a novel idea and only the early adopters were using it. As time went on more and more people added it to their lives, and now e-mail has become a utility many people, not just the computer types, would hate to be without. Many people believe the Internet is following a similar path.

Given the number of home and office desktops that Microsoft already has "won" and the way the Internet will migrate into main-stream computing, one cannot underestimate Microsoft's ability to pull ahead of Netscape in the Internet server market between now and the end of this century.

OPEN MARKET

With the de facto standards for Internet browsers being established by Netscape and Microsoft, a great deal of attention is being focused on the creation of very robust Internet servers. In the early days of Web-based shopping, a Web server consisted of one computer. Today, the most aggressive systems are multiple computer systems requiring complete suites of software. Open Market is a leader in this market.[4]

Open Market offers three products which enable companies to perform secure electronic commerce over the Internet: OM-Transact(TM); OM-Axcess(TM); and OM-Securelink(TM).

OM-Transact is a high-end, complete commerce application which enables companies to offer secure payment, complete order management, and online customer service over the Internet. This product is targeted at three types of customers:

1. commerce service providers (CSPs) who want to offer third party Internet commerce services to multiple other small and medium enterprises and require scalability to large numbers of content servers;
2. large companies who want to conduct business-to-consumer commerce over the Internet;
3. large companies who want to conduct business-to-business commerce over the Internet.

OM-Transact is built on an open systems approach. It supports all HTTP browsers, including those that support security protocols SSL or PCT.

OM-Axcess is an access management and reporting solution for Web applications. It is designed to a simple and cost-effective way of building authentication, authorization and session tracking into Web-based applications and content. By centrally managing the authentication and authorization of end users, OM-Axcess™ provides single sign-on access to proprietary information distributed across the Web. OM-Axcess is ideal for companies and system integrators who want to provide information in an environment, forge business partner relationships, foster collaboration among distributed work environments, and position companies who are building an infrastructure for commerce transactions.

OM-SecureLink is an enabling technology for OM-Transact and OM-Axcess applications which allows a business to quickly and easily turn existing Web content into a commerce-enabled site. SecureLink connects existing content to the shared services provided by a Commerce Service Provider or IT department.[3]

Open Market Inc. uses a formal model for transacting business across the Internet or any other open network, with specific attention to purchase and sale of products that can be delivered over the network. Although Open Market sells a full line of commerce products for the Internet and the World Wide Web, including a secure server (supporting S-HTTP and SSL), their most interesting contribution is their comprehensive approach to producing an overall "commercial environment." This environment includes transaction services as well as tools for creating online stores (StoreBuilder), and it produces smart links to online products for sale.

---

[3] REPRINTED WITH PERMISSION FROM OPEN MARKET INC. © 1997.

One feature that differentiates Open Market's approach from other vendors' stand-alone secure servers is that they separate the content server from the transaction server. The content server acts as a catalog and ordering station, offering users descriptions and prices on available products, as well as ultimately delivering those products once transactions have been completed. The transaction server processes the transaction, and if authorization is permitted, passes on notification to the content server.

The process begins with a customer browsing a content server. The customer initiates a transaction by requesting product information — an offer — from the content server. The model requires that this offer include the following information:

- A pointer to the transaction server handling the transaction
- An identifier indicating who gets paid when a sale is made (the merchant making the sale)
- Product price
- Product description, which points at the digital product's URL (this can also be a description of a physical product)
- A time limit on the validity of the offer being made
- The merchant's digital signature on the offer

When the customer decides to make a purchase, he or she clicks on the appropriate purchase button and connects to the transaction server. At this point, the transaction server can request a user ID and password to identify the user or prompt the user to set up an account. Further authentication at this point is optional, but in any case the transaction server has the option of denying service to "problem" customers at this point.

Assuming the customer has passed this point, the authorization process begins. This will vary depending on how payments are being made. For example, if a credit card is being used, the transaction server can connect to an external financial processing network, pass along the transaction information to the network, and receive an authorization number (if the payment is authorized).

Other options are available, and payment methods could include digital currencies, payment systems, or even alternative "currencies." Open Market has a working relationship with CyberCash and supports CyberCash and CyberCoin payment processing. For instance, a system could be set up to exchange frequent-flier miles online.

Once the transaction has been authorized, the transaction server sends back a "confirmation ticket" to the customer. This provides access to the digital product being purchased, and can include the following information:

- The product being purchased and the name of the content server it resides on.
- Some identifier to limit delivery to the purchaser. This could be the buyer's Internet (IP) address, or a public key, or a shipping address.
- A time limit on the fulfillment of the purchase. This can be used to provide online subscriptions.
- A digital signature on the confirmation ticket, so the content server can authenticate the ticket.

This is the model on which Open Market builds its commercial services. Additional services include special gateways that may be available for linking the transaction server to financial networks or other payment authorizers. Also, both the merchant and the customer receive digital statements of their activities.

This model, illustrated in Figure 7-10, is useful because it demonstrates that simply having a secure World Wide Web server may not be sufficient to perform online commerce. There must be some means of keeping track of transactions and authorizing payments. Although it is possible to do these functions by hand, in the same way that telephone orders are handled, this becomes unwieldy when the number of orders is large—and it fails to capitalize on the benefits of automation that Internet commerce promises.

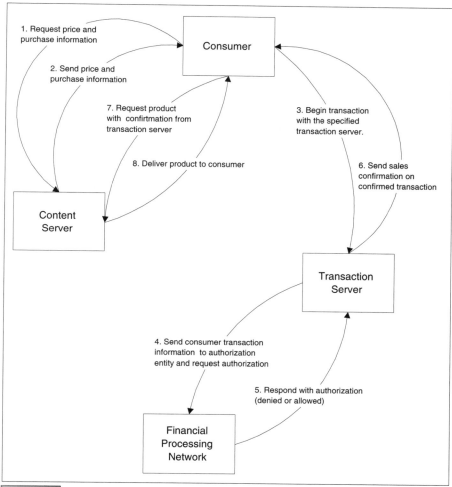

FIGURE 7-11 *Open Market's softgoods transaction model allows customers and merchants to buy and sell online.* REPRINTED WITH PERMISSION FROM OPEN MARKET INC. © 1997.

Open Market has enjoyed tremendous growth. Much of this is due to the fostering of strategic relationships with business partners and several major companies selecting Open Market products to deploy Internet and Intranet projects. A partial listing includes the following:

- Joined with RSA to conduct SET Transaction testing
- Vanguard Investments chose OM-Axcess to offer its shareholders secure Web account access
- Disney Online is using Open Market software for The Disney Store Online
- AT&T's SecureBuy service has teamed with Open Market
- Houghton Mifflin Interactive selected Open Market for its Internet commerce solution
- Novell licensed Open Market technology to support electronic commerce on intranets and the Internet
- Barron's Online selected Open Market's innovative Internet commerce software

EIGHT

DIGITAL
CURRENCIES

Sing a song of sixpence, pocket full of rye...

— NURSERY RHYME

The very idea of individuals being able to exchange values electronically using a digital currency seems impossible — how could the physical component be removed from the exchange of currency? And yet this is already happening, in small ways, and has been for some years. For example, certain public facilities accept coinlike tokens — mass transit systems in particular, but also many toll-collecting authorities. Some mass transit systems require the use of "farecards" which store value in a magnetic strip, instead of coins or tokens. Some toll road authorities place "tags" on your car that can be scanned at low speed so a complete stop at the booth is not required. Prepaid telephone cards represent another digitized currency.

Digital currencies are differentiated from electronic payment systems in two very important ways:

- Digital currencies can be used to maintain the anonymity of the customer in an online transaction, whereas users of online payment systems are usually identifiable, at least to the service they subscribe to.
- Digital currencies themselves can support an actual transfer of value by themselves, without linking to some third-party credit provider or financial institution for authorization to complete the transaction.

The use of standard encryption and digital signature technologies makes it possible to safely and reliably transmit payment information between customer and merchant, or between customer and online payment service provider. Encryption, particularly public key encryption, makes the contents secure from prying eyes, while digital signature techniques ensure that forgery is not possible. However, both encryption and digital signature need to be two-way processes: If Alice and Bob are to exchange encrypted messages, they must identify each other with an encryption key. More critically, digital signatures work only if you can trace the public key of the person signing.

Actual cash transactions can be completely anonymous. When you purchase a sandwich from a restaurant, you exchange currency for the sandwich. The cashier does not ask you for any kind of identification, and as long as the currency you use does not appear to be counterfeit, your payment is accepted without question. Pay with a check or a credit card, and the process is considerably different: You may be asked for identification, for addresses or phone numbers, and your signature may be compared to the one on your driver's license.

More to the point, that transaction becomes a matter of record. The restaurant can keep track of what kind of sandwiches you've been buying, and so can the credit card company. More frightening, the credit card company can build a fairly comprehensive consumer profile based on all your purchases over time: what kind of food you eat, how often you travel, how much gasoline you buy, whether your automobile is serviced regularly or adequately, and much more.

There is no reason why anyone but you should know how often you change your car's oil, and you may wish to keep an anniversary gift secret from your spouse. While consumers who use several different credit cards to avoid having any significant profiles built up by the financial institutions might be viewed as paranoid, there are some who feel strongly about this issue. Cash is an excellent solution. Electronic currencies, fully negotiable and fully anonymous, are another.

DigiCash has been a ground-breaking organization in developing electronic currencies, and their electronic cash trial program, called Ecash, is discussed in this chapter. Ecash does not have any intrinsic value, nor is it exchangeable for any real currency, but since October 1994 one million CyberBucks have been placed into circulation for the purposes of beta-testing DigiCash's electronic currency application. This chapter discusses the principles underlying this electronic currency and explains how it works.

How Digital Currency Can Work

Let's say you wanted to start your own Internet currency. You could run an electronic bank, or e-bank, taking cash deposits from customers and giving them some kind of electronic manifestation of cash on demand. They could spend that manifestation by giving it to others, who could in turn spend it themselves, or they could turn it back in to the e-bank for real money. This manifestation of value is what we'll look at in this section.

Using just the methods discussed in Chapter 2, this service should be fairly simple to provide. Whenever a customer wants to withdraw money from their account, the customer comes up with a randomly generated serial number and signs it digitally. This the customer sends to the e-bank, which uses the customer's public key to certify the serial number as coming from that customer.

The e-bank then digitally signs this serial number using a different public key varying by denomination: A one-dollar signature would be different from a twenty-dollar signature. The resulting signed serial number is sent back to the customer. And of course, the e-bank debits the amount being withdrawn from the customer's account.

These manifestations of value are called digital coins, because each one represents a discrete amount of value. When shopping, the e-bank customer can present a digital coin to a merchant in payment for goods or services. The merchant can certify that the digital coin is, in fact, currency and that it has a certain value by checking the e-bank's digital signature: The signature itself identifies the denomination, and if the signature is valid, the currency can be accepted for payment. The next step is for the merchant to submit the currency to the e-bank for payment into her own account. The e-bank credits the merchant's account for the amount and sends back a receipt to the merchant.

Each of these procedures can generate its own signed receipt or notification, so the e-bank customer gets unforgeable notification from the e-bank whenever a withdrawal is made, the e-bank gets an unforgeable withdrawal notification from the customer, and the merchant gets unforgeable notification that a deposit has been made.

Double-Spending, Part One

Unlike a piece of paper currency, serial numbers on digital coins change every time they change hands. Paper currency gets its legitimacy from the fact that each individual bill represents a certain amount of money. The physical presence of the bill determines whether or not it can be spent: If you forget your billfold at home, you cannot use any of the bills inside it. You cannot have your partner fax you a copy of a twenty-dollar bill to pay for lunch.

Digital currency, on the other hand, eliminates this limitation. In fact, it is in large part the reason why digital currencies have been invented: the ability to transfer values with no physical interaction.

Digital coins can be transmitted by e-mail, or fax, or over the phone, or by any other method of communication. The downside to this is that while a merchant can independently certify that a digital coin represents some value simply by checking its digital signature, the issuing e-bank must be contacted to make sure that the coin has not already been spent.

Double-spending is a real concern of digital currency designers. There are many different ways it could be done, from submitting the same digital coin for payment simultaneously to different merchants, to intercepting someone else's digital coins while they are en route to online merchants. Unlike traditional currency, digital coins can be, and are intended to be, copied effortlessly; thus, requiring online and immediate authentication through the e-bank goes a long way toward reducing the risk of double-spending.

When the merchant, or anyone else taking a payment with digital coins, notifies the e-bank of the receipt of a digital coin, the e-bank can check its records to ensure that coin has not already been spent.

More will be said about double-spending later, after digital currencies have been explained in greater detail.

What's Wrong with This Picture

The system described here would work, but is not significantly more attractive as a system than other online payment systems. Specifically, there is no anonymity at all. As the e-bank keeps track of transactions, it collects information about the specific transactions made by each of its customers. When the merchant's deposit is credited, that transaction inevitably points back to the original customer who made a purchase from that merchant. The result is that the e-bank can accumulate a lot of information about its customers' spending patterns, habits, and inclinations.

There are many who would claim that privacy and anonymity of transactions are necessary only for those who wish to circumvent the law. They argue that only those with something to hide would want their transactions kept private. The issue of criminal payments is taken up in the next section, but whether or not the desire for privacy is a culpable matter, there are many individuals who prefer to keep their business matters private between themselves and the people with whom they do business.

The fact is that anonymous transactions are possible using digital currencies, and customers can retain their anonymity even if both their merchant and their e-bank attempt to break it. This of course assumes that the customer uses an online identity (nom d'Internet) and does not provide merchants with true identity information.

Adding Privacy

To create truly anonymous digital currencies, it is necessary to add some method that allows the bank to certify serial numbers without knowing what those serial numbers are. This is relatively easy to do by having the customer add what is called a blinding factor to the serial numbers chosen for the digital coins.

Remember that the serial numbers are chosen by the customer at random. In the discussion above, this number could be clearly linked with the customer generating the serial number, since the number accompanies account transactions: The request for digital coins must be linked to the account to be debited.

However, the customer can generate a set of serial numbers and then apply some other random factor to those numbers. In effect, the serial numbers are multiplied by some other number. The resulting (large) number is a product that cannot be easily factored (remember that factoring large numbers is difficult). This number can be signed digitally by the bank and sent back to the customer. The customer can divide the resulting signed number by the blinding factor, and the result is still digitally signed, but unrecognizable to the e-bank.

The result is a digitally signed digital coin with a serial number unknown to the bank. The coin can be certified by checking the e-bank's digital signature. When the coin is spent, the e-bank verifies that the signature is valid, and pays the coin amount to the person or merchant presenting it. When the coin is spent, the serial number is checked against a list of serial numbers of coins that have already been cashed. If the number is already on the list, that coin has already been spent; if the number is not on the list, it is paid out and the serial number added to the list.

Anonymity is added to the system because the e-bank never knows actual serial numbers on digital coins until those coins are spent, and the e-bank is never able to connect any serial number to the person who spent it.

Breaking the Law

A merchant who accepts digital currency may ask for your name and address, but you can retain your anonymity by withholding any personal information from the merchant. The merchant cannot trace you based on the serial numbers you use in your digital coins, for the same reasons the e-bank cannot link you to your coins. Only you can prove that you spent a particular digital coin, but only if you choose to disclose the relevant information, such as who you paid it to and when.

Opponents of digital currency object that anonymity can protect anyone who wants to transfer cash from one place to another for objectionable purposes: tax evasion, drug dealing, bribery, extortion, or any other criminal purpose. However, only the person spending digital currency remains anonymous; the person receiving a payment is not anonymous. That person must still go through the e-bank to receive payment, and the person making the payment can incontrovertibly prove that the payment was made.

These features make digital currency inappropriate for receiving payment for criminal enterprises. For example, a drug dealer's customer could give proof that payments had been made to that person; similarly, with extortion or bribery payments, the person making the payments could easily implicate the person receiving the payments.

The result is that digital currencies might be attractive to people wishing to purchase illegal goods or services, but not to those who are selling them. On the other side, law enforcement agencies involved in "sting" operations would be unlikely to accept digital currency payments, since they guarantee anonymity to the person making the payments and would therefore not yield acceptable evidence.

Double-Spending, Part Two

As should now be clear, the risk of double-spending a digital coin is significantly reduced by requiring the recipient of a coin to authenticate it online directly with the e-bank. In this way, the e-bank can make a note of the serial number after certifying its digital signature. If the same serial number is submitted for payment again, the transaction is not permitted.

Additional refinements are possible that further reduce the risk of double-spending. It is possible to embed information that can point to the owner of an account in digital coins issued from that account, without having this information accessible in the normal course of events. This identifier is used in creating the digital coin, but cannot be determined unless the owner of the coin attempts to spend that same coin with more than one merchant.

The way this works is that the account holder's account number, along with the digital coin serial number, can be combined mathematically with some random number. If you know the random number being used in combination with the account number, and you know the resulting combination, you can easily figure out the identification.

Now, when a digital coin is generated, some random numbers can also be generated and combined with the account holder's identification. If you add a simple challenge/response to the purchase process, you can maintain anonymity of the account holder, but identify any account holder who attempts to double-spend. The merchant can ask the customer to give one of two pieces of information for each of the compound numbers described earlier (the mathematical combination of the account ID and some random number). For example, if there are ten of these numbers, the merchant will request ten pieces of information, either:

- The random number, or
- The combination of random number and account ID information

The result will be a list of ten numbers, some of them random numbers, some of them account information essentially encrypted by some set of random numbers. Whether the merchant requests one or the other may itself be randomly determined, or it may be determined by giving every entity capable of accepting payments its own unique query pattern.

If the coin is spent once, the information acquired remains useless. However, if an attempt is made to spend the coin twice, the identity of the double-spender will be divulged. This is how: Because everyone accepting digital coin payments will select a different combination of the two values indicated above, there will be at least one instance where both the random number (essentially an encryption key) and the mathematical combination of account ID and that random number (essentially that information encrypted using the random number as a key) will be available.

The result is that trying to double-spend means fingering yourself as a criminal. This also means that the digital currency does not necessarily have to be authenticated online and immediately, since any attempt by the owner of the account to spend a coin twice will immediately point to that person.

Academic discussions of digital currency have been going on for some time, and there are many more subtleties involved in implementing it, but they are beyond the scope of this book.

DigiCash Ecash Trial

The topics discussed so far in this chapter derive from work done by David Chaum, founder of DigiCash. In fact, these digital coins are more often referred to as Chaumian coins. While there have been other proposals for digital currencies that use other types of mechanisms, no other method has received as much attention—and no other mechanism has been tested as extensively and publicly on the Internet.

Starting in October 1994, DigiCash made available for testing purposes a digital currency client called ecash, a trademark (as is DigiCash). Users who requested a client from DigiCash were given a password and user ID that allowed them to download a copy of the software. Another password/ID pair entitled the user to 100 free CyberBucks (another trademark). No more than one million CyberBucks were to be issued, and these would be exchanged by participants in the experiment.

While there is no value behind a CyberBuck, other than its scarcity, participants have offered various products, including software, documents, pictures, and other items. Some participants asked for donations of CyberBucks, while others set up electronic casinos accepting CyberBucks for wagers. And some participants have offered physical products of one kind or another in exchange for CyberBucks.

Like ordinary currency, digital currency can be exchanged between individuals, or used to make purchases from merchants. Since ecash is a peer-to-peer system, client software can handle the receipt or payment of funds. As a result, the ability to accept payments is not significantly more difficult or expensive to add than setting up to make payments. Although the exact form a digital currency implementation takes will surely be at least slightly different from the ecash software, there is no question that ecash offers a very interesting view of how digital currency can work.

USING ECASH

To get a copy of the ecash software, participants filled out a request form with their name, e-mail address, and information about their systems and their intended use for the ecash client, and waited for DigiCash to reply with user-name and password information. Equipped with these, the participant could connect to the DigiCash server and download software and instructions. Installing this software proved to be no more difficult than any other Internet application; the software was intuitive and easy to use.

Ecash Client Software

Using ecash required an Internet connection; otherwise, supported platforms included Microsoft Windows, Macintosh, and UNIX line mode, as well as UNIX X Window System. Installation under Windows was typical of other similar products. The ecash setup program installed the program files, offered the option of installing with or without sound support, allowed the user to specify a directory to install the program, and finished with a reminder that the ecash required a WinSock 1.1-compliant network link. When the installation was complete, an ecash folder was set up with an icon for the ecash program and a file containing release notes. Double-clicking the ecash icon started the program up.

The first step when first running ecash is to accept the DigiCash license agreement, followed by entering personal information: your full name and your e-mail address. The next panel prompts the user for an account ID and a password for opening a new account. Once this information has been entered, the software begins generating a digital signature key. Once this key generation has begun, a small "digital wallet" appears and a very small animation in the corner of the display indicates that activity is taking place. Once the key is generated, the user is prompted for a password to protect this key.

Because there is communication between the e-bank and the ecash client at this point, the initial registration of keys and setting up of accounts must be done with a live connection to the Internet. If the connection is down, an account cannot be set up. During the trial, each user received 100 CyberBucks, but in actual use some other currency or currencies will be used and some acceptable mechanism for activating accounts will be necessary.

Ecash Client Features

Using ecash once the software is set up is simple. When the ecash client is running, it appears as a small rectangle, with five icons on the bottom third and the upper two-thirds displaying the amount of currency being held in the local client next to a DigiCash symbol.

Click on any of the icons to interact with ecash. The first icon on the left looks like a bank building and is used to withdraw or deposit money to the ecash bank account. There are three options:

- Withdraw from ecash bank account
- Deposit to ecash bank account
- Withdraw from credit card

Only the first two options are available in the ecash trial client; the third is grayed out and cannot be selected. It does suggest that one way of "filling up" an ecash account might be through a credit card advance.

The next icon appears to be a flying banknote: Click here to handle an ecash payment. The same panel is used for paying money out and for receiving an inbound payment. When a user interacts with an ecash shop, the information in this panel is automatically transferred between the ecash clients, but this manual payment method is available, too.

The third, and middle, icon appears to be a notebook with a dollar sign on the cover. This is the ecash payment log. It lists the payments made to or from the account. Deposits to the ecash account are signified by a red arrow; other payments get a green check mark. Each entry in the log includes the following information:

- Payment number (starting from 1 and continuing sequentially)
- Amount of the transaction
- Date and time of the transaction
- The result of the transaction (for instance, whether the payment was verified, or paid into an account, or accepted)
- A description of the transaction (deposit or withdrawal, or a brief description of the shop or individual on the other end of the transaction)

Payments made (money paid out) are kept separate from payments received (money paid in) and are viewed separately.

The fourth icon appears to be a wallet or purse, with a dollar sign on the side and a banknote and coin sticking out at the top. This icon produces the ecash account status, displaying the account ID, the bank address, the amount of ecash in the bank account, and the amount of ecash in coins in the digital wallet.

The last icon, or the first on the right, is a small pliers crossing a screwdriver: configuration tools. Click on this icon to set ecash preferences, including the default amount to withdraw from the e-bank, method of connection, passwords, and type of currency in use.

Ecash Transactions

Ecash exchanges through ecash-accepting shops on the World Wide Web become fairly automated and standardized. Whether the exchange is a payment to an ecash merchant (for example, to make a purchase), or whether it is a payment from an ecash merchant (for example, a refund or a payment on a wager), an ecash request panel appears.

A shop making a request for a payment sends an incoming payment request to the customer. This request includes the account ID of the shop in question, the amount being requested, and a very brief description of what the payment is for. The panel includes the question, "Make this payment?" along with No and Yes buttons. Another button, labeled Policy, can be clicked to see and set a standard policy for making and receiving payments: For example, all incoming payments could be accepted without prompting, or all requests for payment could be automatically denied.

Once an outgoing payment is authorized, the digital coins are exchanged. If exact change is not available, the ecash client offers to exchange money at the e-bank. If the client doesn't have enough to make a payment, it offers to make a withdrawal from the e-bank.

Setting Up a Shop Accepting Ecash

In the ecash trial, setting up a store that can accept ecash payments was relatively simple. An ecash shop is essentially the combination of a standard World Wide Web page, through which your product can be distributed, with ecash payment software, through which payments are managed.

The payment software can run directly on the same system that handles the Web page, or the shop can use a remote server to handle payments. Installing the payment software locally requires running script files on the Web server, something that not everyone is permitted to do on supported systems that can run scripts, and something that no one can do on unsupported systems or systems that cannot run the scripts.

The way it works is that when a BUY Web link is selected, the server starts the ecash software and passes it the product price and description, and the address of the requesting ecash client. With this information, payment is negotiated by the ecash software on both systems: If the client has enough ecash available, and if the user agrees to make the payment, the transaction is completed. The ecash payment software on the server then can allow the Web server to pass along the requested product.

For those who cannot run the ecash payment software on their Web servers, or prefer not to, DigiCash maintains a remote shop server. This requires that the files for sale on the shop's Web server be restricted to access only from the DigiCash Internet domain; customers wishing to make a purchase then are referred to the DigiCash server, which collects the payment on behalf of the shop, passes the payment along to the shop's ecash account, and passes the desired files along to the customer after debiting the customer's account.

Ecash Implementation

According to DigiCash's World Wide Web documents, the company wishes to license the banking software to organizations interested in running electronic banks. They have also stated that they are in the process of negotiating such agreements. As of mid-1995, more information was not available, but it is reasonable to expect that ecash-like systems will be available before very long. Issues that probably remain to be resolved may include the following:

- It is not clear how the sponsoring bank or financial organization would charge for the service.
- It is not clear how much the service would cost the customer.
- Governments almost certainly will involve themselves in the way this type of service is implemented, for the same reasons that they are involved in other banking and financial services.

Once these issues, and any others, have been resolved, however, expect to see the DigiCash software in more general use under license to financial institutions.

SMART CARDS

The majority of our discussions in this text have focused on computer-based solutions to exchanging value. On the surface, the use of smart cards may seem out of context in this text, but is not.

Smart cards look very much like a traditional credit card with one major exception — there is a tiny microprocessor or computer chip on the face of the card. Smart cards are being offered to consumers for small purchases, normally less than US$10.

Outside of North America, smart cards have enjoyed great exposure for several different applications. Most notable is the use of smart cards as prepaid telephone cards. Simply slide the card in to the phone, read the value, and talk as long as the value on the card will allow. This is a very portable, quick, and easy way for you to use your money without fumbling with exact change. The point, which must not be overlooked, is that your money is on the card. It is not a credit card, it is not a check card, and it is not some sort of device representing money sitting in a bank. The most notable difference is that if you load the card with cash and you lose the card — you've lost your cash. Furthermore, to the merchant, once the transaction is complete, they have their money. There is no waiting to settle with the bank.

All over the world consumer and merchant trials are beginning to see how consumers will change from using physical cash in paper and coin form to using a smart card. Some projects are already testing the addition of smart-card technology and function to drivers' licenses and college identification cards.

The Chip

The focal point of the Smart card debate is the function of the chip on the face of the card. Potential applications for the card range from use as a simple prepaid telephone card, to the loading of digital currency, to the complex loading and executing of computer programs for use by the holder, to the collection of data every time you visit a certain merchant, earning you points that you can redeem later.

The financial world is beginning to form alliances around which methods will be employed to manage cash on the cards. For example, MasterCard has purchased 51% of Mondex and is building products around the basic premise of smart-card transactions not requiring any central settlement like the traditional credit-card settlement process. Visa is working with smart cards as well. However, the Visa Cash program will be focused on settlement of the transaction data by a central server, much like current credit card transactions.

Mondex

In 1990, Tim Jones and Graham Higgins of NatWest, a major bank in London, were looking for a way to exchange digital cash. Their idea was the first step in creating Mondex International. Mondex International is responsible for the assignment of Mondex licenses around the world and the development of new products based on Mondex. Mondex International is also responsible for ensuring interoperability among Mondex licensees around the world, security and risk-management issues, and the certification of all Mondex equipment for use around the world.

In late 1996, Mondex USA was formed with seven U.S. corporations to promote smart-card–based electronic cash in the United States. The list includes AT&T, Chase Manhattan, Dean Witter, Discover (Novus), First Chicago NBD, MasterCard, Michigan National Bank, and Wells Fargo Bank. Mondex USA has two groups: Mondex USA Services for promoting commercial development in the United States, and Mondex USA Originator, responsible for originating Mondex Cash to U.S. financial institutions and ensuring that U.S. participants maintain the standards set by Mondex International.

Smart Card Security

Security is focused on the chip embedded in the card and the software which controls the movement of value between smart cards. For example, the Mondex chip is a highly customized security application using the Hitachi H8/310 smart-card microprocessor, which was designed specifically to thwart unauthorized disclosure and modification of data. The cards are "personalized" with cryptographic keys, which sets limits on the card's use.

Mondex has programmed the chip with the Mondex Value Transfer Protocol (VTP) software. This software uses sophisticated encryption to protect value as it passes from one Mondex card to another. Mondex cash can only be stored on or transferred between Mondex cards. The VTP operates in two steps, both transparent to the user. First, two cards "validate" each other. This ensures that only registered cards receive value. Second, using digital signatures to authenticate both payment and receipt, value is transferred and the transaction completed. Each transaction has a unique sequence number.

Transactions

As mentioned earlier, the smart card transaction is normally less than $10. A cup of coffee, a newspaper, lunches, or bus fare are typical smart-card transactions. Simply go to the register, or ticket booth, select your purchases, and use your card. At that moment, the money is transferred from your card to the merchant. There is no delay waiting for an authorization or signing a receipt.

The merchant will require a device to transfer the money off of your smart card. Most merchants will use a device very similar to the card reader used for your traditional credit card, and many have one device capable of processing smart card and credit card transactions.

We have used the term "wallet" in Chapter 6 to describe the way CyberCash manages your money with software on your computer. With smart cards, wallets regain a physical meaning. However, a smart-card wallet is more like a small calculator used for peer-to-peer transactions. Assuming we were to exchange money, the party who owes would insert his or her smart card into a wallet, enter the PIN, and then enter the amount to be exchanged. The first card would be removed from the wallet and the second card would be inserted, a PIN would be entered, and the transactions would be complete.

Putting It All Together

Some smart cards will be programmed for use until the original face amount has been spent, and others will be programmed for reloading. Devices used to reload smart card will include ATM-style machines. Additionally, some smart card trials are exploring the use of telephones and personal computers—equipped with devices capable of reading and writing to smart cards for reloading value to the card.

It is quite probable that when I send my young child off to school in a few years, the school cafeteria will accept smart cards. When my child needs more money for lunch or snacks after school, I will access my bank account with the phone or personal computer, insert the smart card, and download money right to their card from my home.

Much sooner than that, I will probably complete an online purchase by placing my smart card in a device hooked to my phone or personal computer and pay for goods and services on the Internet by transferring money off of my smart card.

Since we have the ability to complete a secure Internet transaction with SSL technology and the smart card has encryption built in for managing the specific task of exchanging money, the risks for me, my bank, and the merchant are very limited.

ELECTRONIC DATA INTERCHANGE

The majority of this book has focused on developing or recently deployed standards and methods for conducting electronic commerce over the Internet. Electronic Data Interchange, or EDI, on the other hand, has been available for years as a method for exchanging business documents between companies. EDI could be considered one of the first truly electronic commerce applications as it uses computers and software standards to manage the flow of business transactions.

Electronic data interchange is generally described as the transfer of business documents between computers. Many businesses choose EDI as a fast, inexpensive, and safe method of sending purchase orders, invoices, shipping notices, and other frequently used business documents.

EDI Basics

From a high level, the first requirement for using EDI is for a company to sign a trading agreement with the companies they wish to exchange EDI documents with. The second step is to subscribe to a value-added network (VAN) who, acting as an electronic mailbox, manages the flow of your EDI documents. You will also need a translator or software to interpret the message and integrate into your existing software. The final step is for you to create the EDI documents and send them to your trading partner via the VAN.

After you, or the software hooked to your company's computer system, create a document it is placed in an electronic or EDI envelope. The VAN is contacted with a modem and the envelope and message is "uploaded" to the VAN for distribution to your trading partner. You will also receive EDI messages addressed to you from your VAN. Depending on the size of your company and the complexity of the computer system used to manage this process, the EDI message will either be created with a standalone piece of software entered one at a time or will be automatically generated from the computer system of a large company.

Documents that can be sent via EDI cover the entire spectrum of today's business world, ranging from a simple purchase order and acknowledgment to health care laboratory results, and from college transcripts to government documents like customs forms.

EDI versus the Internet

EDI has a lot in common with the Internet. EDI relies on standards to make sure that information can be passed between trading partners regardless of the computer and software that is used by each trading partner. Like the Internet, the EDI industry also has a non-profit organization, the ANSI Accredited Standards Committee, who manages the development and publishing of EDI standards.

The biggest difference between the Internet and EDI is that EDI is more of an application than it is a network. The VANs are the "network," although they are traditionally closed systems and are not directly connected to the Internet.

EDI costs can range from free to several thousands of dollars per month depending on your needs, volume of transactions, and your position in the trading relationship. Most EDI vendors charge an annual maintenance, mailbox fee and transmission/transaction fee.

EDI Over the Internet

Since an absolute requirement of any EDI transaction is absolute security and guaranteed delivery of the EDI message, the Internet was not initially used as a part of the EDI process. However, with the continued development of Internet security protocols and systems capable of confirming e-mail messages, the Internet and EDI will continue to overlap. This overlap is being fueled by a constant flow of new Internet-based EDI solutions.

For example, Premenos Corporation (http://www.premenos.com) has introduced several products that utilize the Internet to exchange EDI messages.

It is hard to predict what portion of EDI business will migrate over to the Internet, but it will continue to grow.

NINE

STRATEGIES, TECHNIQUES, AND TOOLS

"Give us the tools and we will finish the job."

— WINSTON CHURCHILL, RADIO BROADCAST,
FEBRUARY 9, 1941)

The raw building blocks of a new Internet commerce are falling into place: protocols and standards for exchanging values electronically, secure Internet information servers, cryptographic tools necessary to keep transactions secure and safe, business services necessary to support online commerce.

There is a continuous flow of information discussing the strategic issues of marketing on the Internet. Given that marketing on the Internet was once considered to be unthinkable, at least among the Internet community, it should be obvious that there are no time- and market-proven methods of selling products on it. While estimates of the size of the Internet range as high as 70 million users in 90 countries, the actual number of users who can profitably be considered to be "on the World Wide Web" may be considerably lower, at least for now. The higher estimates include anyone with any type of Internet connectivity, which can include those with e-mail–only connections, as well as those whose links are mediated through mainframes or other multiple-user systems that don't offer any kind of graphics capability—and that may not even have World Wide Web browsers implemented or installed.

The room for growth in use of the Internet is still huge, and the commercial uses of the Internet are still being developed. That said, there is still much to be said about strategies, techniques, and tools that have been proven over time and are available to merchants as well as customers.

INTERNET STRATEGIES

The Internet is a network of networks, and by its nature is the result of a cooperative effort of all participants. This statement can be applied to at least two different levels of meaning:

- At a very basic technical level, any internetwork depends on every connected network cooperating with every other network.
- At a content level, from the start there has been a feeling that people who use the Internet, particularly for gathering information, should also "give back" something by sharing information when they have something of interest to others.

Cooperation was considerably more important at all levels before the commercialization process began in earnest. For example, some organizations provided Internet connectivity to other organizations simply by allowing them to connect their networks together, and routing traffic properly.

When the focus of Internet participation was the use of newsgroups and e-mail distribution lists, where interaction between and among groups is the primary objective, cooperation was critically important: Participants might request information, which other participants would provide if they had it. The rule was that as long as you were willing to share the results of your queries, others were happy to share information.

Why Share?

Acceptable-use policies once restricted the use of the Internet for any commercial activities, and newsgroups on virtually every topic included at least some discussion of what was acceptable and what was not. These were usually prompted by an inappropriate posting, which may have been as innocuous as a new product announcement from a networking company in a newsgroup devoted to networking. Now, however, individuals and companies are generally free to pursue their activities without apologizing for any attempts to make a living using the Internet.

However, attempting to make every bit you send across the Internet pay off is a self-defeating strategy. Similarly, attempting to cost-justify Internet expenses, particularly in the short term, will very likely fail to capture the value gained from Internet activities. Consider that no executive would ever require a cost-justification study to determine whether a new plant should be equipped with telephones, although what kind and how many telephones is definitely open to discussion. Similarly, customer service is a requirement for virtually any organization selling a product to customers, but the form that support will take can vary.

The bottom line is that potential customers are already paying some kind of access fee to an Internet service provider before they even know about online merchants' World Wide Web sites: attempting to make them pay up front for nonessential services can be counterproductive.

Success Stories

Consider the Yahoo World Wide Web site. Originally started by two students at Stanford University as a free service to the Internet community,

Yahoo became one of the most popular sites on the World Wide Web. At first it was maintained on systems to which the students had access, but the very high traffic it generated made it a drain of resources even though it offered an important service. One obvious solution, making Yahoo a for-pay service, turned out to be completely inappropriate. Setting aside the technical difficulty of limiting access to subscribers, billing those subscribers, and doing it all at a reasonable cost both to the customer and the service operators, there was a feeling that paying subscribers would be much more demanding, while many users would avoid the service altogether.

Another option was to charge a listing fee to the sites listed in the catalog and continue to offer access to the links for free. This, too, raises problems, particularly in terms of sites that offer very important information, but that are operated by individuals or by nonprofit organizations. Charging fees for listings would tend to drive out hobbyists and charitable organizations while making "better" listings (bigger sections or listings under more categories) available to those with deeper pockets.

Free access to both users and maintainers of Web sites was retained by offering corporate sponsorship of the site, along with paid advertisement links. The advertisements do not interfere with the operation of the catalog, but do give the advertisers exposure on one of the most accessed sites on the World Wide Web. The costs of maintaining Internet links sufficient to provide fast and consistent access are taken on by the sponsors, and what was a resource drain becomes a potential profit center. Yahoo is, so far, a success story.

Making It Work for You

The Internet has been, in many ways, a demonstration that certain types of altruism can be in the individual's self-interest as well as the interest of the community. However, setting up a digital storefront does not absolve the merchant from providing responsive, personal service whenever necessary, nor does it absolve the merchant from the responsibility of keeping that storefront current and up-to-date. Getting customers in the door is of no use if, once in, they find nothing of value. Some important points that merchants and vendors do not always consider as they set up an Internet presence include, but are certainly not limited to, the following:

- Putting an electronic version of a corporate brochure online is useful, as long as there is more information available online as well.
- Using automatic mailers referenced on a Web site to e-mail copies of the documents published on the Web site is generally a waste of time.
- Your business cannot run by itself, and there will be potential customers who need to speak with you. The more they need to speak with you, the more likely you are to want to speak with them — for example, the customer who needs 10,000 licenses of your software, or the one who needs your product today and will pay a premium for it.
- Giving your World Wide Web site appeal for anyone who might want to buy your product will bring them back, and will give you increased market awareness.
- The Internet is an ideal way to get up-to-the-second information to your customers; if your online catalogs are a year old, it is worse than having no presence at all, since it makes you look bad and costs you sales of your newer products.

There are many forums for discussing marketing techniques and strategies, including Internet mailing lists as well as World Wide Web sites, magazines, books, and organizations. Some of these are referenced in Appendix B, but the reader is urged to check Internet search engines and mailing lists, since the available resources change constantly and new ones appear daily.

INTERNET TECHNIQUES

Techniques for using the Internet are documented practically everywhere, from daily newspapers to the thousands of books being published to articles in mainstream magazines. And of course, even more material is available online on the Internet itself as well as the online services. Attempting to reproduce all this information in this chapter would clearly be unreasonable. Instead, a small selection of techniques useful to online merchants and customers will be presented here.

Shopping Techniques

Online shopping seems to be breaking down into two categories: commodities and specialty items. In the past, commodities were mostly raw materials which were available with minimal differentiation from any number of different sources. For instance, coal or wheat or sugar are essentially the same no matter where they come from, and pricing is usually about the same from any source. There are many more differentiable products that can now be considered commodities, simply because they are available from many different sources and differ only in price from one source to another.

Specialty items, on the other hand, include anything that cannot be bought elsewhere. Specialties could simply be a piece of information or software not sold anywhere else, or special chocolates, or practically anything else sold only in one place.

Buying Commodities Online

Many computer products are sold as commodities: No matter where you buy a Whizzo XT-10 Ethernet card or a Praxiteles 20″ color monitor or a copy of Word-O-Rific Writing Wizard 5000 word processing software, the products themselves will be essentially the same, with the same documentation, service, and support. Shopping for name-brand products like these is generally done on the basis of price, delivery, and availability. Many different merchants, both online and offline, are competing for your patronage.

If you are shopping for this type of product, there are certain things to keep in mind:

- Do your research first. Determine the vendors, product numbers, and options you want ahead of time — the quality and detail of online merchants' product descriptions vary widely. Check other sources for pricing, as well, if that is important.
- Low prices are important, but another one of the greatest benefits of shopping online is instant gratification. Find out how products are delivered, and how much shipping and handling will cost.
- Keep track of what you order. Merchants selling hard goods online should send you e-mail confirmations of your order, as well as shipping information. Save your e-mail confirmations, and keep them backed up, so you can verify credit card bills.
- If the product you want has to be special-ordered, consider dealing with a local merchant to avoid additional shipping costs. Overnight delivery of a product that won't be in for two weeks may be an expense you can do without.

Don't be surprised to find prices online consistently lower than prices in magazine or newspaper advertisements, particularly for computer products. Print ads must be submitted well in advance to publications, while World Wide Web sites can reflect the absolutely latest prices.

Finally, the online customer should exercise the same or greater caution in choosing an online trading partner as in choosing a mail or telephone order merchant. Even with the development of SET and other security measures, common sense should be used in picking any trading partner either online or driving down the street.

Buying Specialty Items Online

Buying commodity items online is much like buying them in person: The customer has many opportunities for comparison shopping, and impulse purchases may not predominate. Purchase of specialty items, however, may be more impulsive. The greater challenge is finding the merchant if there is only one source.

Merchants with unique products can be found by chance, or by looking for them using any of the many Internet catalogs, or by browsing related Internet sites. Word of mouth is another way to locate specialty merchants.

Keeping security issues in mind, as well as local regulations, is about all you need to consider when buying something you want or need. Logic and common sense should be your guide: Purchases of military secrets, criminal services, and bootleg versions of copyrighted or patented materials should be avoided online as well as in person.

While military secrets and criminal services will usually be readily identifiable (and avoidable), it might be more difficult to determine when intellectual property rights are being violated. If there is any question about ownership of information, you may want to think twice about buying it. Some cases of piracy will be clear-cut: If someone other than the publisher is offering scanned copies of a best-selling book for a fraction of the cover price, that merchant may be a pirate.

Online Selling Techniques

Simply having a World Wide Web page is not sufficient for making sales online. Even if it is equipped to take online orders through a payment system like CyberCash or First Virtual, or through a secure World Wide Web server, or both, sales will not automatically follow. There are many issues involved with online marketing, and although this is not a marketing text, there are a few guiding principles that will help the Internet merchant.

Make Your Store Easy to Reach

Every Internet URL is, at least in theory, as easy to retrieve as any other. In practice, however, there are many factors that will affect the accessibility of your Internet store. You should make it as simple as possible for potential customers to reach your Web site. This includes making it simple for them to refer to your store, as well as making it easy to see what you have to offer, and to order products.

The first step in making your store accessible is making sure that potential customers know your store's URL. Include it in your advertising materials, on your company letterhead, on your business cards—anywhere you would include your business telephone number or address.

Another important technique is to get as many links to your Web site as possible. Listing in Internet catalogs like Yahoo, Lycos, and others is akin to listing in business directories or the Yellow Pages business telephone directory. Look, too, for other Web sites that are relevant to your products, and request reciprocal links. Consider links and ads in special Web sites that may charge for the privilege. Depending on the cost, your product, and the audience these sites can deliver, your investment may be worthwhile.

Once your potential customers have arrived at your Web site, make sure they don't leave right away by providing the best service you can afford. Customer performance will vary depending on many variables over which you have no control, but if your Internet connection is slow, your customers may suffer. Likewise, if you are sharing a Web server with other popular Web pages through an Internet presence provider, your customers may have a hard time getting through.

If you anticipate high demand for access to your Web site, make sure you can handle it. If it takes five minutes to download your page, you'll lose a lot of customers who would rather not wait that long.

Make Your Site Easy to Use

People don't like to wait for Web pages any more than they like waiting for anything else. Make sure you deliver your message fast and concisely up front. For example, if you are selling classical music CDs online and you accept CyberCash only, make sure that is clear up front. Otherwise, customers may spend half an hour browsing your site, find half a dozen CDs they want to buy, and then never return when they realize they can't buy them right away. If you put that information up front, along with a pointer to the CyberCash site, your customers will thank you.

Another common method for cutting down on waiting time without upgrading your Internet link is to cut down on graphic images, or give customers the option of viewing text-only.

Avoid using too many unnecessarily nested menus. Don't make the customer wade through half a dozen submenus with a few options on each if you can use one big main menu with lots of options all together.

Finally, learn as much as you can about Web site design by browsing other sites as well as by taking courses and reading books. Observe how successful Web sites succeed, and how unsuccessful Web sites fail.

Make Your Products Easy to Buy

If you plan to sell your products online, make sure that customers can get everything they need to make a purchase. That means considering all the questions a typical customer might have, and providing the answers, which might include the following:

- Product specifications
- Prices
- Delivery information
- Product options
- Complete product description
- How to use the product
- Testimonials from satisfied customers
- References to product reviews and press coverage

Of course, ordering information must be included; this should be as simple as adding a BUY button to the Web page that points at an online order form.

Making online ordering possible is not always desirable. For example, any product that must be customized to the individual customer pretty much requires direct contact. However, if you do not make online ordering available, you should provide some way to initiate a sales contact online. Simply using an automatic e-mail responder is not enough, especially if the response is simply a version of the same information available through the Web site. There should be some way for the potential customer to directly contact a merchant representative with questions about the product. If e-mail is not practical, at least include a telephone number or postal address.

If you do choose to sell online, be sure you accept as many different methods of payment as practical and possible for you. For the near term, this may mean accepting different credit cards online through a secure server, as well as accepting CyberCash or some other payment system. However, as other payment methods like Internet checking and digital currency systems become more common, you will need to accept some of them. Just as important, you should also include telephone and mail order information for those who prefer to do business that way.

INTERNET TOOLS

In a strict sense, tools are those things which are necessary to create some result: A carpenter would use a hammer and saw to create furniture, a programmer would use a compiler and a program editor to create software. However, transacting business online is a much more broadly defined pursuit, and the tools you must use cover far wider ground.

The most basic, and most important, tool you can put at your disposal is a connection to the Internet and software to use that connection. A good World Wide Web browser, electronic mail client, file transfer software, and the underlying networking software necessary to make it all run are requirements to get at the information available online. With these tools, you will be able to locate information about practically any other Internet tool or technique, including HTML tagging and translation software, secure transaction software, consulting services, World Wide Web server and browser tools and packages, industry organizations, consultants, and vendors of services.

Choosing a Browser

If you can use only one Internet application, a World Wide Web browser is probably the most logical choice. It is the easiest Internet interface to use; it can support other Internet applications, including Telnet, FTP, Gopher, and e-mail; and it is widely implemented on different platforms.

At the moment, the personal computer browser market is dominated by Microsoft with the Internet Explorer and Netscape Communications with the Netscape Navigator browser. Both products are readily available for download from many different locations — as long as you already are online. You can also purchase Navigator packaged with Internet connectivity software through computer software and hardware retailers.

Other Internet Client Software

Electronic mail has been an essential application for decades, from the time it first became available on mainframes in the 1960s to the present. An electronic mail client should be able to save messages sent and received, should allow file attachments, preferably using the MIME standard, and should be almost completely intuitive to use.

Organizations may prefer to continue using their existing e-mail client by implementing an Internet gateway to their existing e-mail server. Individuals may wish to purchase a package like Eudora or others. Microsoft includes e-mail client software with its Windows 95 and Windows Plus! products, as well as other Internet applications software (see next section).

FTP, or File Transfer Protocol, defines procedures for transfer of files between Internet hosts. This protocol is often invoked when transferring files from World Wide Web sites, but can also be used on its own. While FTP-only sites used to be fairly common, they are becoming less common as more sites move their published data to Web sites, or at least to Web interfaces. FTP may be implemented very much like a Windows file manager program, including drag-and-drop file copying. Look for it to be included with complete TCP/IP packages like those from Wollongong, FTP Software, and many others.

Telnet, a remote terminal session application, is less frequently used. It is included with complete TCP/IP packages; Microsoft includes a Telnet implementation with Windows 95.

APPENDIX A

INTERNET GLOSSARY AND ABBREVIATIONS

The Internet has spawned its own vocabulary, mostly consisting of acronyms. Furthermore, there is considerable overlap between different meanings given to the same term, and two terms are often used interchangeably—sometimes correctly. For example, *router* and *gateway* are often used to mean the same thing, a special-purpose computer providing a link between two different networks and passing data intended for destinations on either network as needed. However, *gateway* may also refer, properly, to a computer translating data from one application implementation to another, as in an e-mail gateway.

This glossary provides definitions of some of the more basic Internet terms necessary to understanding commerce applications. The interested reader is directed to other texts for more detailed information about the terms presented here, and for more information about other terms not included.

agent
A system acting on some other system's or individual's behalf. Agents can be used to do comparison shopping, for example.

anonymous ftp
An implementation of the file transfer protocol software that allows users to access files without having accounts on the ftp server.

API

Application Programming Interface; a set of standard routines used to make standard functions available to custom-designed programs.

application

A program providing some network function to end users or systems.

application layer

The top layer in the standard Internet Protocol network architecture conceptual model. This is the level at which interaction takes place between the end user and the application.

ASCII

American Standard Code for Information Interchange; refers to the "standard" alphanumeric character set.

asymmetric cryptography

See **public key cryptography**.

AUP

Acceptable use policy. Often refers to a policy of permitting only non-commercial uses for traffic carried by an Internet service provider subsidized by the U.S. government.

backbone

A special type of internetwork intended specifically to connect other internetworks to the Internet, or used to connect internetworks across wide geographic areas.

bandwidth

The amount of data that can be carried by a communications link in a given time. Usually measured in bits. A typical telephone link is capable of about 28.8 Kbps (thousands of bits per second).

bit

The smallest unit of binary information, represented as either "1" or "0."

bridge

A special-purpose computer that connects two networks of the same type. It reproduces transmissions from one and sends them to the other connected network.

browser

Usually refers to a World Wide Web client program. Browsers are capable of requesting data from Web servers and processing data received in response to these requests.

byte

A basic unit of data, consisting of 8 bits.

card-not-present transaction

A credit card transaction where the merchant receives the credit card number but cannot physically link the card to the purchaser. This includes telephone and mail orders, as well as on-line transactions.

CGI

Common Gateway Interface. A specification for creating programs that accept information acquired through World Wide Web pages and pass it on to other programs, or take information from other programs and make it accessible through World Wide Web pages.

CIX

Commercial Internet Exchange. An industry organization for Internet service providers.

cleartext

Text that has not been encrypted.

client

A computer or system that makes requests for some kind of network service from another computer or system acting as a server.

cracker

An individual who uses computers for criminal pursuits. This term is not yet in general use, but is current among computer professionals and academicians. See also **hacker**.

cryptanalysis

The study of cryptographic processes with the intent of finding weaknesses sufficient to defeat those processes.

cryptography

The study of mathematical processes useful for keeping data secret by encryption, guaranteeing its provenance, or guaranteeing that its content has been unchanged.

daemon

A program or process running on a server that listens to the network for requests for its service.

data link layer

The bottom layer in the standard Internet Protocol network architecture conceptual model. This is the level at which computers connected to the same physical wire (LAN) communicate with each other.

datagram

The basic unit of network transmissions under TCP/IP. A basic unit of network transmission in connectionless services.

decryption

The process of reversing encryption; application of a mathematical process to encrypted data to restore it to its cleartext version.

DES

Data Encryption Standard. A private key encryption standard approved by the United States government for the encryption of data when implemented in hardware. Uses 56-bit encryption and is generally accepted as sufficiently secure when correctly implemented.

DHCP

Dynamic Host Configuration Protocol. A protocol used to automatically configure Internet nodes when they initiate their network connection.

digital signature

The result of the application of a cryptographic process to the digital document being signed. The signer uses his or her private key (of a public/private key pair) to come up with the signature, which is a sequence of characters. The document can be verified as coming from the signer by using the signer's public key to verify the document.

DNS

Domain Name System. A distributed database system implemented across the Internet for the purpose of linking Internet host names (used by people) with Internet Protocol addresses (used by computers).

e-mail

Electronic mail.

EBCDIC

Extended Binary Coded Decimal Interchange Code. This is the data representation standard used by IBM mainframe computers. Most other systems use ASCII representations.

EDI

Electronic Data Interchange. Refers to the exchange of business information, including purchase orders and invoices, between computers used by cooperating companies.

EFT

Electronic funds transfer.

encapsulation

The use of headers to "surround" network data for the purpose of handling its proper routing across a network or internetwork. The result is a network transmission unit directed to some destination host, with some unspecified content that will not be accessed until it arrives at its destination.

encryption
A reversible process of modifying cleartext for the purpose of keeping it secret from anyone other than its intended recipient.

Ethernet
A baseband networking medium, initially developed in the 1970s by Robert Metcalfe.

FAQ
A list of frequently asked questions (with answers) pertaining to a mailing list, Usenet newsgroup, product, or activity.

FDDI
Fiber Distributed Data Interface. A network standard for fiber-optic media.

file server
A computer connected to a network and capable of offering other users on that network access to its file system.

finger
A TCP/IP application used for retrieving a list of currently logged-in users on a specific system or for getting information about some specific user of that system.

firewall gateway
A special construct for the prevention of attacks on an organizational internetwork originating from the global Internet. The firewall may include one or more gateways or routers and may comprise separate network segments, as well as software filtering and other mechanisms for protecting corporate network resources.

ftp
File Transfer Protocol. The set of specifications, or the program itself, for transferring files between two computers on the Internet.

gateway

A special-purpose computer for internetwork connectivity. Often refers to a **router** (see entry). Often refers to a system mediating between protocols, as with e-mail gateways that accept e-mail from the Internet and translate it to the appropriate e-mail protocol on the internal LAN.

gigabit

1 billion bits.

gigabyte

1 billion bytes.

Gopher

A character-based Internet information publishing application, developed at the University of Minnesota.

hacker

A term applied to individuals interested in computers and computing. This term is often used popularly to refer to individuals involved in criminal pursuits such as breaking into computers without proper authorization. Many purists prefer its original meaning, referring to individuals who have deep interest in as well as understanding of computers. See also **cracker**.

handshake

The process of negotiating a connection between two hosts. The initiating host waits for acknowledgment from the destination host, which in turn waits for acknowledgment of its own response.

home page

The opening document of a World Wide Web site. It may also refer to the Web document that an individual user's Web browser points to on start-up.

host

Any device connected to a network that can send or receive requests for network services.

HTML

Hypertext Markup Language. An Internet standard for creating World Wide Web documents, based on the Standard Generalized Markup Language (SGML). Markup languages create plain-text files using tags to set off functional sections of the document, which are interpreted appropriately for display by the document-viewing software.

HTTP

Hypertext Transfer Protocol. An Internet standard defining the interaction between World Wide Web clients and servers.

IAB

Internet Architecture Board. Part of the Internet Society, the IAB oversees the IESG and the IETF.

IANA

Internet Assigned Number Authority. A group organized through the Internet Society for maintaining assigned numbers relating to the Internet Protocol suite.

ICMP

Internet Control Message Protocol. A protocol used to exchange reachability and routing information between hosts and routers on the same LAN.

IESG

Internet Engineering Steering Group. A steering committee overseeing the activities of the Internet Engineering Task Force (IETF).

internet

See **internetwork**.

Internet

The network of networks connecting tens of millions of users around the world.

internetwork

Literally, a network of networks. Any network consisting of two or more discrete networks connected by routers and capable of supporting seamless interoperability between hosts connected to any part of the internetwork.

InterNIC

The Internet Network Information Center. InterNIC administers and assigns Internet domains and network addresses.

interoperability

The ability of disparate computer systems to send and receive requests for network services across disparate networks, seamlessly and transparently to the end user.

IP

Internet Protocol. A protocol defining the interaction between hosts communicating across an internetwork.

IP address

A numerical address assigned to a computer connected to an internetwork that uniquely identifies it on that internetwork.

Ping

Internet Protocol, Next Generation. Another name for **IPv6**.

IPv6

Internet Protocol, version 6. The next revision of the Internet Protocol, to be implemented in the second half of the 1990s. In addition to various new features, IPv6 increases the size of Internet addresses from 32 bits to 128 bits, thus increasing the number of available network and host IP addresses. This is necessary to accommodate continued exponential growth in Internet connectivity.

IPX

Internetwork Packet eXchange. An internetwork protocol used by Novell NetWare and other LAN operating systems.

ISDN

Integrated Services Digital Network. A type of telephone service providing high-speed (128 Kbps and up) and digital services (multiple phone lines on a single link, conferencing, and many others).

ISOC

The Internet Society. A professional organization supporting Internet standards processes as well as other activities.

Kerberos

A method for securely authenticating users to networked hosts, developed at MIT. Kerberos uses special servers to maintain user passwords and mediate the exchange of session keys between users and hosts.

key

A quantity of data used in cryptographic procedures to encrypt, decrypt, or authenticate other data.

LAN

Local area network. A network connected computers in the same general area, on a single network cable (or a set of cables that emulate a single wire).

latency

The delay between the transmission of a piece of data and its reception at its destination. Latency is one measure of network connection performance; **bandwidth** is another. High-latency links will be very responsive and work well with interactive applications such as terminal emulation even if the transmission rate is low.

MAC

Message Authentication Code. A quantity of data based on the contents of a message, used to confirm that it has been received as transmitted.

MBONE

Multicast Backbone. A special network backbone used to transmit multicasts (including coverage of standards meetings and other content, in real time) over the Internet.

MIME

Multipurpose Internet Mail Extensions. A specification for the linking and transfer of nontext files with Internet e-mail and other IP applications (including Usenet news).

multicast

Transmission of network traffic to some, but not all, hosts connected to the network or internetwork.

multihomed host

A system connected to an internetwork on two or more different individual networks. Routers and gateways are, by definition, multihomed hosts, since they link two or more separate networks.

NetWare

A commercial network operating system available from Novell Inc. offering network resource services across the IPX network protocol.

network

Any system of interconnected systems. In particular, the system defined by computers connected to the same communications medium in such a way that each can communicate with the other connected computers.

NFS

Network File System. A TCP/IP network protocol developed by Sun MicroSystems, Inc., for sharing resources between connected workstations. Originally implemented mostly on UNIX systems, NFS implementations are now available for most platforms.

NIC

Network information center. An organizational resource devoted to providing information about a network.

NNTP

Network News Transfer Protocol. A TCP/IP protocol defining the exchange of Usenet news between servers and clients.

NOC
Network operations center. An organizational resource devoted to supporting the day-to-day operations of a network.

node
A device connected to a network; more specifically refers to the network interface itself, so a multihomed host may represent multiple nodes.

nonrepudiation
The ability of the recipient to prove who sent a message based on the contents of the message. The quality can derive from the use of a digital signature on the message, which links the sender to the message.

NOS
Network operating system. A software product that allows hosts on a LAN to share network resources, including disk storage, programs, and peripherals connected to the LAN.

NSF
National Science Foundation. One of the most important organizations involved in development and research in TCP/IP internetworking, NSF funded NSFNET, which ultimately evolved into the Internet backbone.

octet
A term used to refer to an 8-bit byte of data, usually in the context of internetworking.

out of band
Using a medium of exchange different from the primary medium of data exchange. Most commonly refers to the practice of exchanging keys or other sensitive information to be used for network communication by telephone, by hard copy, or in person.

packet
A unit of network transmission; specifically may refer to the unit of data transmitted across a packet-switched network (such as the Internet).

PCT

Private Communication Technology. A protocol specification released by Microsoft in late September 1995, describing mechanisms for secure communication between individuals on the Internet, providing encryption and authentication.

PEM

Privacy Enhanced Mail. An Internet standard defining a protocol for the secure, authenticable, and nonrepudiable transmission of electronic mail.

PGP

Pretty Good Privacy. A freely distributed program implementing public key cryptography for e-mail, and also sometimes used for electronic commerce purposes.

ping

Packet Internet Groper. A simple TCP/IP network application in which the originating hosts sends a signal to a destination host to determine whether or not the destination host is reachable through the network.

PPP

Point to Point Protocol. A protocol defining the connection of a single host to another host over a bidirectional link (such as a telephone line), and connection to network resources.

private key

Of the two keys used for public key cryptography, the one that must be kept secret, so the owner of the key can decrypt messages encrypted with the public key.

protocol

A set of rules defining the behaviors of interacting systems, particularly when applied to rules for exchanging of information between networked systems.

280   APPENDIX A

public key

Of the two keys used for public key cryptography, the one that can be made public, so that senders can encrypt messages.

public key cryptography

The cryptographic system in which encryption is done with one key and decryption is done with another.

RFC

Request for Comments. The generic term for Internet standards documents. Originally, researchers and academicians working on specific internetworking projects published their work as RFCs to solicit further comments from others working in the field, as well as to identify errors and problems.

router

A multihomed host (connected to at least two networks) that is able to forward network traffic from one connected network to another.

S-HTTP

Secure Hypertext Transfer Protocol. A protocol that defines security additions to the HTTP protocol, developed within the traditional Internet standards process. S-HTTP operates strictly at the application level, adding encryption and authentication to World Wide Web client/server communications.

secret key

A key that must be kept secret. The term is sometimes used to refer to the private key in asymmetric cryptography (public key cryptography), but more properly refers to a shared secret between parties who use the same key to encrypt and decrypt messages.

server

Any computer connected to a network that offers services to other connected systems on the network.

SLIP

Serial Line Internet Protocol. A method of connecting a single computer to the Internet through a telephone link, SLIP is generally considered less desirable than PPP for this purpose.

SMTP

Simple Mail Transfer Protocol. The set of rules defining the transmission of electronic mail between users.

SNMP

Simple Network Management Protocol. This protocol defines functions used to monitor and manage network resources across internetworks.

SSL

Secure Sockets Layer. A protocol first developed by Netscape and subsequently provided to the rest of the Internet community to add encryption and authentication at the network layer just below the application level.

STT

Secure Transaction Technology. A protocol specification released by Microsoft and Visa International late in September 1995, intended to define the interchange of credit card payment information across public and private networks.

TCP

Transmission Control Protocol. The protocol defining the way applications communicate with each other across the Internet. TCP is a reliable protocol, meaning that all transmissions between applications must be acknowledged by the recipient.

TCP/IP

Transmission Control Protocol/Internet Protocol. The description of any network using the Internet protocols, named for the two dominant protocols used on the Internet.

UDP
User Datagram Protocol. A protocol defining a connectionless, unreliable transport-layer service between applications on the Internet.

URL
Uniform Resource Locator. A protocol for defining the exact location of a World Wide Web resource, and for identifying the method of access, the host on which it resides, and the path and filename of the resource.

WWW
World Wide Web.

APPENDIX B

ELECTRONIC COMMERCE ONLINE RESOURCES

The best resource for information about any aspect of the Internet is the Internet itself. Sometimes the Internet is too good a resource, particularly since there is such a wealth of material on-line with very little quality control. It seems as if there are thousands of organizations and individuals presenting themselves as "Internet experts," complete with Web pages full of their "articles" and extracts of talks, courses, and seminars. More useful, in general, are the Web sites maintained by mainstream vendors, financial institutions participating in the digital marketplace, and organizations devoted to supporting the Internet and electronic commerce such as the Internet Society and CommerceNet.

The companion CD-ROM to this book includes URLs pointing to scores of different World Wide Web sites relating to electronic commerce. The reader is directed to these sites for the latest information about everything discussed in this book, as well as information that appeared too late to be included. The links in the CD-ROM are described here (as they are on the CD-ROM itself).

Other Internet resources include e-mail distribution lists and Usenet news groups. Some relevant ones are listed in the last section of this appendix.

Although every effort is made to ensure accuracy and completeness, the state of the Internet is such that rapid change is inevitable. Neither this nor any other printed guide can hope to be up-to-date for any substantial length of time. As a result, although most of these links should be accurate and useable, the reader may prefer to search for more up-to-date links directly on the Internet if one of the cited links does not connect to the expected resource.

WORLD WIDE WEB RESOURCES

There are hundreds of thousands of information sources of all types available online, with many of them accessible through the World Wide Web. This section offers links and descriptions of some of those relating to electronic commerce, divided by categories.

Electronic Commerce Companies

These companies make information available online about their products and services, all of which are directly related to electronic commerce. Many of these companies work together in strategic partnerships, licensing arrangements, consortia, and other arrangements. Some of the listed organizations are in the process of acquiring others, while some of the listed organizations may have been spun off from other companies. The point is that these URLs should be considered starting points for searches, rather than authoritative addresses.

BroadVision, Inc.
http://www.broadvision.com

Developing software to support foundations for electronic buying and selling.

Cardservice International
http://www.cardsvc.com

Offers credit card services to Internet merchants.

Checkfree Corporation
http://www.checkfree.com/

Provider of electronic payment services.

ClickShop Com
http://clickshop.com/

Offers electronic shopping cart software called Shopping 770 to be added to electronic-shop Web pages.

CyberCash, Inc.
http://www.cybercash.com/

Provider of payment services for the Internet.

Cylink Corporation
http://www.cylink.com

A licenser of public key cryptography algorithms.

DigiCash bv
http://www.digicash.com/

Developers of digital currency systems.

Enterprise Integration Technologies
http://www.eit.com

Sells software and services in support of WWW commerce; was involved in the creation of CommerceNet, as well as the Secure HTTP specification.

First Virtual Holdings Incorporated
http://www.fv.com/

An information-only Internet payment system.

Hewlett-Packard
http://www.hp.com

A leading provider of hardware and software in many vertical markets, including electronic commerce.

Internet Shopping Network
http://www.internet.net

Internet shopping services, offering computer-related products as well as online catalogs, floral arrangements, gifts, and more.

Mecklermedia Corporation
http://www.iw.com

Publisher and trade-show sponsor with strong Internet orientation; provides much current information on this Web site.

MegaWeb, Inc.
http://www.dynamicweb.com

They offer the Dynamic Web Ordering System for setting up online storefronts.

Microsoft Corporation
http://www.microsoft.com

The software giant has big plans to get involved in electronic commerce and released a specification for online transactions jointly with Visa International in September 1995.

Mondex USA
http://www.mondexusa.com

The U.S. branch of an international digital currency and smart cards supplier.

NetMarket
http://www.netmarket.com

Produces secure Web server package using PGP.

Netscape Communications Inc.
http://home.netscape.com/

The latest information from the Web browser/server publisher.

PaylinX Corporation
http://www.paylinx.com/

Provides real-time secure credit authorizations and settlement.

Premenos
http://www.premenos.com

Pioneering EDI company, offering software for IBM multiuser systems.

RSA Data Security, Inc.
http://www.rsa.com

A licenser of public key cryptography algorithms.

Sun MicroSystems
http://www.sun.com

Internet pioneer Sun offers network security solutions among many other products.

Surety Technologies
http://www.surety.com

Offers "digital notary" services.

Terisa Systems
http://www.terisa.com

A joint venture of Enterprise Integration Technologies and RSADSI, Terisa was launched to market, license, and support technologies for secure Internet transactions.

The Internet Group
http://www.tig.com

Provider of electronic commerce consulting and services.

Verifone
http://www.verifone.com

Leader in transaction automation industry; is acquiring EIT for its electronic commerce division.

Verisign, Inc.
http://www.verisign.com

A spin-off from RSADSI, Verisign provides public key certificates to individuals and companies.

Financial Institutions

The number of banks offering some type of service over the Internet, from simple information services to actual banking services, is growing rapidly. These are just a few of the first to get online; more will certainly be there by the time you read this.

Bank of America
http://www.bofa.com/

Currently offering information services online.

Bank of Montreal
http://www.bmo.com/

Canadian bank with WWW services.

BankNet Electronic Banking Service
http://mkn.co.uk/bank

First bank to allow deposits online, in United Kingdom.

Barclays Bank
http://www.barclays.co.uk/

Major U.K. bank offers information services online.

Citibank
http://www.citibank.com/

Major bank offering global services; site provides information about services.

CyberBank
http://www.webshop.com/cbank/

A service for trading certificates of deposit online.

KeyBank
http://www.keybank.com/

Major financial services and banking company.

MasterCard International
http://www.mastercard.com

International payment services organization, including credit and debit cards.

NationsBank
http://www.nationsbank.com/

Major financial services and banking company.

NORWEST Corporation
http://www.norwest.com/

Major regional financial services institution serving U.S. Midwest.

Security First Network Bank
http://www.sfnb.com

A pioneer in Internet-based banking

Visa International
http://www.visa.com

International payment services organization, including credit and debit cards.

Wells Fargo Bank
http://www.wellsfargo.com/

Major bank, offering actual online services as well as information.

General Catalog and News Services

These general catalog services should be the first stop in tracking down new information sources. The interested reader will find some of them invaluable for tracking down the latest and most updated sites for electronic commerce, as well as other topics. Also included here are some sites that are neither comprehensive nor catalogs, but that are maintained (usually by individuals) to provide pointers specifically to topics related to online commerce.

All-Internet Shopping Directory
http://www.all-internet.com

A directory of sites offering items for sale over the Internet, including e-mail sales.

Altavista
http://www.altavista.digital.com

A very robust search engine provided by Digital Computer.

AT&T 800 Number Directory
http://www.tollfree.att.net/dir800/

Access AT&T's directory for toll-free numbers.

Galaxy
http://www.webcrawler.com/

An Internet catalog operated by TradeWave.

InfoSeek
http://www.infoseek.com/

A for-pay Internet search service, covering more than just World Wide Web sites, including Usenet news searches as well as commercial/premium databases.

Lycos
http://www.lycos.com/

One of the most comprehensive Internet catalog sites.

Pathfinder (Time/Warner)
http://www.pathfinder.com/

Links and more, including a Catalog 1, for buying from your favorite mall stores and more — all online.

The NandO Times
http://www2.nando.net

An online, 24-hour Internet "newspaper."

WebCrawler
http://www.webcrawler.com/

Another Internet catalog site, operated by America Online.

WWW Business Resources List
HTTP://sbe.d.umn.edu/resource/resource.html

A list of links to businesses, retailers, and other business resources on the World Wide Web. Maintained by a faculty member at the University of Minnesota, Duluth.

Yahoo
http://www.yahoo.com/

One of the most popular Internet catalog sites.

Yahoo/Electronic Commerce
http://www.yahoo.com/Business_and_Economy/Electronic_Commerce/

Links to hundreds of sites relating to electronic commerce, online sales, marketing, electronic currencies, and online transactions.

Online Commerce Organizations

Trade and industry groups are an important set of resources for any industry, but particularly for a new industry.

CommerceNet
http://www.commerce.net

The trade association for online and Internet commerce. See the end of this section for more details on CommerceNet.

Data Interchange Standards Association
http://www.disa.org

A standards body for Electronic Data Interchange (EDI).

Electronic Commerce Association
http://www.globalx.net/eca/

An organization based in Canada dedicated to providing support to the electronic commerce industry and participants.

Electronic Commerce Resource Center
http://www.ecrc.ctc.com/

A U.S. government-supported resource center for promoting use of electronic commerce technologies by industry.

Financial Services Technology Consortium (FSTC)
http://www.fstc.org/

A nonprofit consortium of financial services companies and academic and research organizations working toward the goal of enhancing the competitiveness of the U.S. financial services industry.

NAFTAnet
http://www.nafta.net/

NAFTAnet, Inc., provides services relating to electronic commerce as it relates to international trade and NAFTA — the North American Free Trade Agreement.

The EM-Electronic Markets Newsletter
http://www-iwi.unisg.ch/iwi4/cc/em/emnewsl.html

A quarterly technical journal published out of Switzerland covering the electronic commerce technologies.

World Wide Web Consortium
http://www.w3.org/pub/WWW/Consortium/

Consortium dedicated to development of the World Wide Web.

Online Marketing, Buying and Selling

There are literally hundreds of electronic malls on the Internet. This list is hardly comprehensive, but gives pointers to a few of the more interesting Web pages devoted to buying and selling, as well as some of the more typical digital malls.

For a more complete and current listing of digital malls, check one of the Internet search engines.

Amazon.com
http://www.amazon.com

A major online bookseller.

America Online
http://www.aol.com

The online service provides numerous opportunities for shopping using their own software interface, as well as linking members out to the Internet for Web-based shopping.

CompuServe
http://www.compuserve.com

In addition to their online service, CompuServe offers private network applications for their customers looking for ways to transact business in a "closed-circuit" environment.

CyberSource Corp.
http://software.net

A product center for software vendors to market Windows 95 software products for online sales.

IndustryNet Online Marketplace
http://www.industry.net/

A members-only service (but membership is free) providing information and links to products and information.

Internet Shopping Network
http://www.isn.com

Online shopping for electronics and other products.

Yahoo/Shopping Centers
http://www.yahoo.com/Business_and_Economy/Companies/Shopping_Centers/

Literally hundreds of pointers to Internet shopping centers.

Specifications and Standards

One of the most important reasons the Internet is so rapidly moving to become a medium for commercial transactions is that it is a system with open standards. Here are a few places to look for the open standards being proposed and developed by some of the participants in the electronic commerce marketplace.

First Virtual Protocols (Green Commerce, others)
`http://fv.com/tech/index.html`

This is an index to technical specifications and standards for use with the First Virtual Internet Payment System.

Internet standards and proposed standards
`ftp://ds.internic.net/`

This is a central repository for all Internet standards as well as for drafts and reports from Internet workgroups. Look here for specifications of Secure HTTP, HTTP, HTML, URL, and many others.

Secure Electronic Transaction Protocol (SET)
`http://www.mastercard.com/set/`
`http://www.visa.com/cgi-bin/vee/sf/set/downloads.html?2+0`

MAILING LISTS

By limiting participation to subscribers, mailing lists can focus discussion within a group sharing interests. Subscribing is usually as simple as sending an e-mail message to the list server. Specific list rules and "administrivia" are almost always sent to new subscribers, describing how to unsubscribe from the list, how to submit messages to the list, and how to reach the list manager in an emergency.

These are a few lists dedicated to electronic commerce topics. Although there is a wealth of information in these lists, it often flows too copiously for working people to keep up with. For example, the Cypherpunks list may generate well over a hundred messages daily.

Cypherpunks

Subscribers to this list discuss cryptography and its implementation in current software, as well as many other topics related to security and privacy issues. To subscribe, send e-mail to:

```
majordomo@toad.com
```

No subject is needed; put the following in the body:

```
subscribe cypherpunks your@email "Your Name"
```

You must substitute your own e-mail address where it says `your@email` and your own name where it says `Your Name`.

Before subscribing, remember that this is a very high volume list. You may get well over 100 messages from the list daily, so if you can't handle that volume you may prefer to subscribe to one of the cypherpunk digest services.

Cypherpunks Lite

A moderated and edited version of the Cypherpunks list is available for $20 per year from COMSEC Partners. Only the more important, interesting, or relevant posts are forwarded to subscribers. You can look at what previous selections were made by checking archived files at this site:

```
ftp://ftp.crl.com/users/co/comsec/cp-lite
```

Files at the site are compressed using gzip. To subscribe, send payment to COMSEC at:

COMSEC Partners
1275 Fourth Street, Suite 194
Santa Rosa, CA 95404 USA

Be sure to indicate your e-mail address, and whether you prefer the digest version (multiple postings are batched and sent together in a single message).

WWW-buyinfo

The WWW-buyinfo list is for discussion of methods of using the World Wide Web to buy and sell products. To subscribe, send e-mail to:

```
www-buyinfo-request@allegra.att.com
```

The body of the message should include:

```
subscribe www-buyinfo
```

It is not necessary to include a subject for the message.

Internet Marketing

The Internet Marketing list discussions are mostly about marketing activities using the Internet. To subscribe, send e-mail to:

Include the following in the [body/subject] of the message:

It is not necessary to include a [body/subject] for the message.

EDI List

The EDI-L list is for discussions about Electronic Data Interchange issues of a general nature. To subscribe, send mail to:

```
listserv@uccvma.ucop.edu
```

Include in the body:

```
subscribe edi-l Your Name
```

Substitute your own name where indicated; it is not necessary to include a subject for the message.

IETF-EDI

The IETF-EDI working group works to produce specifications for the use of EDI standards over the Internet, with an initial focus on the transport of EDI via Internet e-mail.

To subscribe to this list, send e-mail to:

```
listserv@byu.edu
```

Include in the body of the message:

```
sub ietf-edi Your Name
```

Substitute your own name where indicated; it is not necessary to include a subject for the message.

HTMARCOM

HTMARCOM stands for High Tech MARketing COMmunications. This list discusses that topic as it relates to Computer and Electronics products and services.

To subscribe to this list, send e-mail to:

```
listserv@rmii.com
```

Include this in the body of your email message:

```
SUBSCRIBE htmarcom you@domain.name
```

Substitute your own e-mail address where indicated; it is not necessary to include a subject for the message.

COMMERCENET

CommerceNet is a nonprofit organization created to help businesses and consumers use the Internet for buying and selling, with the specific purposes of improving efficiency of transactions, reducing costs of ordering and delivering goods and services, and speeding goods and services to market. Member organizations include networking service vendors, consultants, software publishers, hardware manufacturers, Internet service providers and consultants, and many other organizations with an interest in the development of electronic commerce over the Internet.

CommerceNet Charter

The CommerceNet charter includes the following goals:

- Operate a World Wide Web server offering access to directories and other information useful to opening an electronic marketplace for business-to-business interaction.
- Increase the speed with which electronic commerce is implemented on the Internet through the use of pilot programs in areas including secure transactions, digital payment services, digital catalogs, EDI over the Internet, and others.
- Add electronic commerce features to existing Internet services and applications, and encourage development of new services.
- Encourage organizations of all sizes to participate in electronic commerce, and support programs to publicize CommerceNet facilities.
- Provide an information infrastructure for Northern California, and interface that resource with other national and international resources.

The entire enterprise is oriented toward the goal of making electronic commerce a superior alternative to paper-based commerce.

CommerceNet Participation

Participation in CommerceNet can take the form of full corporate member, for large organizations; however, this option may cost $35,000 per year. Associate memberships are available for as little as $5,000 annually for smaller businesses (those with less than $10 million in annual revenue).

For those who do not need or wish to participate as members of the CommerceNet consortium, subscriptions are available for $400 annually, with a $250 initiation fee. Subscribers are entitled to inclusion in CommerceNet directories and Internet software and information packages, among other benefits. Subscribers may also purchase Internet host services from third-party Internet service providers at special rates.

What CommerceNet Offers

CommerceNet offers a forum for industry leaders to discuss issues and deploy pilot applications, and from these to define standards and best business practices for using the Internet for electronic commerce. Through these efforts, CommerceNet will help this emerging industry evolve to common standards and practices so that users will see a seamless web of resources.

Participating companies get additional assistance from CommerceNet, including the following:

- Access to Internet connectivity through BBN.
- Directories to CommerceNet members and subscribers, as well as pointers to other electronic commerce organizations and activities that are available online.
- Access to information provider and Internet presence software tools.
- Access to commerce security mechanisms supported within commerce applications (including authentication, encryption, digital signature, and public key certificates).
- Educational opportunities for small businesses to learn about publishing on the Internet.

APPENDIX C

GUIDE TO THE CD-ROM

The companion CD-ROM included with this book includes everything you need to get started with Internet commerce.

- The Microsoft Internet Explorer browser software.
- The complete text of the Secure Electronic Transaction (SET) Protocol in MS Word and PDF formats.
- The Adobe Acrobat Reader software for both Windows 3.1 and Windows 95.
- The CyberCash digital cash electronic payment system that works with your Internet browser.
- Links and pointers to scores of different electronic commerce, digital currency, and online transaction sites and Internet resources.

This appendix describes how to install and use these materials.

NOTE: If you already have Internet connectivity and a World Wide Web browser, it may not be necessary to install the Microsoft Internet Explorer software. Please skip to the last sections to read about accessing the World Wide Web links document and protocol specification documents using your existing software.

NOTE: If you already have Internet connectivity and a World Wide Web browser, but do not have a CyberCash digital wallet, skip to the third section to read about installing the CyberCash client to work with your existing Web browser.

MICROSOFT INTERNET EXPLORER

Microsoft Internet Explorer software for both Windows 3.1 and Windows 95 users is provided in case your current Internet browser software does not support SSL and the related security features discussed in the previous chapters. As the size of these files continues to grow, so that downloading them takes even more time, this software is provided to get you going quickly.

This section is offered to help you locate the software on the CD and begin the installation process. The installation wizards are very complete and self-explanatory, with context-sensitive help.

WIN 3.1

To install the Microsoft Internet Explorer for Windows 3.1, use File Manager to locate and execute the file `d:\MSIE\WIN31\SETUP.EXE`.

You may wish to visit the Microsoft Web for the latest information on Microsoft Internet Explorer for Windows 3.1 at

`http://www.microsoft.com/iesupport/`

WIN 95

To install the Microsoft Internet Explorer for Windows 95, use Windows Explorer to locate and execute the file `d:\MSIE\WIN95\MSIE302M95.EXE`.

You may wish to visit the Microsoft Web for the latest information on Microsoft Internet Explorer for Windows 95 at

`http://www.microsoft.com/iesupport/`

THE ACROBAT READER

As mentioned earlier, the SET documentation is included on the CD in two formats: Microsoft Word version 6.0/7.0 and PDF format.

In case you do not have easy access to a word processor, we have included the Adobe Acrobat Reader 3.0, which can be used to review the PDF versions of the SET documentation.

Adobe Acrobat Reader 3.0 automatically installs a plug-in that allows it to work with Netscape Navigator 2.0 or 3.0, and an ActiveX control that allows it to work with Microsoft Internet Explorer 3.0 or greater. This reader does not have an expiration date.

For complete details on the reader, please refer to the Adobe Web site at:

`http://www.adobe.com/prodindex/acrobat/readstep.html`

Software Versions

Adobe Acrobat Reader software versions for Windows 3.1 and Windows 95 are included separately.

WIN 95

On the CD provided with the book, you will find the file `ar32e30.exe` in the `d:\acrobat\win95\` subdirectory. Before running the program, it is important to close any Web browsers you may have running. You can use the Windows file manager to locate and run the program. Simply double-click on the file `d:\acrobat\win95\ar32e30.exe`. The installation program will provide complete installation information as the installation process proceeds.

If there is a failure at any point during the installation of Acrobat Reader 3.0, the installer performs a complete uninstall. For this reason, it is important not to close the installer application by using its close box in the upper right corner of the background window after clicking the "Thank You" dialog box that appears at the end of the installation. If you wait for a second or two, the installer will automatically close the background windows after the installation is complete.

The installation procedure will ask you to read and accept the Electronic End-User License Agreement.

Minimum Hardware Requirements
- i386, i486, Pentium, or Pentium Pro processor-based personal computer
- Microsoft Windows 95, or Windows NT 3.51 or later
- 8 MB of RAM (16 MB for Windows NT) for Acrobat Reader
- 10 MB of available hard-disk space

Recommended Hardware Requirements
- Pentium processor-based personal computer
- Windows 95
- 16 MB of RAM
- 10 MB of available hard-disk space

Windows 3.1 and 3.11

On the CD provided with the book, you will find the file `ar16e30.exe` in the `d:\acrobat\win31\` subdirectory. Before running the program, it is important to close any Web browsers you may have running. You can use the Windows file manager to locate and run the program. Simply double-click on the file `d:\acrobat\win31\ar16e30.exe`. The installation program will provide complete installation information as the installation process proceeds.

If there is a failure at any point during the installation of Acrobat Reader 3.0, the installer performs a complete uninstall. For this reason, it is important not to close the installer application by using its close box in the upper right corner of the background window after clicking the "Thank You" dialog box that appears at the end of the installation. If you wait for a second or two, the installer will automatically close the background windows after the installation is complete.

The installation procedure will ask you to read and accept the Electronic End-User License Agreement.

Minimum Hardware Requirments

- i386, i486, Pentium, or Pentium Pro processor-based personal computer
- Microsoft Windows 3.1 or Windows 3.11 or later
- 8 MB of RAM for Acrobat Reader
- 5 MB of available hard-disk space

Recommended Hardware Requirements

- Pentium processor-based personal computer
- Microsoft Windows 3.1 or Windows 3.11 or later
- 12 MB of available hard-disk space

CyberCash Digital Wallet

The companion CD also includes the CyberCash digital wallet software. Using either your Windows Explorer or File Manager, you can install CyberCash by executing `d:\CYB_CASH\WINCYBER.EXE`.

CyberCash software requires at least an 80386 25-MHz PC running Windows 3.1 or higher or Windows 95. It also requires at least 2 MB of free hard-drive space and 4 MB of RAM.

This version of the CyberCash software includes the CyberCoin features that will allow you to use your software to make micropayments (i.e, less than $10).

We take a very thorough look at the installation process in Chapter 6.

You can also check the CyberCash Web site at `http://www.cybercash.com/` for the latest information on CyberCash and the wallet software.

WORLD WIDE WEB LINKS DOCUMENT

The CD-ROM includes a special file containing links to the World Wide Web resources referenced in Appendix B. If you already have World Wide Web connectivity, you can go directly to any of these sites by opening this file with your Web browser program. To do so, put the CD-ROM in your CD-ROM drive, start your Web browser, and point the browser to the following URL:

```
file:d:///commerce/links.htm
```

Once loaded, you should be able to click on any of the links to reach the referenced electronic commerce Web pages.

> NOTE: The Internet is a rapidly evolving environment, and although every effort has been made to ensure that the URLs included in this book and CD-ROM are accurate and current, some will undoubtedly change over time. In the event that a listed site is not accessible, the reader is urged to search for it using an Internet search site or some other mechanism.

SET PROTOCOL DOCUMENTS

The CD-ROM also includes the documents detailing the Secure Electronic Transaction (SET) protocol published in June of 1997.

The SET documents are organized into three books:

Book 1	Business Description	Contains background information and processing flows for SET. Intended as a primer on software that both interfaces with payment systems and uses public-key cryptography.
Book 2	Programmer's Guide	Contains the technical specifications for the SET protocol. Primarily intended for use by software vendors who intend to create cardholder and merchant software.
Book 3	Formal Protocol Definition	Contains the formal protocol definition for SET. Primarily intended for use by: • cryptographers analyzing security, • writers producing programming guides, and • system programmers developing cryptographic and messaging primitives.

NOTE: Standards and specifications are updated and upgraded regularly, to reflect changes and improvements. These documents, as well as many others, are available online through links defined in the World Wide Web links document described earlier. If in doubt, please refer to the online versions of these documents rather than the versions included in this CD-ROM.

SET files have been published in two document formats: Microsoft Word (`d:\set\word`) and PDF (Adobe Portable Document Format) (`d:\set\pdf`) based on the format in which they were prepared.

Microsoft Word Files

If you are using a word processing program that can view a Word 6.0 file, start your word processor and open files in the `d:\set\word` subdirectory on the CD-ROM.

The Word version of the SET documents is spread over several Word files. All the files for each book are contained in a single directory for each book.

Book 1 is contained in the directory d:\set\word\book_1, which contains the following files:

```
ReadMe.txt        Set_Bk1.DOC
SEC41.DOC         SEC42.DOC
SEC43.DOC         SEC44.DOC
SEC45.DOC         SEC46.DOC
```

Book 2 is contained in the directory d:\set\word\book_2, which contains the following files:

```
ReadMe.txt        Part1.DOC
Part2.DOC         Part3.DOC
Appendix.DOC
```

Only one file contains Book 3; it is found in d:\set\word\book_3:

```
SET_BK3.DOC
```

PDF Files

If you do not have access to a word processing program that can view a Word 6.0 file, you can use the Adobe Acrobat Reader software discussed earlier.

Once the reader is installed, run the Acrobat program. Use the File and Open commands to open files in the d:\set\pdf subdirectory of the CD-ROM.

The PDF version of the SET documents is contained in three files.

- To view Book 1, select d:\set\pdf\set_bk1.pdf
- To view Book 2, select d:\set\pdf\set_bk2.pdf
- To view Book 3, select d:\set\pdf\set_bk3.pdf

Index